For Freedom's Sake

Women in American History

Series Editors
  Mari Jo Buhle
  Nancy A. Hewitt
  Anne Firor Scott
  Stephanie Shaw

A list of books in the series appears at the end of this book.

For Freedom's Sake:
The Life of Fannie Lou Hamer

Chana Kai Lee

University of Illinois Press

Urbana and Chicago

First paperback edition, 2000
© 1999 by the Board of Trustees of the University of Illinois
All rights reserved
Manufactured in the United States of America

∞ This book is printed on acid-free paper.

Library of Congress Cataloging-in-Publication Data
Lee, Chana Kai, 1962–
For freedom's sake : the life of Fannie Lou Hamer / Chana Kai Lee.
p.   cm. — (Women in American history)
Includes bibliographical references and index.
ISBN 0-252-02151-7 (cl. : acid-free paper)
ISBN 0-252-06936-6 (pbk. : acid-free paper)
1. Hamer, Fannie Lou. 2. Afro-American women civil rights workers—United
States—Biography. 3. Civil rights workers—United States—Biography. 4. Afro-
American women civil rights workers—Mississippi—Biography. 5. Civil rights
workers—Mississippi—Biography. 6. Civil rights movements—United
States—History—20th century. 7. Civil rights movements—Mississippi—His-
tory—20th century. 8. Afro-Americans—Civil rights—History—20th century.
9. Afro-Americans—Civil rights—Mississippi—History—20th century. I. Title.
II. Series.
E185.97.H35L44   1999
973'.0496073'0092—ddc21   98-58017
[B]
CIP

1 2 3 4 5 C P 5 4 3 2 1

In Loving Memory of Althea Martin and Maletus Alexander

Contents

Preface

Biographies of the poor make generous offerings. They teach us just as much about the empowered as they do about the dispossessed and disfranchised. Life histories of the privileged are rarely as kind. Invariably, a humbling possibility grabs our attention: on some abstract, symbolic level, oppressed individuals ultimately *can so* reclaim value and garner just rewards from their historic battles against devaluation and exclusion. After all, it is what they have done and said during the fight that warrants our writing about them. In this sense and others, the meaning and consequences of a poor person's life stretch far beyond the scope of that life, and far beyond the limits that others had set for it. It makes sense, then, that a poor woman's story—a poor, black southern woman's story—could speak so thoroughly to a central theme of American history: the fight for political and economic freedom.

This is such a story. It is one account of the life and times of the civil rights activist Fannie Lou Hamer. It is at once the story of a major social protest movement and of a remarkably dedicated black woman from the Mississippi Delta. The last of twenty children born into a sharecropping family, Hamer drew strength and inspiration from poverty and racism and went on to become one of the most respected leaders of her day.

Early influences on Hamer's character were everlasting. A bold and attentive mother shaped Hamer's understanding of race, class, work, and sex in the South. Through her mother's words and actions, Hamer came to appreciate the individual power that flowed from clever, self-affirming responses to injustice. Psychologically, she had to, for vulnerability was an onerous reality for black girls and women in the Jim Crow South. Unquestionably, Hamer's identity was also shaped by sexualized racial violence—her grandmother's rape, which Hamer learned of as a girl, and the involuntary sterilization and sexual molestation that Hamer experienced as an adult. These experiences took up meaningful space in her inner life; the agony and anger were constant. In addition, beginning as early as age six, Hamer led a hard, uncertain existence as an exploited sharecropper. For much of her life, deprivation defined her material existence.

The summer of 1962 marked her formal entry into the civil rights movement. Arrests, bombings, and job dismissals followed, but Hamer continued working as a field secretary with the Student Nonviolent Coordinating Committee (SNCC) throughout the early sixties. She conducted door-to-door canvassing and taught citizenship classes throughout the rural South. As a dynamic speaker and moving singer, Hamer also contributed significantly to the organization's fund-raising. Through her work with SNCC and the Mississippi Freedom Democratic Party (MFDP), an organization she cofounded, Hamer helped bring thousands of blacks into an institutionalized political process, an important step in African Americans' quest for improving life-chances.

Among her many contributions, Hamer is remembered most for the stand she made at the 1964 Democratic National Convention in New Jersey. There, Hamer led an MFDP challenge to unseat the all-white Mississippi delegation. The highlight of the convention came when Hamer delivered a passionate account of the 1963 police beating in Winona, Mississippi, that left her partially blind. It was at this point that Hamer rose to national prominence.

Beginning in 1965, Hamer began concentrating her efforts on economic self-reliance through the Mississippi Freedom Labor Union, Head Start programs, and the Freedom Farm Corporation, a cooperative venture she established to feed, clothe, and house Mississippi's poor. In many ways, the building of the corporation was largely a one-woman effort. Hamer traveled thousands of miles to raise funds for the farm, making numerous speeches and conducting intensive letter-writing campaigns. Thousands of people were fed and clothed in Sunflower County, and similar projects sprang up in surrounding areas. Throughout the 1970s, Hamer combined all of her strategies for change—she ran for office, participated in party conventions, boycotted stores, initiated school desegregation law suits, and spoke out on the lead issues of her time, from the Vietnam War to abortion.

Accounting for her actions and reactions, both political and personal, demands recognition of the shifting social contexts for Hamer's life. These contexts gained meaning from the general configuration of race, sex, and class hierarchies of Hamer's time and place, and from the relative positioning of Hamer in her various social settings. As a worker, Hamer spent most of her adult life as a destitute farmer charged with supervising others and keeping records for the plantation. In her marriage, Hamer was a take-charge woman who never allowed her civil rights activities to be circumscribed by the demands of family and marriage, a fact that she kept private—apparently because of her conflicting feelings concerning what participation in the movement meant for her marriage. In her public life, Hamer was the outspoken, indignant grass-roots leader who was highly respected and sometimes even feared. Most people in the civil rights movement respected her leadership largely because, in her public persona, she was the quintessential victim of racism and poverty who chose to stand tall and unbroken in the face of ever-present defeat. Yet, it was this same position that was partly responsible for keeping her outside the circle of mainstream, middle-class, "more respectable" civil rights leaders, many of whom regarded her plainspoken, abrasive manner as too much of an embarrassment in the real world of politics. Combined, these roles represented a curious sort of status for Hamer the wife, mother, farm worker, and political activist. They created a duality of being that, on one hand, allowed her much leverage and influence but, on the other hand, often left her angry, unfulfilled, wanting, and confused. As a plantation timekeeper, grass-roots leader, and self-directed mother and wife, Hamer assumed positions that became their own sources of authority for her, sources that occasionally allowed her small doses of agency in her political and private worlds.

Although personal tragedy and political disappointment were constant, Hamer's life is not a story of complete victimization or defeat. Neither is it an example of complete triumph over all odds. The impact of her experiences falls somewhere in between. Her civil rights struggles brought many rewards, but they also resulted in enormous personal pain, disappointment, and exhaustion. In the end, after movement activity had waned and the national attention had discovered a new focus, she was left virtually alone to assess the consequences of her sacrifices made in a quest for freedom. This book is as much about the collective journey as about the personal costs.

Hamer was just one of a number of black women leaders in the civil rights movement. Black women played pivotal roles in every significant stage of the movement. It was Daisy Bates who led the 1957 challenge to desegregate the all-white Central High School in Little Rock, Arkansas. Septima Clark, a longtime educator, engineered the first citizenship schools, which encouraged and trained local leaders throughout the South. Moreover, had it not been for Ella Baker, a veteran activist, the youthful energy of the movement might never have found the effective organizational base that SNCC provided. Black women afforded the civil rights movement a style of leadership that contributed greatly to its success, and it was the destitute sharecropper Fannie Lou Hamer who rose up and gave this style of leadership its broadest appeal.

Through her leadership, Fannie Lou Hamer represented a necessary left-wing tendency within the civil rights movement. She functioned as both symbol and worker. She was truly one of those well-respected individuals in the movement who walked others through rough times by mere example and by actual hands-on help. To many, she was one of those "mamas" in the movement. According to Charles Sherrod, a SNCC member, "the 'mamas' were usually the militant women in the community—outspoken, understanding, and willing to catch hell, having already caught their share." This study is an effort to document the life experience of one of those women, a woman whose share of hell was undeniably convincing testament to the power of the human spirit.

Acknowledgments

I give thanks to many for support of this project. I am grateful to the institutions that gave generous financial support: Duke University and the Andrew W. Mellon Postdoctoral Fellowship; the University of Florida and the McKnight Dissertation Fellowship; and Indiana University and the Summer Faculty Fellowship Program. I especially appreciate the comments and interaction provided by the participants of the year-long seminar "Think Globally, Act Locally: Women's Leadership and Grassroots Activism," sponsored by the Andrew W. Mellon Foundation and the Duke University–University of North Carolina-Chapel Hill Center for Research on Women. Special thanks to Nancy Hewitt, Annie Valk, and others for making this experience possible.

My research was made much easier due to the gracious assistance of various librarians at institutions around the country: the Moorland-Spingarn Research Center, Howard University; the Zenobia Coleman Library, Tougaloo College, Tougaloo, Mississippi; Jackson State University, Jackson, Mississippi; the Library of Congress, Manuscript Division; the Martin Luther King Jr. Library and Archives in Atlanta; the Mississippi Department of Archives and History; and the Fort Wayne Public Library, Genealogy Division, Fort Wayne, Indiana.

I owe a debt of gratitude to many colleagues in the workplace. I received loads of advice and unending support while at the University of Florida. I thank especially Robert Zieger, Steven Feierman, Jane Landers, David Chalmers, Hunt Davis, Eldon Turner, and Susan Kent. At Indiana University, several colleagues also offered helpful direction. Ellen Dwyer, Larry Friedman, Judith Allen, Richard Blackett, John Bodnar, and Steven Stowe gave suggestions on organization, argument, and source material. Leah Shopkow shared useful insight and readings on biography and historical theory. For their timely gestures of solidarity and friendship, I also thank Ann Carmichael, Phyllis Martin, M. Jeanne Peterson, Wendy Gamber, Jane Rhodes, Lynn Hudson, Chalmer Thompson, Audrey McCluskey, Eileen Julien, Carol Polsgrove, Leon Pettiway, and Patricia Fox. A special group of graduate students at Indiana rejuvenated me at pivotal moments. I thank them also: J. Ogbonna Green Ogbar, Richard Pierce, Daphne Cunningham, Damon Freeman, Lynn Pohl, Susan Ferentinos, and Lydia Murdoch.

Several colleagues and acquaintances across the United States supported this effort through examples of their own work and an occasional much-needed kind word: Jacquelyn Hall, Elsa Barkley Brown, Barbara Ransby, Gerald Horne, Earl Lewis, Rosalyn Terborg-Penn, Stephanie Shaw, Cynthia Griggs Fleming, Robin Kelley, George Lipsitz, Deborah Gray White, Blanche Wiesen Cook, Gerald Gill, Bruce Schulman, Paula Giddings, Vicki Crawford, Leslie Brown, Karen Brodkin, and Steven Lawson. A special expression of thanks is owed Clayborne Carson and Charles Payne, two scholars who have deeply enriched our understanding of civil rights activism among youth and the rural poor. Both have treated these historical groups with the careful attention and utmost respect they deserve. I hope that this dimension of their influence on civil rights studies is readily noticeable in this biography.

Ellen Carol DuBois and Nell Irvin Painter certainly have made their marks on this work and my professional life generally. I have so much to thank Ellen for, but mostly I thank her for believing. Her love, faith, and toughness have meant more to me than she probably knows. Similarly, Nell walked with me through the many personal and professional struggles that became the context for this work. I am grateful to her for thoughtful advice on researching, writing, and teaching history, especially biography. She has been ever charitable in her support.

John Dittmer was especially steadfast and generous with his support. A beacon and guide, John read the raw, uncut dissertation for the University of Illinois Press and offered his honest assessment of its promise. He remains one of my biggest cheerleaders. I am not sure where any of us would be without his work on Mississippi. If what I have done here meets his approval only partially, then I am more than satisfied.

The University of Illinois Press showed an early commitment to this project. For this, I offer sincerest thanks to Karen Hewitt and Richard Wentworth. I am also grateful to Carol Bolton Betts for her wonderful editorial care and patience. My deepest gratitude is reserved for Nancy Hewitt and Anne Firor Scott, two editors of the Women in American History series. Nancy read and carefully commented on many drafts of this work, from unwieldy dissertation (everyone else's description) to the finished manuscript. She remained amazingly efficient and thorough throughout this long process. Drawing on her vast knowledge and experience, she taught and encouraged at every step along the way. She was simply the best, a first-time author's dream editor. I am more than a little fortunate to have had her as an editor and a friend through this experience; she has been a godsend. In her own special way, Anne Scott made this entire experience a wonderfully rewarding and instructive one. I have benefited enormously from her clear, detailed advice on style. Her genuine kindness and steady confidence in this work have carried me a long way. In addition, Beverly Guy-Sheftall graciously agreed to read the manuscript for the press and offered helpful comments and a glowing endorsement. I deeply appreciate her close reading and validation.

Completing this book would have been a far more difficult task without the cooperation of a special community of folk. I am most grateful to the Hamer and Townsend families for their gracious assistance with interviews and other information during my travels to Mississippi: the late Laura Ratliff, Jackie Hamer, Lenora Hamer, Sylvia Townsend, and the late Perry Hamer. I thank them for sharing their company, food, and shelter, and for driving me around Ruleville and other parts of Sunflower County. I also thank the many activists who shared their memories and otherwise encouraged my efforts, especially the late Septima Clark, Lawrence Guyot, Unita Blackwell, and Zoharah Simmons.

The love and support of two dear sister-friends, Ula Taylor and Tera Hunter, inspired me to keep pushing along when my inner resources became depleted. With her sense of humor and healthy homegirl perspective, Ula kept me laughing at life's absurdities and encouraged focus on the things that matter most in and outside of academic life. A smart and devoted historian, Ula offered an example of discipline and integrity that I drew on constantly as I struggled through my research and writing. I cherish the wholesomeness of our connection. A black woman could not ask for a more loyal and dedicated friend.

Certainly it has been spoken and written in other places: Tera Hunter is one of the most conscientious and generous individuals in this profession. An outstanding and hardworking scholar, Tera read the entire manuscript, and with her usual care and intelligence, she offered numerous suggestions for improvement, always stopping to affirm the strengths of my work and person.

Through many e-mail messages, phone calls, and letters, she constantly made herself available to me. My debt to her is enormous.

Other friends shared in this process as well. I thank especially Joycelyn K. Moody and Evelyn C. White for substantive discussion and direction on the larger themes of this work.

The blessings of a large family have kept me fortified. I thank my parents, Ylga Lee and Isaac Lee, for abiding love and generosity, and my good-natured brothers, Nye and Dwan, for friendship and devotion. For everlasting support, I hold close to my heart the words and deeds of Althea Martin, Gilbert Martin Sr., Julie Bell Lee, Mary E. Wood, and Maletus Alexander. Special loving thanks go to my aunt Beverly Buford, my uncle Ken Buford, and my late aunt Wanda Helm for providing transportation, food, housing, and fun conversation during my travels to Mississippi and Washington, D.C. Ever a source of affection and perspective, other kindred also gave unconditional comfort and good cheer: Dwight Martin Sr., Freddie Martin, LaVerne Martin, Cynthia Martin, Lavatryce Benjamin, Youree Kay Martin, Brenda Laster, Barbara Moore-Lee, Octavia Lee, Gilbert Martin Jr., and Gary Martin. The most inspiring source of family support has been the joy and sweetness provided by six small children, the loves of my life: Nye Jr., Nytavia, Roman, Shaina, Asya, and Randi.

Finally, I offer a special heartfelt thanks to A. Baghad for helping me respond in gentle, self-nurturing ways to my soul's clamor. Our paths crossed, and I am a better person indeed. I am confident that this work reflects that much.

For Freedom's Sake

one

I ain't good lookin' and my hair ain't curls.
I ain't good lookin' and my hair ain't curls.
But my mother she give me something,
It's gon' carry me through this world.
—Billie Holiday

Delta Daughter

Fannie Lou Hamer's path to civil rights leadership was not inevitable or pre-ordained. But perhaps nothing could have put her more effectively on a direct path to political activism than her own agonizing childhood. Hamer's involvement in the civil rights cause was more than a function of generic identification with the collective suffering of her race, class, and sex. What seemed an insurmountable combination of poverty and racism to many sharecropping families was, for Hamer, an inspiration to relentless effort.[1]

Hamer was born Fannie Lou Townsend on October 6, 1917, in Montgomery County, Mississippi. She was the child of two sharecroppers, James Lee and Lou Ella Bramlett Townsend, both well up in age at the time of Fannie Lou's birth.[2] The Townsend family already included fourteen boys and five girls. In addition to sharecropping all of their lives, James Lee and Lou Ella had other responsibilities. According to Hamer, her father worked as a Baptist preacher and bootlegger in the community while her mother, like most black women sharecroppers, also labored in white homes as a domestic servant.[3]

Both Lou Ella and James Townsend were natives of Mississippi, as were her parents and his father. (James Lee's mother was born in South Carolina.) The Townsends married on September 4, 1891, in Choctaw County, Mississippi, and sometime between 1891 and 1910 they moved to Montgomery County, where they stayed for a time with James's brother, Ben Townsend.[4] Subsequently, while thousands of black families made that "Great Migration" out of the rural South—settling first in southern urban areas and ending up in the Northeast and Midwest—the Townsends relocated to nearby Sunflower County (sixty miles west of Montgomery) on E. W. Brandon's Ruleville plantation.[5] Fannie Lou was two years old at the time.

In her autobiographical accounts, Hamer frequently depicted her parents as self-sacrificing and resourceful. Her recollections accented the full extent of her parents' efforts to provide for the Townsend family. In the case of her father, Hamer seemed to see no contradiction in his being a man of the cloth and of spirits. She never spoke publicly about his bootlegging in a critical way. It was indeed almost a source of pride. James Lee was simply doing what needed to be done to help the family to survive, and after his death, Hamer took over the bootlegging operation for a brief time. In this regard, Hamer's thinking and living, like that of her parents, were guided by a moral economy that blended a Christian worldview with southern realism. One did what one needed to do in order to survive, within the limits of one's own value system.

For the Townsends and other sharecroppers in predominantly black Sunflower County, hard work, poverty, exploitation, and violence were stark realities. Sharecropping, a postbellum system designed to replace slavery as a cheap source of labor, was the lowest rung on the ladder of farm tenancy. Sharecroppers worked an assigned section of plantation land. The landlord provided tenants with housing, food, seed, fertilizer, and farm equipment from the plantation owner's company store, usually at outrageously high interest rates, and took half or more of the crop.

Located in the heart of that cotton-rich, fertile flatland between the Yazoo and Mississippi Rivers commonly referred to as "the Delta," Sunflower County was the home of the "ruralest of the ruralest and poorest of the poorest," in Fannie Lou Hamer's words. Such a characterization captures the harshness of life for the Townsends and their neighbors during the 1920s and 1930s. Workers' wages averaged anywhere from $1.25 to $3.00 a day. Hamer recalled times when her mother worked for as little as "25 and 30 cents per day." Many black families during this period subsisted on as little as $300 a year, struggling against widespread disease, poor or nonexistent education, inadequate medical care, and malnutrition.[6] Political disfranchisement of African Americans and the social indignities of Jim Crow made matters even more hopeless for Afro-Mississippians.

Children experienced such conditions in immediate ways. Hamer recalled that her childhood was "worse than hard." Although the Townsends made fifty to sixty (and sometimes as many as seventy) bales of cotton per year, they still had difficulty surviving, a fact they were constantly reminded of during meals.[7] Dinner often consisted of unseasoned greens and flour gravy. At other times, the family had only bread and onions. According to Hamer, "It was horrible!" There was never enough food to satisfy her hunger. Sometimes that food was little more than "maybe some corn meal and an onion cut-up with some salt on it."[8]

In her memories, which were probably nearly as painful as the actual experiences, Hamer was always careful to juxtapose deprivation against what she perceived to be elements of privilege in her own very limited environment. In her autobiography, Hamer told of recurrent dreams of relieving hunger with a piece of cornbread or the Townsend family's special Christmas treat, oranges and apples. Adequate clothing was hard to come by as well. Hamer, who claimed that she was a "big girl" before she received her first pair of shoes, remembered that "Mama tried to keep our feet warm by wrappin' them in rags and tying them with string."[9]

At the age of six, Fannie Lou joined her brothers and sisters on the plantation—chopping cotton twelve to fourteen hours each day, from the proverbial "can see to can't see." Her lifelong work in the cotton fields began when a conniving plantation owner encouraged her to try her hand at cotton picking, an experience that was probably her first direct encounter with the unjust order of the American South.

Hamer told this particular story often, emphasizing the deceptive landowner's gesture as a "trick," an example of fate and treachery: One day while Fannie Lou was playing by a gravel road near her family's home—a patched, tin-roofed wooden shack—the plantation owner drove up and asked if she could pick cotton. The youngest Townsend child responded honestly by saying she did not know. The owner suggested in a most optimistic and encouraging tone that she could. He then piqued her interest by offering the child a "reward" of sardines, a quarter-pound of cheese, some Cracker Jack, and a gingerbread cookie called a Daddy-Wide-Legs, all in exchange for picking thirty pounds of cotton in a week.[10]

With this promise in mind and the ever-present hunger pangs in her stomach, Fannie Lou rushed out onto the field and told her mother and father about her conversation with the landowner. Her parents did not discourage her. Instead, they told her that she would have to pick her own cotton for the goodies promised by the owner; they would not give her the thirty pounds that they had worked for. With the eagerness of a naive six-year-old, Fannie Lou strapped on a cloth flour sack and began filling it up with cotton as fast as she could. At the end of the week, she had given it her best effort and successfully completed the task by picking thirty pounds. Fannie Lou was taken to the store and given each item the landowner had promised. With hunger so often on her mind, she enjoyed the "treats" so much that she later recalled never stopping to think that now she would be expected to work every day.

By the end of the second week, she had graduated to a larger croaker (or grass) sack and doubled her efforts by collecting sixty pounds of Mississippi's precious fiber.[11] But this time there were no rewards; there was not even comparable pay for comparable work performed (if there was such a thing under sharecropping). Seven years later, at the age of thirteen, the teen-aged Fannie Lou found herself picking as much as two hundred to four hundred pounds of cotton a day, for which she would receive only a dollar.[12] In 1968, before an astonished and admiring church congregation in Ohio, Fannie Lou Hamer sized up her cotton-picking prowess by remarking, "I[t] had become an art." Like some of her peers, Hamer developed a love-hate relationship with the crop. Even though it came to symbolize her suffering, her individual yield was also a source of pride.[13]

It was not until she became an adult that Fannie Lou realized that she had been exploited. In a 1965 interview, she recalled of her initiation into fieldwork: "So I picked the 30 pounds of cotton that week, but I found out what actually happened was he was trapping me into beginning the work I was to keep doing and I never did get out of his debt again."[14] Hamer's experience has elements of tragedy, of superhuman strength and stamina, and of childhood and racial vulnerability occasioned by deprivation and longing. In her account, Hamer made little reference to less-dramatic, more-practical issues that might help explain why she entered the fields so early, such as her family's need for additional labor. Nonetheless, this story has become a central feature of the Fannie Lou Hamer lore. It provides evidence that her childhood experiences—and memories—were central to her later political commitments.

Hard work was becoming a constant in young Fannie Lou Townsend's life, as she picked two hundred to three hundred pounds per day alongside family members. They all labored incessantly in the burning sun as the wealthy landowner watched from his porch in comfort. In recalling the increased work demanded during land-clearing time, Hamer often described cutting stalks "like men." Just before beginning her stint as a field-worker, Fannie Lou had a frightening bout with polio, which left her with a limp that plagued her for the rest of her life—a limp that did not, however, keep her from the fields. Physically challenged or not, Fannie Lou kept returning to the fields, tagging along with her parents and siblings, dragging behind her a cloth bag nearly as large as she was.[15]

For the Townsend family, life was not always a cycle of work and starvation.

When there was recreation or rest time, the family usually spent it roasting peanuts and laughing at their father's jokes to the point of pain. When bedtime rolled around, the family crawled into beds that "rattled like flaps of paper" because they were made of dry grass and corn shucks.[16]

Because of the long, hard hours that Fannie Lou Townsend spent in the fields, she generally attended school after the harvest was completed, which meant that her schooling, in a one-room shack on the plantation, lasted only four months out of the year—December through March. The black school year was three months shorter than the average school year for whites. Such inequities were to persist for decades in Mississippi (see table 1), another factor in the emergence of Fannie Lou Hamer as a political activist. Because the Townsend children never had adequate clothing or shoes, the inclement weather that typically occurred during these months became yet another obstacle to receiving a decent education.[17]

As if seasonal labor and bad weather were not enough, schools for young black Mississippians were segregated and woefully underfunded; the black educational experience was a cruel joke. During Fannie Lou's school-age years (approximately 1924–30), school expenditure per black child averaged a little less than 20 percent of that for each white child in the state. Depending on the size of a county's black population, sometimes disbursements for black students were as low as 3 percent of white expenditures. This was the case in DeSoto County. These statistics are even more appalling when we consider the fact that these same black children constituted well over 50 percent of the state's school-age population.[18] What is more, a deluge of racist propaganda in school textbooks dampened the black educational experience. As a third-grader, Fannie Lou had more than one encounter with the Sambo-type character Epamdinandus, a little black boy whose stupidity transcended the boundaries of human imagination and brought constant shame and danger to the adult members of his family, particularly his mother and grandmother.[19]

When Fannie Lou did attend school, it was often a rewarding experience. One of her favorite teachers, Thornton Layne, made it so. Layne was a black man noted for such comical idiosyncrasies as putting his shoes on the wrong feet whenever the heels wore down, so as to, as he put it, "let the heels straighten out."[20] For the most part, Fannie Lou loved school and it showed in her performance. She gradually developed a reputation as a skilled speller, winning a number of spelling bees. She also drew much praise from the adults in her community for her ability to recite poetry. In this regard, she heeded her mother's words of wisdom: learn to read because "when you read, you know— and you can help yourself and others."[21] However, economic pressures forced

Table 1. Selected Socioeconomic Characteristics of White and Black Mississippians, 1960

	All Mississippians	White Mississippians			Black Mississippians		
		Number	Percent of All Mississippians	Percent of All Whites	Number	Percent of All Mississippians	Percent of All Blacks
Family income							
Median ($)	2,884	4,209			1,444		
No. below $3,000	258,549	111,589	43.2	34.5	146,960	56.8	82.9
No. above $10,000	25,924	25,149	97.0	7.8	775	3.0	0.4
Receiving public aid							
All categories	115,462	44,272	38.3		71,190	61.7	
For dependent children	20,898	3,937	18.8		16,961	81.2	
Education (adults)							
Median (years of school completed)	8.9	11.0			6.0		
No formal schooling	40,640	8,444	20.8	1.2	32,196	79.2	8.4
Four years of high school or more	317,100	288,085	90.8	42.2	29,015	9.2	7.6
Four years of college or more	59,273	52,523	88.6	7.7	6,750	11.4	1.8
Home equipped with a bathtub or shower							
Yes	355,282	308,084	86.7	73.1	47,198	13.3	22.7
No	273,663	113,250	41.4	26.9	160,413	58.5	77.3

Sources: U.S. Bureau of the Census, 1960 Census of Population. Vol. 1, Characteristics of the Population, Part 26, Mississippi (Washington, D.C.: Government Printing Office, 1963); United States Commission on Civil Rights, Hearings Held in Jackson, Mississippi, 2:355–73. (Adapted from Frank R. Parker, Black Votes Count: Political Empowerment in Mississippi after 1865 [Chapel Hill: University of North Carolina Press, 1990], 19–20.)

Fannie Lou to leave school for good at the age of twelve. Later she joined the Strangers Home Baptist Church, where she continued developing her reading skills through Bible study, a road to literacy taken by a great many slaves and ex-slaves.[22]

As a child, Fannie Lou enjoyed making her people proud and happy, and she was anything but bashful. Family members would sometimes stand her on a table and she would break into her rendition of "This Little Light of Mine," a song for which she became famous during her years in the civil rights movement. It bothered her to let others down and so she always tried to do something for people.[23] This concern for other people's miseries and discontent also found a place in her adult character. It was these same qualities (along with Hamer's Christian background) that inspired her to perform service for others in her later years through civil rights activities and personal sacrifice.

But Fannie Lou was not always everybody's little darling. In fact, she earned a reputation among her family members for being quite mischievous. Her older sister Laura Ratliff later attributed this fact to her sister's birth position and her parents' relative old age: because Fannie Lou was the spoiled, youngest child of middle-aged parents, she got away with outrageous, annoying behavior. In an interview, Ratliff cited one particular incident to prove her point. One day Fannie Lou was at home with Laura, who was responsible for making the meals and taking them to family members in the field. While watching her big sister prepare the food, Fannie Lou decided that she was going to help. After ignoring Laura's order not to bother a newly purchased twenty-five-pound bag of rice, Fannie Lou grabbed a small bucket, filled it to the top with water and rice, and put it on the stove to cook, or to watch the water "sweat and sweat [boil]," as Ratliff later recalled. As Fannie Lou stood there and watched the bucket boil over, Laura resolved that she was not about to clean it up. She was sick of her little sister's unruly ways. When their father entered the house, he cried, "Laura, what's all this water doing on the floor?" Without hesitation, Laura replied, "Papa, I told Fannie Lou to leave it alone." When Mr. Townsend turned toward Fannie Lou, she immediately made for the door and ran out into the cotton field. As she ran down one row, her father gave chase in the row beside her, trying to cut her off. Just as he would nearly catch up with her and attempt to cross over to her row, Fannie Lou would change direction and head back the other way. This went on for a while before Papa Townsend caught her and started back toward the house with her in his arms. As he was approaching the house, he screamed to his wife, "Ella, bring me that shotgun 'cause I'm gon' kill this son of a bitch." Lou Ella immediately intervened and demanded that her husband not touch her youngest child. In reflecting on this incident, Laura Ratliff noted, "And that's how it was most of the time: Papa would want to whip Fannie Lou because she was just too bad, but Mama wouldn't let anyone touch her." Whenever Fannie Lou wanted a piggyback ride, Lou Ella would demand that the other children give her one, even if they weighed much less than Fannie Lou, as was the case with Laura. James Lee, in turn, would demand that the older children not give in to the youngest and threatened to spank all involved if he caught them going against his wishes.[24]

It is not clear whether Hamer had an abusive or decidedly negative relationship with her father. Since Papa Townsend knew of Lou Ella's protectiveness of her children, especially Fannie Lou, we can be certain that he was exaggerating his plans to punish Fannie Lou for the rice incident. However, even when we consider the prominent place held by profanity in southern discourse, the language he used is still abusive and threatening in any context, especially when directed at a child by its parent. Incidents such as these may account for the fact that James Lee does not figure prominently in Hamer's public recollections. James Lee the fair-minded disciplinarian did not hold the same place in Hamer's heart as Lou Ella the overly protective, self-sacrificing mother. The overwhelming influence of Mother Townsend overshadowed other adults' influences, and no other grownups loomed as large in Fannie Lou's heart and mind. In addition, the profound impact of Lou Ella's slow, tragic death only magnified her influence in Hamer's memory. Hamer left us few memories of her father and many of her mother.

Fannie Lou was born to a woman of legendary courage and astounding resourcefulness. What Lou Ella Townsend lacked in material necessities she compensated for with strength of character and ingenuity. Lou Ella was young Fannie's "main inspiration." She nurtured her daughter with determination and faith, and her affirming influence provided her child a special weapon in the battle against self-hatred and shame.[25] While Hamer underwent extensive formal training during her days in the civil right movement, her development as a leader began some forty years earlier as she picked cotton in the fields of Sunflower County under the watchful eye of her mother.

Like her own children, Lou Ella Townsend grew up in a dehumanizing social environment. She was born of slave parents from Mississippi. Her mother, Liza Bramlett, spoke often about the horrors of slavery, and the Townsend children listened closely when Lou Ella passed these remembrances down. Fannie Lou remembered names and other details about Liza Bramlett's life, but she held little appreciation for the significance of such experiences until she grew older. In her autobiography, Hamer recalled of her grandmother: "She was a slave and she used to tell us how she was first a Gober and then a Bram-lett. I didn't know what to make of it as a child."[26]

Lou Ella was born into a huge family that included twenty-three children. Twenty of Lou Ella's siblings were the offspring of violence—the products of rape. Lou Ella was one of only three children in the family whose father was not a white man who had forced himself on Liza Bramlett. Reputedly, the fa-ther of the three was a black man with whom Liza had a consensual relation-ship. According to Laura Ratliff, their grandmother spoke often to the girls about "how the white folks would do her." In explaining how "they sho' done Grandma bad," Laura recalled that "this man would keep her long as he want to and then he would trade her off for a little heifer calf. Then the other man would get her and keep her as long as he want—[she was] steady having ba-bies—and trade her off for a little sow pig."[27]

Fannie Lou Hamer referred often to this aspect of her family history, speak-ing from her own informed position. At the NAACP Legal Defense Fund In-stitute in 1971, she proclaimed of her grandmother's treatment, "It's been a special plight for the black woman." Finding equal parts humor and hypocri-sy in the hysteria of antimiscegenationists, she noted that it "tickled" her to hear others sound the alarm about racial integration. She had good reason to ridicule such fears. She said that "I'm very black, but I remember some of my uncles and some of my aunts was as white as anybody in here, and blue-eyed, and some kind of green-eyed—and my grandfather didn't do it, you know. So what folks is fighting at this point is what they started."[28] In her remarks, Hamer alluded to what the historian Neil McMillen refers to as "Jim Crow's most vexatious problem." Clearly Hamer was amused by the absurd fear that integration would instigate unprecedented race mixing.[29] Her family's expe-riences proved that this social fact of southern life had very deep roots. Of all these experiences, Liza Bramlett's ordeal loomed large in Hamer's family his-tory.

We can only speculate about any other details surrounding the conception and birth of Liza Bramlett's twenty-three children. The specific circumstances are not known, nor do we know about Liza Bramlett's psychic and social re-sponses to her reluctant encounters. But the pain and anger that the Town-send granddaughters expressed in their recollections are undeniable. Most relevant to this story are the ways that Bramlett's personal history helped to shape Fannie Lou Townsend's identities of race and gender.

The tale of Liza Bramlett's life socialized Hamer for black southern wom-anhood. It contained invaluable lessons and a painful truth that Hamer and her sisters could not afford to forget: A black woman's body was never hers

alone; there were often times when she had little say-so over her own reproductive destiny. The consequences of somebody else's "crime" were hers to
bear alone and in shame. More often than not, there was no recourse for violated women forced into sexual encounters, and certainly no punishment for
the perpetrators. Violence and vulnerability filled black female lives with terror. How frightening this must have been for a young child to learn. Some
adults could not protect themselves or their children from other adults, simply because they were not equal in status, by custom or by law.

Much of what Fannie Lou Townsend learned to appreciate about her mother had to do with Lou Ella's very painful and confusing personal experiences.
As Hamer came to have similar experiences in her own adult life, identification with her mother's person and individual history probably intensified.
Fannie Lou Townsend was deeply inspired not only by Lou Ella's sad past but
by the efforts her mother made to ensure that the Townsend family could survive physically and spiritually. Lou Ella Townsend was indeed the quintessential "outraged mother," moved by anger and determined to "make a way out
of no way," if only for her children's sake.[30] Through her life, Hamer was deeply
impressed with her mother, whom she often referred to as "a strong woman."

In addition to being a very attentive mother, Lou Ella Townsend worked
when and wherever she could find employment outside the home. Most often this work included picking cotton, killing hogs, and cleaning the homes
and clothes of white landowning families after putting in exhausting hours in
the fields. Fannie Lou often accompanied her mother on her rounds as a domestic worker, and she would watch her mother intently, as "Mama Townsend"
scrubbed clothes so hard that the scrub board would blister her already worn
hands. As Lou Ella Townsend worked, she sang to Fannie Lou, sometimes
making her youngest daughter feel sad and lonely.[31]

Learning how to survive required ingenuity and resourcefulness, which Mrs.
Townsend had in abundance. For instance, one way that the Townsends earned
a living when the cotton crops did not yield enough money was by "scrappin'
cotton." They would walk sometimes twenty miles a day in subfreezing weather
to each plantation in the area, asking the landowners for their leftover cotton
plants. After getting the landowners' approval, Mrs. Townsend would direct
her family to "scrap" the cotton, or pick the plant until it was clean. With feet
wrapped in rags and "froze[n] real hard" because they could not afford shoes,
the Townsend family would work through as much as twenty-five to thirty
acres a day until they had scrapped a full five-hundred-pound bale of cotton.
They would then haul their bale to the gin, where they would sell it and get
some cash for food.[32]

Along with "scrappin'" cotton, Mrs. Townsend would go from house to house offering to kill hogs. In exchange for her labor, Mrs. Townsend was able to bring home a portion of the animals' remains, most often the intestines, feet, or head. Mrs. Townsend also would try her hardest to supplement her family's diet by making their garden yield as much as possible. "I seen my mother go out in the garden and she would get tops off of greens; she would get the tops off of white potatoes. She would get the tops off of beets and all this kind of stuff. And she would cook it," Hamer once recalled.[33] Although this wasn't much, it augmented their regular meals of greens and flour gravy, enabling the Townsends at least to survive.

Lou Ella Townsend was known not only as a diligent worker but also as a fighter in every sense of the word. She never let anyone harm her children. [34] She would even strike back at whites who attempted to abuse them. One day when the "bossman" on the plantation hit her youngest son in the face, Townsend responded by warning him not to do it again. Amused by the warnings of this lowly woman sharecropper, he burst out in laughter and proceeded to swing her around. She responded in like measure by holding his arm while they wrestled to the ground. In spite of the danger involved, she had apparently gotten her point across, for after their duel this man never again bothered the Townsend children.[35] However, this incident prompted community members to wonder about Mrs. Townsend's seemingly foolhardy ways. Many black people were afraid for her. Some concluded that Lou Ella was just crazy because she "didn't have sense enough to be afraid of white folks," while many others reasoned that she was "just too busy to be afraid."[36] Similar statements would be expressed about her youngest daughter as she stepped up to engage in political struggle on behalf of the have-nots of her world.

Even before she reached adulthood, Fannie Lou had begun imitating some of her mother's courageous ways, and she demonstrated the same kind of boldness toward her playmates and peers. One day when seven-year-old Fannie Lou was outside playing with a young white girl, the girl's brother approached and demanded that this "dirty nigger" not play with his sister. Without hesitation, Fannie Lou balled up her fist and punched the boy in the mouth.[37]

Yet, even Fannie Lou wondered about her mother as she watched her go to the fields every day. She noticed that her mother would leave with a pan on her head and a bucket in each hand. One bucket would always be covered. One day, out of curiosity, Fannie Lou took a peek in the covered bucket only to find that her mother had a 9 mm Luger stowed away. As Hamer later described Lou Ella, "She was a deeply religious person, but she didn't allow anybody to mess with her children." Even as a young girl, Fannie Lou knew that there was just cause for her mother's peculiar ways. One day a white man, riding his big black horse named Charley, approached Mrs. Townsend in the field and announced his intentions of taking her young niece Pauline back home with him, but he was "goin' to give her a good whipping first." Looking back on that moment with a sense of pride, Hamer recalled, "My mother just stood there, popped her cork and said, 'You don't have no Black children and you not goin' to beat no Black children. If you step down off of that horse, I'll go to Hell and back with you before Hell can scorch a feather.'" Not willing to test the woman, the shamed horseman simply rode away without Pauline or anybody else in Mrs. Townsend's charge.[38]

Certainly, much of Mrs. Townsend's behavior stemmed from her own childhood observations of the most extreme expressions of racism and sexism in violence against black women. The painful knowledge of her own mother's being "passed around" from one white man to the next certainly impressed upon her the need to protect herself and her family from attack, using the most effective and innovative means at her disposal. One can read Hamer's recollections of her mother—for example, her observation that her mother "didn't allow anybody to mess with her children"—as part reality and part wish or desire. Clearly the issue of power was of paramount importance in Fannie Lou Hamer's life. She needed to feel and believe in her mother's strength and ability to exert control, especially in a setting where personal power or the perception of it was the only real clout or privilege that black sharecroppers had. This was probably especially true for sharecroppers' children, who were even more powerless than their parents.

Mrs. Townsend played a special role in helping Fannie Lou feel good about being black. She encouraged Fannie Lou to be decent and to respect herself as well as other black people, especially whenever her youngest daughter expressed a desire to be white. By the time she was ten, Fannie Lou had concluded that whites were the people who appeared to suffer least in society, and they also seemed to have everything that she did not, and for this reason she "wanted to be white." For the youngest Townsend, there was a direct link between race and access to resources. Just as whites seemed to have everything, blacks had little of anything, despite their hard labor. Fannie Lou noticed that "the people that wasn't working, which was the white folks, they had food and they had clothes and everything." She had difficulty locating the fairness in this reality. After all, she "worked every day, hard work" and "never did have food." As both protest and plea for perspective, she asked her mother "why I wasn't white, so that we could have some food." Lou Ella admonished her youngest to never speak that way again: "Don't feel like that. We are not bad because we're black people."[39]

Lou Ella Townsend reinforced her wisdom soon afterward by making Fannie Lou the first and only child in the community to own a black doll.[40] Upon giving her the gift, she advised Fannie Lou that she might not understand the importance of the gesture at her young age, but that some day it would have meaning for her. Whether Fannie Lou understood immediately was immaterial. She needed to begin practicing and living self-respect as soon as possible in her life. "I want you to respect yourself as a Black child, and as you get older, you respect yourself as a Black woman," Lou Ella Townsend counseled her, adding, "If you respect yourself enough, other people will have to respect you." By Hamer's own account, Lou Ella Townsend certainly "was a woman who believed deeply that Black was beautiful and not a shade less than beautiful."[41] For Lou Ella, passing along these lessons to little Fannie Lou constituted an act of survival and resistance—an activity characteristic of black mothering since African women were brought to America.[42] Soon after receiving her mother's advice, Hamer began reflecting on some of her community and family experiences. As if she had stumbled upon an important revelation regarding racial inequality, she began realizing, "It wasn't because this cat [the white man] was the best, but it was because of the kind of crook that he was, you know, the white man was such a crook."[43]

In spite of her family's poverty, Lou Ella Townsend tried hard to keep her children decently clothed, even at the expense of appearing less so herself. One of Fannie Lou's last childhood memories of her mother was seeing Lou Ella Townsend "wear clothes that would have so many patches on them, they had been done over and over and over again."[44] In this remembrance, as well as in others regarding her parents, Hamer emphasized self-sacrifice and self-effacement, along with self-respect and self-love in racial terms.

In addition to the value of self-respect and self-sacrifice, Fannie Lou's mother also taught her the futility of hatred, a lesson reinforced through the Christian church. During the civil rights movement, Hamer drew on one particular lesson whenever called upon to explain her position on black separatism or her reaction toward the violent ways of white supremacists: "Ain't no such of a thing as I can hate and hope to see God's face."[45] This and other Christian beliefs were reinforced by her father, a "deeply religious man," and by her mother, who faithfully dropped to her knees every night and prayed that God would let her live to see the Townsend children reach adulthood.[46] One of the few fears that Lou Ella Townsend had was the possibility of having to leave her children to be cared for by others. Although Hamer does not mention it in recollections of her mother, it seems reasonable to suggest that Lou Ella Townsend was also fearful of simply losing another child. Census records for 1900 reveal that the Townsends had four children by that year, but that Lou Ella Townsend had given birth to six by the age of twenty-four, two of whom died. While many women during this period may have lost far more than two children, losing even one had a lasting impact.[47]

Another way Mrs. Townsend instilled positive values in her children was through song. In this way she built on an African tradition of using music to socialize the young, build a sense of community, pass on important messages, and allow a release for pent-up emotions and frustrations.[48] She taught her family the value of enduring rough times and the need to work diligently. As she worked the fields as a young child, Hamer noticed that her mother "would express herself and other people would express themselves by sanging some of the songs and look like we could work harder."[49]

As a leader of the civil rights movement, Hamer also used songs to teach and inspire, which helped make her a charismatic leader and a dynamic mobilizing force for the movement. In this regard, her mother influenced not only the message brought forth by Hamer, but also the method by which it was expressed. Lou Ella Townsend, Hamer, and others taught and inspired through song, though they did not treat music as a coherent, explicitly developed didactic narrative. Instead, the song, as Hamer and her mother used it, was a composite of emotional reaction and social commentary, all designed to create an impulse, a feeling upon which to act. Sacred and secular songs alike conveyed a sense of purpose, and as such gave the impression of control and direction over one's life or the lives of one's community. The effect of such presentations was enhanced by various musical styles or qualities, including repetition and allusion.[50] Thus, from Lou Ella Townsend, young Fannie Lou acquired another of the skills of cultural protest that became a distinguishing feature of the leadership she later provided the movement.

In large measure due to her mother's influence, Fannie Lou began to show signs of a well-developed sense of right and wrong as a teenager. She always vowed to her mother that if she ever got a chance to change conditions she would. It was not long before she was truly beginning to understand the wisdom her mother had passed along to her.[51] In the company of her peers and family members, she questioned their everyday lives, much as she had come to question the vast differences between blacks and whites in the rural South. As she approached adolescence, she challenged others to share in her outrage: "Now what you think?" she confronted them, "Black people work so hard, and we ain't got nothin' to show for it. The white folks don't do nothin', and they be drivin' they cars, and wearin' fine clothes and eatin' them some fancy ribs and grits." With a measure of indignation that soon became her signature as an adult, she declared, "You know one thing: that ain't hardly right."[52]

Early in her life, Fannie Lou became aware of how the inequities in the system led to a host of personal tragedies for her mother and family. Whenever she was later interviewed about her childhood years, Hamer always recalled the one tragedy that never left her memory: the murder of the family's farm animals by a white man terribly unsettled by the mere thought that some black people were making too much progress. This was an especially disheartening event because it occurred when the Townsends were almost "getting ahead."

Sometime between 1928 and 1929, James Lee Townsend and his family momentarily broke the cycle of perpetual indebtedness and cleared enough to purchase their own wagons, cultivators, plows, and even livestock—three mules (Ella, Bird, and Henry) and two cows (Mullen and Della). In fact conditions had improved so rapidly that the head of the household even bought a car, made arrangements to rent some land, and started making improvements on the family home.[53] For most farming families, sharecropping was not a static condition. Along with indebtedness, geographic and economic mobility were also characteristic features of sharecropping in the South. The average sharecropper moved around frequently—from plantation to plantation, from owner to owner, and from one rung of the agricultural ladder to another. In this regard, the Townsend family was typical of most tenant families.[54]

Evidence of the Townsends' upward mobility was no secret to the members of the community, including its white members. Late one evening a white man sneaked up to their animal trough and poured into the stock feed a gallon of poison known as Paris green, a bright green insecticide containing arsenic. The Townsends were staying away that night in temporary housing because they had not yet completed repairs to their permanent residence. When the family members arrived at the scene, they found one mule already dead and the other two mules and cows with swollen stomachs and no chance for survival. Soon after, the remaining animals died. The poisoning dashed any hopes the family had of achieving self-sufficiency. Enraged, James Lee Townsend turned to thoughts of immediate retribution: "I would be willing to just join hands with any man that would do anything that dirty and just shoot it out with him," he said.[55] The tragedy was especially painful for twelve-year-old Fannie Lou; one of her favorite cows, Della, was among the animals killed. Della was a favorite, in part, because the Townsend children loved to quench their thirst and hunger by taking turns sucking milk from her teats.[56]

Life became increasingly difficult after this tragedy. As Hamer recalled, "after that white man killed off our mules, my parents never did get a chance to get up again."[57] Soon afterward, the family went back to sharecropping (or "halving," as they sometimes called it). Fannie Lou had to drop out of school at the end of the sixth grade and began full-time, year-round fieldwork to help her family survive.[58] In spite of the tragedy, according to Hamer, the Townsends mended their spirits and continued on, but all was not forgotten in her heart. She remembered, "I watched them [her aging parents] suffer and I got angry."[59]

Like her experience with the deceptive landowner who lured her into picking cotton at age six, the poisoning incident became a staple in Hamer's public recollections. She told the story over and over, framing it in the same terms she used in characterizing her entire life: hardship and persecution met endurance and resolve. In emphasis and interpretation, Hamer seemed to be offering justification or rationale for her activism. By noting that she "watched" and "got angry," Hamer conveyed the sense that her life moved inevitably toward participation in the civil rights movement.

Even before the Townsend family tragedy, young Fannie Lou was moved by another incident that demonstrated the dangers faced by sharecroppers who sought to improve their condition by taking what they deemed rightfully theirs. When Fannie Lou was eight years old, another incident of violence and injustice unfolded in the nearby Delta town of Drew—one that ended far more tragically than the poisoning.

Drew was the home of Joe Pulliam, a sharecropper who was killed in a dispute involving outstanding remuneration for work he performed for a plantation owner. One day the landowner offered Joe $150 to recruit some families to work on his plantation. Pulliam agreed, took the money, and decided instead to use it to fix up his house and acquire whatever else he needed since the owner had never paid him for his previous work. As Joe saw it, the money was not for work yet to be completed but for work already performed in the field. After it became apparent that Joe had no intention of bringing back families or returning the money, the white plantation owner, accompanied by another white man, tracked down Joe in his home and shot him in his upper torso. Not seriously injured, Pulliam ducked away, got his Winchester rifle, and fired back, killing the landowner in the exchange. Meanwhile, the other white man "outrun the word of God" (as Hamer put it) back into town and rounded up a group of his friends to avenge the landowner's death. Anticipating that a lynch mob had assembled to track him down, Pulliam had already started on his getaway to nearby Powers Bayou, where he hid in a hollow tree. Upon being discovered and fired upon, Joe Pulliam engaged his pursuers in a wild and deadly shootout. The battle ended only after the mob set an overpowering gasoline fire that forced Pulliam to crawl out from his makeshift bunker. Pulliam collapsed, but before he died he single-handedly killed thirteen and wounded twenty-six of his pursuers, according to Hamer.[60]

In overkill typical of southern racial violence, mob participants tied Pulliam's heels to the back of a car and dragged him through town for all of the black community to see. Upon reaching their final destination, they cut off his ear and placed it a jar of alcohol to showcase in a store window in Drew. Afterward, as Hamer recalled, "Mississippi was a quiet place for a long time."[61] The impact of such events on Hamer's developing political awareness was profound: "All of those things, when they would happen, would make me sick in the pit of my stomach and year after year, every time something would happen it would make me more and more aware of what would have to happen in the state of Mississippi."[62]

These experiences were typical manifestations of the brutally virulent racism that shaped rural black life. Such violent, inhumane acts often occurred without provocation and were aimed at upholding the existing racial and economic order. They tore at the social fabric of the American countryside and made peaceful living an elusive reality for more than twenty million of its citizens. Sadistic landowners and their "lesser accomplices" constantly inflicted undue hardships on black people, leaving them no recourse but to struggle and suffer.[63] Neither of the major tenant farming organizations—including the Sharecroppers Union and the Southern Tenant Farmers Union—ever established a real presence in Mississippi largely because of such violence.[64] And needless to say, blacks found no redress through formal political participation. This would have to wait.

In 1939, James Lee Townsend was overcome by a stroke and his general health began to deteriorate rapidly. He died soon afterward. One of Hamer's biographers, Susan Kling, notes that this was a "time of travail" for young Fannie Lou Townsend.[65] This was also the period during which Lou Ella had a severe accident: as she was clearing land for cultivation (a process known as deadening), all for a measly $1.25 a day, a piece of wood flew into her eye. As Hamer remembered, "She was using an axe, just like a man, and something flew up and hit her in the eye. It eventually caused her to lose both her eyes and I began to get sicker and sicker of the system there."[66]

The death of her father is one of many mysteries in Hamer's recollections of her early life. In her self-constructions, Hamer makes no reference to how this affected her life, economically or emotionally. Probably, with her father's death and her mother's injury, the family faced an even greater struggle to survive. This would have been true even if most of the Townsend children had already moved out, which was likely the case by 1939, when most of them were well into adulthood. Fannie Lou Townsend was among the last to leave home, according to the recollections of her sister Laura Ratliff. Between James Lee's death and Lou Ella's disabling injury in 1939 and Fannie Lou Townsend's departure from home in 1944, it is not clear what her family and economic experiences were like. Though these years were undoubtedly an important and difficult period, her recollections ignore them and focus only on leaving.

Around the age of twenty-seven, Fannie Lou Townsend fell in love and married Perry (Pap) Hamer, a farmer and tractor driver who was five years her senior. Fannie Lou and Pap had been eying each other for a long time in the fields until finally they struck up a friendship, which led to their marriage sometime in the early 1940s. It seems possible that Fannie Lou was not Pap's first wife or partner. He already had a daughter by another woman at the time he began a serious courtship with Fannie Lou. There is some confusion as to the exact date of their marriage. Some short biographical sketches of Hamer record a marriage date as early as 1942, and some document it as late as 1945. (Hamer often cited 1944, but there are no marriage records that document this claim.).[67] Some individuals have suggested that perhaps theirs was a common-law marriage. Certainly this could explain the differing dates and lack of conclusive documentation. If they were in fact common-law spouses, then this was nothing out of the ordinary since common-law marriages were not unusual among sharecroppers and were first recognized under the Mississippi Constitution of 1869.[68]

After getting married, Fannie Lou moved on to W. D. Marlow's plantation in Ruleville, where Pap had worked for twelve years, and the couple farmed the land together.[69] During this time she also took up the duty of timekeeper, which involved maintaining records on working hours, the number of bales picked by each fieldhand, and the amount of pay due each person. If Hamer found "spare" time, generally it was consumed by domestic chores in the owner's house. To make ends meet, especially during the winter, the Hamers ran her late father's juke joint, from which they sold bootleg liquor. They also fished, and Pap hunted rabbits and squirrels to supplement the couple's regular meals. But despite all their efforts, they remained poor.[70]

Hamer worked at least three different jobs as an adult, and two of them were especially important in helping her establish an important community presence. In addition to farming and domestic work, she worked for a time as an insurance saleswoman.[71] She was handpicked for this job because of her ability to handle numbers and because it was known that she was a recognized leader among her people. She had earned this reputation by being a fair timekeeper who often jeopardized her own relationship to the boss in her secret efforts to ensure fair returns for other sharecroppers. In looking back on this period of her life during her civil rights years, Hamer identified some of her actions as acts of resistance, an interpretation that clearly resonated well with the immediate historical moment of a protest movement. If her timekeeper experiences counted for something, then she had a long background in civil rights, a background that included daily acts of resistance dating back to the 1940s. As a timekeeper, Hamer worked nearest the scales where cotton was weighed, and she recorded the weights and dollar amounts that defined everyone's livelihood. While doing so, she observed how the owner used deliberate miscalculations and various devices to cheat sharecroppers who came to "settle up" at the end of the season. Of all the field-workers, undoubtedly she was best positioned to intercede on behalf of others—within reason, of course, given her own tenuous position. Eventually she grew disturbed as she watched the owner "beating people like that" and decided on a plan literally to restore the balance. It was an effort to "rebel," as she later described her actions. She began taking her own weighted instrument to the cotton field, and whenever the landowner was not looking or had left the field momentarily, she added her own counterbalance to the scales so that workers got their fair share. She recalled, "So, I would take my pea to the field and use mine until I would see him coming, you know, because his was loaded and I know it was beating people like that." In her mind she acted in defiance; in doing so, instinct and creativity served her well. "I didn't know what to do and all I could do is rebel in the only way I could rebel," she once told an interviewer.[72]

Fannie Lou Hamer once described the home she lived in with Pap as "pretty decent." They had running water indoors (though no hot water), a bathtub, and an inside toilet, though it never flushed, so they still used an outhouse. This outhouse became a constant reminder of the indignities blacks faced, especially after Hamer discovered that the Marlow family's dog, Ole Honey, had his own "bathroom" indoors. One day while cleaning the bathrooms in the Marlow big house, Hamer was interrupted by Marlow's daughter who told her, "You don't have to clean this one too good. It's just Ole Honey's." Soon afterward Hamer discovered that Ole Honey was a dog.[73]

As in her childhood, Fannie Lou Hamer did not have much social or recreational time. When she did engage in non-work-related activities, they usually involved some type of church function or going fishing with Pap. Curiously, Fannie Lou Hamer also loved to "go to the drugstore and pick up detective stories, stories about the FBI and the Justice Department."[74] It is not clear which stories Hamer is referring to in her memoirs. What seems significant about this memory is the point at which she revealed it, in August 1968 during an interview about her general movement activities. By 1968 Hamer already had a "relationship" with the FBI. The bureau had her under surveillance as early as the 1964 Democratic National Convention, if not sooner.[75] Hamer knew about the agency's interest in her activism (as well as that of many other political activists), and she became a very vocal critic of the agency, as were many Mississippi activists who felt the FBI did little to protect them. Did the huge place and importance of the agency in Hamer's political thinking intrude on her memories of detective stories—stories that actually may have been more general in nature? Remembering stories specifically about the FBI may be a case of Hamer's reading back a history for herself. The coincidence of her interest in the FBI some years before her life of activism stands out against other rather uneventful memories from the first two decades of her married life. Her fondness for reading is not at issue here, since throughout her personal papers there are notes (in her handwriting) concerning books she read during her movement years. These were mostly history books used by teachers during the 1964 Mississippi Freedom Summer project, such as Lerone Bennett Jr.'s *Before the Mayflower*.

Fannie Lou Hamer may also have read to others, most notably her mother. In 1951, Lou Ella—now in her eighties, her sight almost completely gone—moved in with Fannie Lou and Pap. The couple continued to care for her until February 1961 when Lou Ella Townsend, completely blind, died at about the age of ninety.[76] Never able to do much about her mother's physical suffering or to help her retire earlier from years of hard labor in the fields and in white homes, Hamer had always promised herself that when she grew up she would at least take care of her mother. To achieve this was the only consolation that she found after her mother's death: "I carried out my vow for when I was grown, I took care of her for ten years before she died."[77] Fannie Lou Hamer would not have had it any other way. The mere thought of putting her mother in a home was inhumane and disgraceful. "There was no way on earth she would ever leave my house to be put off somewhere on somebody that didn't even know her and didn't care," Hamer once remarked.[78] Apparently Perry Hamer supported Fannie Lou's decision, for he was very fond of Mother Townsend. She was really the only mother he had ever known. (His biological mother died when he was around ten years old.) Lou Ella felt close to Perry. In earlier years, whenever he would stop by the home of one of the Townsend children to check up on "Mama," she usually ended up following him back home.[79] Even as Mrs. Townsend was nearing her death, she was still teaching and singing to her youngest. Fannie Lou recalled going to bed at night listening to "songs that would really sank down in me, powerful message songs like, 'I would not be a white man, I'll tell you the reason why. I'm afraid my lord might would call me and I wouldn't be ready to die.'"[80]

By 1954, the Hamers had begun caring for two young girls that they had adopted: nine-year-old Dorothy Jean, the offspring of a single mother unable to care for her, and five-month-old Virgie Ree, a burn victim whose parents were too poor to provide adequate medical care.[81]

Not long after Lou Ella Townsend's death, tragedy again struck Fannie Lou Hamer. In that same year, she went into the hospital to have a small cyst in her stomach removed, only to wake up and find that she had been given a hysterectomy. This is another area of life about which Hamer gives us very few details. In her autobiography, she does not mention this incident at all. Whenever Hamer discussed the event, it was in the context of her public statements against the sterilization of poor women in the South during the 1960s. Motherhood and fertility may have been difficult topics in general for Hamer. Questions remain about her reproductive history prior to 1961: Was she ever pregnant? Did the Hamers attempt to have children between 1944 and 1961? In movement circles, rumors abound that Hamer had miscarried once or twice during her earlier years. One Hamer biographer, Kay Mills, asserts that Hamer had two pregnancies that ended in stillbirths.[82] Perhaps Hamer used her rarely told experience of sterilization to turn attention (hers and ours) away from her earlier attempts to make a family. Maybe Pap experienced sterility himself before her own tragic experience. This is another case of silence in Hamer's recollections. For a woman who used so well the numerous tragedies in her life to give meaning to her political activities, this kind of silence invariably attracts attention.

Hamer's involuntary sterilization was not uncommon in the Mississippi Delta (nor across the nation). A little less than fifty years before Hamer's sterilization, a number of states began passing "eugenic" or sterilization laws aimed at those who were deemed criminals and degenerates. Under these laws, sterilizations reached all-time highs in the 1930s, when as many as twenty-five thousand were performed. In the mid-fifties, numerous new statutes were introduced that targeted welfare recipients and were based on the premise that the state needed to step in and do something to curtail the activities of those who allegedly saw parenthood as a moneymaking venture in the form of increased welfare benefits.[83]

The racism behind these measures was apparent in debates concerning a proposed Mississippi statute that received a great deal of national attention in 1964. The prevailing sentiment was that an increase in Mississippi's black population endangered both the racial purity and economic progress of the great Magnolia State. Presumably, African-American children and their parents would be wards of an ever-growing welfare state, thereby draining the state's dwindling resources. Some white Mississippians felt a need to address such an impending danger by proposing a bill legalizing sterilization, a bill for which they had great hopes. In his forecast of the bill's impact on Afro-Mississippians, Representative Stone Banefield of Kosciusko, Mississippi, remarked: "When the cutting starts, they [black people] will head for Chicago."[84] This bill proposed that it be a felony for a parent on welfare to have a second or subsequent illegitimate child, punishable by serving one to three years in the state penitentiary for a first conviction and three to five years for repeat offenses. This was known as a sterilization bill because in exchange for a jail term, "offenders" could agree to sterilization. Due to nationwide pressure, Mississippi lawmakers eventually abandoned the sterilization idea and reduced the "crime" to a misdemeanor with a three-month maximum jail term. Yet, this same pressure had little, if any, impact on the type of illegal sterilization that Hamer fell victim to and spoke out against.

After the hysterectomy, Fannie Lou Hamer went back to the fields. She continued to speculate that, "hard as we have to work for nothing, there must be some way we can change things . . . there must be something else."[85] She kept hoping and praying and, finally, during the summer of 1962, Hamer seized an opportunity to make change. This was the year the Student Nonviolent Coordinating Committee (SNCC) descended on Ruleville.

two When spider webs unite, they can tie up lions.
—African proverb

Perhaps the primary human task is the establishment of a personal identity, a unique style,
a signature. Of course, this task contains an
irony: one is to attain a sense of self created
largely from the materials given one by others:
family, community and culture.
—Aaron D. Greeson

Black Woman Leader

The Student Nonviolent Coordinating Committee (SNCC) came to Ruleville, Mississippi, in August 1962, and forty-four-year-old Fannie Lou Hamer attempted to vote for the first time. From that point on her life changed dramatically.[1]

The Student Nonviolent Coordinating Committee emerged during an intense period of domestic social upheaval—a period beginning in the late fifties and reaching its peak during the mid-sixties. African Americans and other Americans of like minds let their discontent with the racial order in the American South (and later on in northern areas) be known using a variety of tactics ranging from litigation and boycotting to sit-ins. A civil rights organization originally comprised of college students, SNCC spearheaded the freedom movement of the sixties with its voter registration campaigns in the black-belt areas of Georgia, Alabama, and Mississippi. Its original emphasis included lunch-counter desegregation, but the group's members later reasoned that someone making only twenty-three cents an hour (three dollars a day) could not even afford to eat at a lunch counter. Consequently, the organization shifted its emphasis to gaining political power and combating economic inequalities.[2]

What attracted Hamer to SNCC was its commitment to "local autonomy [as] the basis of sustained militancy," as well as its belief that the movement was best served by building pockets of community leadership. In this respect, SNCC was largely influenced by Ella Jo Baker, the long-time activist who had called the organization together in 1960. Baker held firmly to the conviction that "strong people don't need strong leaders." Fannie Lou Hamer soon became one of the more well known of the local leaders, combining grass-roots support with the power to be heard nationally.[3]

One hot day in August 1962, an individual in Hamer's Ruleville church stood up and announced that a group of young people would be visiting the area to teach people how to register to vote. The visitors were members of the Council of Federated Organizations (COFO), an umbrella coalition of major civil rights organizations—the National Association for the Advancement of Colored People (NAACP), the National Urban League (NUL), the Congress of Racial Equality (CORE), the Southern Christian Leadership Conference (SCLC), and SNCC. The council was established in 1961 for the purpose of promoting cooperation and less competition among organizations with different civil rights agendas in Mississippi. A series of meetings between town folk and COFO representatives, mostly SNCC members, was scheduled to begin the following Monday, August 27, at Williams Chapel Missionary Baptist Church, the only house of worship in the community that allowed voter registration workers a forum.

Mary Tucker notified Hamer about the meeting. Tucker, in her sixties, was a long-time family friend of the Townsends. She was like an aunt to Hamer, who affectionately called her "Tuck." Tucker remembered her friend's not being as eager as Hamer liked to claim in later recollections. When Tucker invited Hamer to her house to hear the youngsters talk about the coming mass meeting and its purpose, Hamer replied, "What for, Tuck?" Tucker offered the reasons that "would mean something to her." Hamer replied with marked disinterest, "Tuck, they taught us that mess in school and that's turned me off like that." Her feelings hurt, Tucker persisted. "I felt real bad but I wouldn't let on," she recalled.[4]

Although Hamer stayed away from the planning meeting at Tucker's house, she considered going to the larger gathering that was to take place at the church. She asked her husband what he thought about the meeting. With few exceptions, Fannie Lou consulted with Perry Hamer on matters regarding her subsequent civil rights activities. In this regard, theirs appeared to be a conventional marriage. Regarding her political activism and its potential effect on her marriage, Hamer once noted that she "always liked to run things by Pap so that he would know that he was still the man of the house."[5] After gaining Pap's approval, Hamer prepared to attend SNCC's first Ruleville meeting. The next evening, Hamer went back to Tucker's house and apologized for being so dismissive: "Tuck, I come to beg your pardon. I never sassed you before in my life and it hurt me so bad when I thought about what I had said to you."[6] They left for the mass meeting at Williams Chapel.

At this COFO-sponsored meeting, the Reverend James Bevel, a staff member with SCLC, and three SNCC members, James Forman, Bob Moses, and Reginald Robinson, informed a fascinated audience of its constitutional rights as citizens of the United States and of the state of Mississippi.[7] Specifically, they told the audience that as adults they were all eligible to vote and, more important, eligible to vote out of office those individuals most responsible for keeping them down. Not the least of these was Senator James O. Eastland.[8] Bevel then delivered a stirring sermon, entitled "Discerning the Signs of Time," based on a Bible passage, Luke 12:54. The sermon called on everyone to recognize the signs of the times and to act on them much as one would see clouds forming in the sky and prepare for coming rain.[9]

The civil rights workers' presentation contained new and exciting information for the group. It certainly lit a fire in Hamer, apparently to the point of helping her to ignore or forget her initial response to Tucker's invitation. In reflecting on the gathering at the church, Hamer noted, "Until then I'd never heard of no mass meeting and I didn't know that a Negro could register and vote."[10] The COFO representatives told the eager group that they would have to fill out voter registration applications, which they were taught to do that night. The SNCC members then asked who would be willing to go to the county courthouse in Indianola to secure this most precious of rights. Eighteen people raised their hands and expressed an interest in testing a longstanding practice of excluding blacks from southern politics and thereby limiting their control over their own destinies. Before leaving the church, the organizers made sure the volunteers signed their names on a list of those who were going to make that historic step the following Friday, August 31, 1962.

Among the courageous eighteen, Hamer emerged as the leader, virtually by consensus; no vote or other actions gave her this position. It was a logical extension of her role as community leader, a position derived largely from her work as timekeeper on a plantation. During the mass meeting, Hamer was not only among the first to commit to go, but she also encouraged others to make that same fateful decision through an impromptu, charismatic personal testimonial.[11] As June Jordan put it, "Her bravery made them brave."[12] Hamer sensed that change was necessary, and her decision was undoubtedly influenced by the excitement she felt at the possibility of realizing a better life—a life in which the needs of the poor ceased going unnoticed. "I could just see myself voting people outa office that I know was wrong and didn't do nothin' to help the poor," Hamer recalled, foreshadowing her central preoccupation with empowering the impoverished. At the end of the mass meeting, she resolved, "I had made up my mind that I was gonna come out there when they said you could go down that Friday to try to register."[13]

Hamer's decision to get involved in voter registration work was not, as she put it, a "bolt out of the blue." The vote symbolized hope and empowerment for the individual. She had reflected and dreamed about its transformative potential. It represented a way out of a seemingly hopeless and permanent situation. It was a concrete response to the perpetual injustice that filled the lives of the southern poor. Voting was a practical answer for a very practical, no-nonsense woman who was exceedingly impatient for something better. In the fields, Hamer had long pondered bringing a change in conditions for herself and those around her, although she was not certain that voting might be a way to do this. Before SNCC came, she talked so much about this that some labeled her the "one . . . [who] didn't have real good sense," much in the same way that folks had talked about her mother when she did whatever it took to protect her children from abusive white men.[14]

At that particular hope-filled moment, Hamer had not given much thought to the dangers involved in trying to realize this basic democratic right. It just all made good sense to her, and she simply knew that she wanted to be a part of this activity. In her recorded "autobiography," she conveyed her enthusiasm by describing her immediate reaction: "When they asked for those to raise their hands who'd go down to the courthouse the next day, I raised mine. Had it up as high as I could get it." It was not until years later, after a number of brushes with death, that she thought about how dangerous this undertaking was: "I guess if I'd had any sense I'd a been a little scared. The only thing they could do to me was kill me and it seemed like they'd been trying to do that a little bit at a time ever since I could remember."[15]

During the town meeting, Hamer found inspiration in the freedom songs. The intense energy and persuasive force expressed through the music reinforced Hamer's conviction that this would be an important moment in her community's history. She began to feel an attachment to these young activists that would remain in place for a long time. The songs eliminated any doubt in her mind: these activists "really wanted to change the world I knew—they wanted Blacks to register to vote! They wanted Blacks to be able to have some small say about their destiny."[16] Most of the movement songs impelled people to action by their visionary, empowering lyrics that foretold the dawning of a new society. Freedom songs like "Ain't Gonna Let Nobody Turn Me 'Round," "We Shall Overcome," "Keep Your Eyes on the Prize," and "This Little Light of Mine" emphasized individual perseverance, while encouraging steadiness of purpose and the elimination of fear. In essence, the freedom songs— whether sacred or secular—must have sounded like direct personal appeals for a deeply spiritual Hamer to draw on two central motifs of her life: struggle and courage.

Later in the week of the town meeting, Hamer and seventeen other defiant members of the Ruleville community climbed aboard an old bus chartered by SNCC and owned by a black man who used it during the winter for transporting local cotton-field hands from Mississippi to Florida and Georgia.[17] It was twenty-six miles from Ruleville to the county seat in Indianola. As the bus pulled into Indianola, Hamer immediately began taking notice of the wild scene outside the courthouse. A crowd had started forming near the bus as the vehicle pulled up to its final destination. Wearing cowboy hats and toting guns, hostile white men and women were gathering around the courthouse, their panting dogs faithfully by their sides. They reminded Hamer of "Judge Clampett [meaning Jed Clampett of the television series 'The Beverly Hillbillies'] and that bunch, but they wasn't kidding down there."[18] And she certainly had just cause for thinking they were serious, for Indianola was notorious as the birthplace of the White Citizens' Council, a supremacist group founded in resistance to the 1954 *Brown v. Board of Education* decision outlawing segregated schools.[19]

Apparently, Hamer was unprepared for the big commotion the efforts to register would cause. In spite of the advice and warnings of the younger, more experienced activists and the record of her own experiences, she was momentarily shocked and puzzled by the scene. It took a minute or two before it dawned on her who and what were the real center of attention. But by the time she figured out what was taking place, she had committed herself too deeply to the task at hand to draw back or to desert her seventeen prospective coregistrants, or the SNCC staff members. As the eighteen marched up to the courthouse and prepared to enter the registrar's office, they were met by a very unfriendly circuit clerk, Cecil B. Campbell. Making sure that these Ruleville citizens did not feel in the least bit welcome, he inquired about the purpose of their visit. In a 1968 interview, Hamer remembered that as the group approached, he snapped, "What do you want?" With little hesitation, Hamer proudly responded, "We are here to register."[20] Campbell then directed them to go back outside and reenter in pairs. Hamer and Ernest Davis stayed inside while the others left the courthouse and waited patiently until they were called.[21]

Hamer and Davis entered and provided their full names. The registrar then directed them to answer twenty-one more questions on their place of employment, employer, place of residence, and even the date of the application itself. Forewarned, Hamer and the others knew very well that this information would

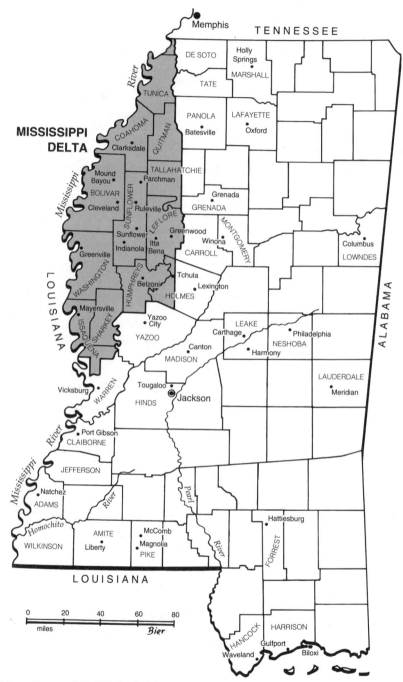

Map 1. Centers of Civil Rights Activity

be turned over to the hostile White Citizens' Council, but they provided the information despite the life-threatening risks involved.[22] Hamer and the others had come to understand the significance of SNCC's presence. They knew that the organizational or structural opportunities for change had presented themselves. Thus, they sought to take full advantage of this brief period in their lives, and Hamer's presence as the leader seemed to motivate the delegation to stand firm.

After Hamer and Davis provided the requested personal information, Campbell administered a literacy test, a test that Hamer described as being "rough." To be sure, the source of such "roughness" was in no small way attributable to the ominous spectacle of rifle-carrying whites strolling in and out of the courthouse as the prospective registrants were being examined.[23] In such a difficult environment, the registrar instructed examinees to read, copy, and interpret sections of Mississippi's state constitution so that he could determine literacy. Hamer's portion of the "exam" required that she read and interpret section 16 of the state constitution, a section that dealt with de facto laws. Later Hamer recalled that this was her first exposure to the actual contents of Mississippi's state constitution.[24] She thought she could certainly copy it, but interpreting it was out of the question. By her own admission, she knew "as much about a [de] facto law, as a horse knows about Christmas Day."[25] But as quickly as she had resigned herself to failure on this first attempt, she had also quietly resolved that she would return as many times as it took until she passed. This was a typical Hamer response during her early movement years.[26] Obstruction seemed to make her feel even more strongly about the moral correctness and necessity of her actions. Oddly enough, in this respect, racist resistance did just as much to define her character as did her own initiative and popular appeal.

After "flunking" the test but surviving what she simply referred to as an "ordeal," she and the others walked back toward the bus and climbed aboard in anticipation of the late afternoon trip back to Ruleville. But just as the group began boarding, Hamer noticed a state highway patrolman driving back and forth by the vehicle.[27] The bus drove off, but it was only a matter of a few miles and brief minutes before this same law enforcement official, accompanied by local policemen, confronted the group with the consequences of its actions. As the bus crossed a bridge leading out of Indianola, the highway patrolman, flanked by the additional officers, flagged it down and directed the driver to come to a halt. The officers then ordered all passengers off the bus. Everyone left the bus and began singing "Have a Little Talk with Jesus." The officers ordered them back on the bus and demanded that the driver return to Indianola, where he was fined one hundred dollars for operating a bus of the "wrong" color and then threatened with arrest because he did not have the money.[28] The bus was a very bright yellow and the officer claimed that it could have been mistaken for a school bus. However, the same vehicle had never been stopped when it was used to transport migrant cotton workers out of state.

When it appeared that the driver would be taken to jail, the eighteen passengers decided that he should not go alone, although many of them, including Hamer, still did not quite understand what was going on. "We didn't know what it was all about[,] but we knowed we should stick with him because he carried us down there," Hamer recalled.[29] Loyalty to someone who had taken a significant risk in the voter registration effort played a major part in the group's decision to stick by its driver. In addition, the riders simply did not have one hundred dollars among them. Their choice to unite behind the driver in his moment of individual persecution netted an unexpected result that seemingly gave all parties involved a safe and relatively convenient way out of a potentially dangerous situation. When it looked as if the entire group would offer to be arrested too, the officer—apparently not wanting to attract any civil rights attention or to deal with the hassle of having such a large group on his hands, in light of the earlier scene at the courthouse—reduced the fine to thirty dollars, which the eighteen passengers gathered up and paid collectively.[30]

Susan Kling identifies this incident as a significant turning point, a stage in Hamer's personal fight against racism.[31] Beginning with the Indianola experience, Hamer moved from being an individual whose sole means of "resistance" was survival to being one who took initiatives to promote collective struggle for real power. As she began resisting on a different level during her SNCC years and after, the stakes and positive consequences grew in direct proportion. When she would place a counterbalance on the scale as a corrective to the planter's outright cheating, and when she countered other, more devious, ways of depriving tenant farmers, she went beyond simply resisting for herself. Her actions increasingly had larger consequences, if only because more people were benefiting from them. However, from another perspective, Indianola was not the beginning of Hamer's real trouble. It was a replay of the injustices with which she had grown up. But now Hamer was encountering injustice in a new form—juridical, which complemented the outright physical violence and theft characteristic of both her earlier and later years. This new experience with injustice resulted from Hamer's effort to realize empowerment on different terms, precisely through exercising her right to the franchise.

There was much that was significant about Indianola. Hamer was introduced to new possibilities via the vote, which at that point she saw as having great potential for making her life better, although she knew that the process would not be easily achieved. She was a forty-four-year-old woman who was familiar with the racist ways of most white Mississippians, although she was constantly amazed at the lengths to which some would go to keep blacks powerless. On another level the Indianola experience helped Hamer realize the strength in numbers for community action. For Hamer the "Indianola 18" was now a collective, an easily identifiable unit of folk bound by common concerns and committed to certain political objectives. And Hamer had a distinctive place in this collective entity, not simply because of her longstanding membership in the Ruleville community, but also because she had begun seeing herself as embodying the potential for both justice and empowerment. By leading the group up to the courthouse and deciding to enter first, Hamer performed an act of leadership that others in the group were expected to follow. Coming out of the fields and boldly walking into a courthouse was unimaginable for these individuals before August 31, 1962. In this regard, the Indianola voter registration attempt was anything but an insignificant gesture. In 1960, blacks comprised more than 61 percent of the voting age population in Sunflower County, yet they made up only 1.2 percent of registered voters.[32]

The act in Indianola was much more than a group of poor disenfranchised black Southerners going up against a rigid system of exclusion to exercise a constitutional right. It also represented a significant psychological transformation: local folk, led by the Indianola 18, were now beginning to believe that they had it in their power to change what had been seen as hopelessly unalterable. Certainly, the mass meeting in Ruleville figured prominently in this transformation—the music, the enthusiastic appeals of the young, predominantly SNCC-led group. For others, this transformation went beyond the introduction of a method of action around which they could imagine a new future; more fundamentally, it may have led some to believe that they deserved better. Such a transformation for Hamer began early with the teachings of her mother, who insisted that her daughter learn to love and value herself in spite of messages to the contrary from the outside world. Certainly this aspect of her personal history eased her transition into leadership for the movement.

■ ■ ■

As Hamer's political work picked up steam after her first registration attempt at Indianola, so did the harassment. In fact, Indianola marked the beginning of a series of politically motivated but ultimately unsuccessful attacks on Hamer's life and livelihood. It seemed that with each new attack or threat of attack,

Hamer resisted with stronger force and deeper commitment to the cause. This was one quality of her leadership that would soon convince others to join the fight.[33]

After the group finally made its way out of Indianola and arrived back in Ruleville, the bus driver dropped everyone off at the church. A fellow Ruleville citizen, the Reverend Jeff Summers, drove Hamer four miles to the plantation, where she had been living (or, as Hamer would make a point of saying, "existing") for the past eighteen years.[34] Coming home, Hamer was met by her daughter, Dorothy, and her husband's cousin. As June Jordan put it, it was only a matter of minutes before "trouble fell into [Hamer's] life like a hammer smashing on her head."[35] Her children quickly informed her that the plantation owner, W. D. Marlow, was "blazing mad and raising sand" and had left a message for her either to go back to the courthouse and withdraw her voter registration application or leave the plantation. Bent on breaking her spirit and weakening her will, the landowner also had warned that her husband, "Pap," was not to go with his wife if she decided to leave or else they would lose all of their furniture, and Pap would find himself looking for another job as well.[36]

Hamer listened without responding as her daughters relayed Marlow's message. She then entered the house, where she sat down on the girls' bed. Meanwhile, Pap remained outside. No sooner had Fannie Lou walked inside than Marlow arrived, demanding to know whether his message had been passed along. Marlow asked Pap, "So did you tell her what I said?" Pap replied with a stiff "Yes, sir." Marlow added swiftly, "I mean that she got to go back and withdraw her registration or she'll have to leave?" Hamer, overhearing the exchange between Pap and Marlow, got up from the bed and stepped outside. Just as Marlow noticed her presence, he asked: "Did Pap tell you what I said?" Hamer replied calmly, "Yes, sir, he did." Evidently unable to restrain the paternalistic impulse within, Marlow continued, "Well I mean that you going to have to tell me whether you going back and withdraw your registration [application] or you going [to] have to leave here. We're not going to have this in Mississippi, and you will have to withdraw. I am looking for your answer, yea or nay?" For a moment Hamer simply stared at him. Marlow then added, "I'll give you until tomorrow morning. And if you don't withdraw you will have to leave."[37]

Beyond the political significance of his effort to keep tenant farmers disfranchised, Hamer was struck on a more personal level by the selfishness of Marlow's reaction. She thought to herself: "What does he really care about us? I had been workin' there for eighteen years. I had baked cakes and sent them overseas to him during the war. I had nursed his family, cleaned his house,

stayed with his kids. I had handled his time book and his payroll. Yet he wanted me out." It was almost as if she expected him to put aside momentarily the
racist constraints and customs of Jim Crow Mississippi. She was offended that
he did not have the decency and consideration to try to understand how she
might have wanted to do something—anything—to better her own condition.
In spite of the very humane ways she had acted toward him, Marlow could not
bring himself to accept her need to do something for herself. Having had about
as much as she could take from Marlow, Hamer declared a commitment to
herself: "I made up my mind I was grown, and I was tired."[38] In a 1968 interview about her showdown with Marlow, Hamer recalled her final response,
"Mr. Dee, I didn't go down there to register for you. I went there to register
for myself."[39] She did not wait around to see what would happen the next
morning. With the aid of Andrew Young and James Bevel of the SCLC, she
moved out that night, leaving home and family for the freedom to act in her
own best interest.

It is not entirely clear whether Hamer had any doubts or fears about leaving at that particular moment—or whether she revised her memories later on.
Her 1968 recollection of this moment leaves the impression that she left with
little regret or hesitation, which was probably not entirely the case given that
leaving meant separation and difficult times for her family. Pap had to stay on
until the end of the harvesting season. Apparently to insure himself against
any more labor losses, W. D. Marlow gave every indication that he would make
good on his threat to take the couple's furniture and car.[40] Although Hamer
made a decision to leave her home, family, and job, there was simply no way
Pap could leave, in light of the family's fragile economic position. That position would now become even more desperate since the family would be without Fannie Lou's contribution. Even though Pap stayed on the plantation after Hamer departed, Marlow was content that he had gotten the best of the
Hamers. To add insult to injury, he fired Pap anyway at the end of the harvest
and confiscated the furniture and car, for which he was still claiming the family owed an outstanding debt of three hundred dollars.[41]

Hamer's decision to leave that night was probably not easy for her to make
or her family to accept. In Hamer's case, as a plantation timekeeper, she was
giving up one of the more desired positions for black plantation workers. It
was a unique position that allowed her a certain degree of leverage and control over her own destiny as well as that of her family and coworkers. Although
a plantation timekeeper was not above exploiting or being exploited, she or
he did have a status with the white landowner slightly above that of a typical
sharecropper. But irrespective of Hamer's relatively privileged station as time-

keeper, leaving was difficult because she also had no clear idea where she would find her next source of income or how long this search would take. Although Marlow framed his ultimatum as a choice between two options, Hamer's departure was anything but an exercise in free will. In leaving that night, she merely anticipated what would surely follow the next morning, and perhaps wisely so, in light of the persecution she soon faced.

Hamer left her home, husband, and children to stay with friends in Ruleville. She first went to the home of neighbors, Mary and Robert Tucker, who were known for housing voter registration activists.[42] The Tucker home was only one of several places where Hamer sought refuge. Everywhere she went, violence followed. It was only a matter of days before Hamer, in attempting to realize the most basic of constitutional rights, was subjected to drive-by shootings, Mississippi style—politically motivated, pointed in intent, and indiscriminate in consequence. A reign of terror was touched off in the small town of Ruleville after the first wave of SNCC-led voter registration attempts, and Hamer emerged as a leading target for persecution. On September 10, 1963, ten days after her eviction from the plantation, sixteen bullets were fired into the Tucker home, fortunately missing all human targets.[43]

Few people were naive enough to regard this shooting and Hamer's recent move as coincidental. It was apparent to many Ruleville inhabitants that a group of white supremacists was after Hamer—the new troublemaker on the block, in the eyes of the many self-appointed guardians of Jim Crow. The Indianola visit, as well as SNCC's activities throughout other parts of the Delta, was stirring up much controversy in the small town of Ruleville, and Hamer (as well as a few of her local coworkers) came to symbolize that trouble in the minds of those determined to preserve the old order.

The same night that the Tucker house was targeted, shots were fired into the home of Herman and Hattie Sisson, critically wounding two young Jackson State women students sitting near a window. Twenty-year-old Marylene Burks received gunshot blasts to the head and neck, and eighteen-year-old Vivian Hillet sustained bullet wounds to the arms and legs.[44] Although Hamer suspected the shots were intended for her, there was certainly enough evidence to suggest that the shots were also meant for Hattie Sisson, who, like Hamer, had become a target after her widely publicized voter registration attempt some two weeks before Hamer's own attempt.[45] That same evening, night riders fired into the home of Joe McDonald, reportedly one of the very few active black registered voters in all of Sunflower County. When the McDonalds heard the initial gunfire, they all jumped into the bathtub, where they remained until the firing ended. Everyone in the McDonald household escaped injury.[46]

Throughout her time on the run, Hamer received much-needed charitable support from Ruleville citizens, oftentimes across class boundaries. For example, Hamer had food to eat in large part due to the admirable efforts of some black schoolteachers sympathetic to her plight.[47]

Hamer had now become a virtual fugitive in her own hometown. She stayed with friends and family here and there as she tried to elude those who diligently sought to eliminate her, politically and physically. Ultimately, she and her husband decided that it would be best that she leave Ruleville altogether. This decision was prompted by a very curious scene in the Marlow plantation office that Pap observed and immediately felt compelled to act on. A little more than a week after the initial retaliation on Hamer, he casually strolled into the plantation maintenance shop and noticed some buckshot shells with plastic covers sitting on top of the table. Immediately he grew suspicious and hurried out to the Tuckers' home, where his wife apparently was staying that night. Pap told Hamer what he had seen in the shop and suggested he would take her out to their niece's place in Cascilla, located in Tallahatchie County, just northeast of Sunflower. His fears were anything but unfounded. Hamer remembered that he reasoned to her, "I believe something going to happen because a man don't buy no buckshot shells this early in the year, you know, not for rabbits or something like this [that]." So Hamer and her two adopted girls proceeded to Tallahatchie where they continued to pick cotton to support themselves. They ended up staying until late October.[48]

It appears that, in her two months in Tallahatchie, Hamer experienced a significant change of heart and attitude. She began reflecting on her condition when the thought came to her not to run away any longer from what was happening, but to return. This plan was spawned by her ruminations over a fact of American life—racial injustice. One Saturday morning Hamer arose and began preparing herself to leave the house. Somehow understanding Hamer was not dressing to go out to work that morning, her niece asked where she was headed. Hamer replied, "Back to Ruleville." Although this announcement rattled the girls, Hamer had done a great deal of reasoning with herself and had concluded that by continuing to lead a life in exile she was complying with an unjust order, which amounted to a slap in the faces of her parents and grandparents.[49] She rejected the notion that she was a criminal who needed to act as if she had done something wrong. When one of her daughters raised the possibility of something happening upon her return, Hamer told them, "But this what you got to look at. I'm not a criminal. I hadn't done one thing to nobody, I went down to register for myself and I got a right to live in Ruleville because its people there have done way more thing[s] than that, they still here, and I'm going back to Ruleville regardless."[50]

In fact her bold decision to return involved much more than her refusal to be treated like a criminal. It also had to do with the familiar theme of economic exploitation. Few unjust conditions enraged Hamer so much as the continued (and unacknowledged) devaluation of her labor and that of her forebears. It seems she could not help but see her return as reclaiming the land she had worked and developed, even if this reclamation was more symbolic than real— as turned out to be the case, since she could not return directly to the Marlow plantation. In her explanation to the girls she added, "My parents helped to make this town and this county what it is today, because it was out of their sweat, tears, and blood that they [white landowners] got as much land that they have here; and I [have] a right to stay here."[51] Although fearing for their caretaker's life, the girls accompanied Hamer back to Ruleville.

This change of heart reflected a variation in Hamer's usual reaction to persecution and harassment. It signaled a moment of transition somewhat akin to a religious conversion. While in Tallahatchie, Hamer had a searching and reflective moment that caused her to resituate herself in relation to the world around her.[52] Although Hamer was resolute, very decisive about her part at the Indianola courthouse, she initially trod with caution when she returned to Ruleville. She and Pap concluded that she had gone as far as she could go in testing the limits of racist reaction. By the time she returned from Tallahatchie, however, Hamer had decided that such challenges, however life-threatening, must be met with a steadfast, more principled opposite reaction. Christian faith and emotional memories of her parents and grandparents triggered and bolstered such a transformation.

Hamer's return to Ruleville was not permanent, however. No sooner was she reunited with her family than she was informed of a sugar refinery accident involving a male cousin in Chicago. He had been injured in an explosion at Chicago Starch, a plant where finely powdered sugar and other confections were processed. Since she had played a role in his upbringing, Hamer felt a special obligation to assist him in his recovery. So, off she went to Chicago the following day, and she remained there for two weeks. Before returning to Ruleville, Hamer stopped again in Tallahatchie County to pick up the rest of her belongings.[53]

During the fall of 1962, Hamer increased her activities in the movement, even though it meant being away from her home base. She attended a SNCC leadership training conference at Fisk University at the invitation of Bob Moses, who dispatched a local activist, Charles McLaurin, to locate her in Tallahatchie and bring her to Nashville.[54] Hamer had been identified by the organization as the "perfect prospect" for local leadership development after her trip to Indianola. Also, SNCC invited Hamer as a way of tapping into the community of the needy because she had served as a leader on the plantation during her tenure as timekeeper, a position in which she often served as a go-between for black laborers and white "bossmen" or landowners. Hamer's residence was often an after-work gathering place for members of the community because of her stature, although Pap was not always happy about this.[55] While at the conference, Hamer participated in the politics and voting workshop, which addressed the topics of nonviolence, communications, and economics. Although this did not mean that she had no interest in other activities covered by conference sessions, her choice indicated the faith she had in effecting change through voting. When asked on the conference application form why she wished to attend the institute, Hamer replied, "To find out what I could do in Miss. to help free my people." Following the conference, Hamer returned home in December 1962 and continued her voter registration canvassing as a field secretary-at-large for Mississippi under the sponsorship of COFO.[56]

When Hamer reunited with her family for good after spending more than two months away from home, she found that peace still was not in store for her. In part this was so because she wasted little time in going back a second time to register. On December 3 the family moved into a new home on Lafayette Street that relatives and friends had helped them to acquire, and on December 4 the seemingly undaunted Hamer was right back at the Indianola courthouse. In a 1975 interview with Howell Raines, Hamer recalled that before taking the voter registration test for the second time, she proudly declared to the registrar, "Now, you cain't have me fired because I'm not livin' in no white man's house. I'll be here every thirty days until I become a registered voter."[57]

Because of the fierce persecution that invariably followed registration attempts, especially in remote areas like the Mississippi Delta, it is unlikely that Hamer made these points in quite the same kind of bold pronouncement that she related in her interview with Raines. The movement gave its participants a good deal of hope and courage, but rarely did their heady faith or confidence translate into the feeling of invincibility that Hamer's statement seems to convey. In public and in private, activists were forever mindful of the many life-threatening dangers that lurked nearby. Certainly this must have been the case for someone with a reputation like Hamer's; drive-by shootings, threatening letters and phone calls, in addition to the off-season appearance of buckshot shells, must have touched off some kind of alert in her mind. For this reason, it is difficult to regard her alleged statement to the registrar as an instance of unmitigated temerity. If in fact Hamer was fudging the truth in her later account, this should probably be regarded as one of many instances in which she was crafting an image of herself as the big, bad, strong and daring black woman. If this is the case, then Hamer, as an historical figure conscious of her own place in public life and history, stands among substantial historical company.[58]

Upon Hamer's return visit, the registrar, Cecil Campbell, questioned her on section 49 of the Mississippi constitution, addressing the House of Representatives.[59] There were a number of reasons why Hamer returned with such determination and sense of urgency. One was the sheer indignation she felt at having been denied the precious right to vote. The rage that Hamer felt and often voiced about her deprivation was constant in her life, and it proved to be a powerful source of motivation. The persistence of injustice and her frustratingly painful memories seemed to ignite her rage periodically, causing it to brew and intensify, as it did during her exile days in Tallahatchie. Second, it is possible that at this point she was beginning to envision a larger place for herself in the civil rights movement, and maybe even in mainstream American politics as well. Most of the local activists who led or encouraged others to make that foray into their respective county courthouses tended to be registered voters themselves. This was not necessarily a SNCC requirement, but it certainly helped one's cause to be a personal example of what could be achieved. Third, Hamer had simply become impatient about determining her own destiny and the destinies of people most like her in matters of race and class.

On January 10, 1963, Hamer returned to the Indianola courthouse expecting to have to take the exam yet a third time. Instead, Hamer learned that she had finally passed. Oddly enough, Hamer attributed her passing partly to preparation on her part. In her interview with Raines, she noted, "I went back then the tenth of January in 1963, and I had become registered. . . . I passed the second one, because at the second time I went back [on December 4], I had been studying sections of the Mississippi Constitution, so I know if I got one that was simple enough that I might could pass it."[60] Although Hamer and other civil rights activists knew that the outcome of the exam was most often subjective and political, they always held out hope that they could demonstrate enough "correct" knowledge and be judged objectively. Hence, activists poured a lot of energy into projects like the citizenship schools instituted by the South Carolina activist Septima Clark and attended and taught by figures like Hamer.

After registering, Hamer was not able to vote immediately because she did not have the two poll-tax receipts that were required in Mississippi and in other black-belt states. One could not qualify as an official elector until these taxes were paid in consecutive years. It was not until May 1964 that Hamer cast her first vote.[61] Despite the legal obstacles and the violence directed against her, Hamer persisted and continued to make her "small" stands for freedom and justice. In doing so she would soon become an important symbol of the movement.

Because Mississippi law then required that the names of all persons who took the registration tests be printed in the local paper for a minimum of two weeks, Hamer's victory subjected her family to retaliatory attacks by angry white citizens and law enforcement officers.[62] Such harassment extended to employment; Fannie Lou and Pap were unable to find work. She had definitely overturned the applecart, and there were plenty of Sunflower County residents who were anxious to remind her of this. By the time Hamer had returned to Ruleville in the winter of 1962, the Hamers, with the help of movement friends and Fannie Lou's sixth-grade teacher, had established their own permanent home (owned by a black woman in Ruleville) at 626 East Lafayette Street. Fannie Lou Hamer was able to live there for the rest of her movement years.[63] Even as they moved, however, so did their tormentors. Carloads of white men armed with rifles circled the home constantly, hurling obscenities at Hamer and her family and threatening to shoot them down. If Hamer or one of her family members decided to leave the house, they would be followed by these same cars, with the hostile passengers continually threatening and cursing. Hamer received the same threats and obscenities through numerous anonymous phone calls or in abusive letters.[64] As usual, Hamer's response was to continue to "work and get our people organized."[65]

Before long, things went "from badder to worse," as Hamer described this period of retaliation. In addition to the wave of terror, official reprisals steadily rained down on her. State law enforcement officers and Ruleville city officials waged their own relentless campaign to strike fear into the hearts of those who would be so bold as to secure a basic democratic privilege in the franchise. Mississippi law enforcement officials often paid Hamer and her husband unexpected visits at unreasonable hours. Between four and five o'clock one morning, a group broke into the Hamer home with their guns drawn and billy clubs positioned high in the air, ready to come down on the first body that moved.[66]

On another occasion, during the Christmas season, Pap Hamer had gotten up one morning to go to the toilet. No sooner had he turned the light out and walked out of the bathroom than he and Fannie Lou heard a knock at the door. As Pap opened the door, in walked Dave Fleming, from nearby Drew, Mississippi, a fearless character commonly called the "Sundown Kid," a moniker no doubt pinned on him for exploits typical of the one he pulled off that morning at the Hamers' residence.[67] Accompanying him on his mission were a few other white men, including the Ruleville sheriff, S. L. Milam. The sheriff was the brother of J. W. Milam, the infamous accused murderer of Emmett Till, the fourteen-year-old Chicago native whose bloated and badly disfigured body was found in the Tallahatchie River. The intruders asked Pap what he was doing up at such an hour. The crew then searched the Hamers' house with flashlights in one hand and cocked guns in the other. They shined their lights around in every room, including the Hamer bedroom.[68] Fannie Lou Hamer recalled this incident with particular distaste because, among other transgressions, it showed total disregard for her as a woman: "I was in the bed [and] they didn't know how they would find me as a woman, in my house, you know, and they flashed the lights around, and they had the guns in their hand, and then they backed out you know, backed out like, you know, we were some kind of criminals."[69]

Many times the Hamers found state-sponsored harassment a much tougher challenge than the isolated but persistent threats of a few mean-spirited individuals. The case of a "delinquent" water bill was one such incident with the authorities. One day Hamer had ventured outside to retrieve some water only to discover that the water line had been turned off. Assuming that it had been turned off by two young boys in the neighborhood who had assisted her in doing this before, Hamer promptly turned the water back on and "caught a bucket full." But later the two boys told Hamer they had not cut the water off. Hamer thought, "Oh [no,] this is some kind of trap."[70] That evening, the mayor, Charles M. Dorrough, sent a night watchman out to the Hamer home to deliver a message summoning her to city hall to talk with him. The next day Hamer took time away from her political work to comply with the mayor's request. Dorrough told Hamer that she was guilty of theft for taking the water because her water bill was delinquent by two days. (It was due on the tenth of the month, and it was the twelfth when she went outside and turned the water on.) It is not clear whether Fannie Lou Hamer ever confessed to the charge; her counter-grievance focused on the original source of the problem: the water bill had been for the outrageously high amount of nine thousand dollars, supposedly for the consumption of six thousand gallons of water. Hamer began disputing the bill, saying that there was no way in the world that her family had used six thousand gallons of water in one month. This bill was even more outrageous given that the Hamers had no running water in the house and all of the family members spent much of their time away during the daytime hours. The children were in school, Pap was usually out hunting, while Hamer would be out in the field canvassing potential voters. Having lost her appeal and obviously unable to pay the amount required, Hamer returned home. Soon the law returned in the person of S. L. Milam, this time to take Pap Hamer to jail.[71] Not long after, he was bailed out by Charles McLaurin, and apparently nothing more serious came of the matter. But the absurdity of the entire incident was not lost on Hamer. While retelling this story in a 1968 interview, she remarked, "Now that's not even funny. . . . When a person drags you down like that then you know this is really something."[72] Such harassment by Ruleville officials (including excessive telephone and electricity bills) continued throughout Hamer's political career.[73]

Hamer certainly was not alone on Mayor Dorrough's political hit list. The mayor also played a leading role in harassing the Williams Chapel Missionary Baptist Church by cutting off its free water service and terminating its tax-exempt status because its property was suspected of being used for "purposes other than worship services." Soon afterward U.S. Fidelity and Guaranty mysteriously canceled the church's fire insurance, causing the church to shut down for a time.[74] Dorrough also fired city employees suspected of having any association with SNCC and its voter registration activities, and he often interfered with the distribution of federal surplus food to Ruleville citizens.[75] Moreover, as SNCC charged in a telegram to Attorney General Robert Kennedy, Dorrough "willfully and maliciously beat a 14-year-old Negro youth" after warning the young activist, "I'm not going to have that mess or any of that integration stuff."[76]

In her autobiography, Hamer described the winter of 1962 as "rough." She recalled not having the opportunity to can any food and that Pap was not able to get a job because everyone knew that he was married to Fannie Lou.[77] Because Pap and Fannie Lou Hamer only spoke fondly of one another in interviews, it is difficult to determine what sort of strain this financial hardship placed on their marriage. To be sure, the Hamers' financial woes continued right through her rise to national and international prominence and on until her death. During the early phase of Hamer's political career, her immediate family subsisted mostly on charitable contributions from other family members, friends, and movement organizations, primarily SNCC. The family also received a little federal relief in the form of food stamps and goods from their local welfare office. In a 1963 letter to James Forman, Hamer asked for "one hundred and fifty dollars" because she had to have "a phone put in and something els [sic] important as I get 24.09 a week."[78] Since no one would hire the Hamers and Fannie Lou was not yet on SNCC's payroll at this point, the cash she referred to was probably part of their relief package.

On one occasion, however, Hamer absolutely denied receiving public assistance. In a 1969 interview with the *Amsterdam News,* she stated proudly:
"When we had hard times, we refused to go to the Welfare Dept. I would not
want my husband to have to leave the home and go through the agony of a
guilty conscience." This contradicts the recollections she shared later with John
Egerton, as he reports in *A Mind to Stay Here:* "and on top of all harassment
we didn't have to work. People brought us food, and we were finally able to
get commodities from the welfare office—the man literally threw it at us. Various people and programs met our everyday bills. And SNCC helped a lot."[79]

Perhaps what we have here is another instance of Hamer's crafting a pub-
lic/historic image for herself.[80] Excessive neediness had a dual and paradoxi-
cal function in Hamer's self-imaging. Most often it served her as an asset
whenever she emphasized themes of survival and triumph over destitution.
Need was the problem to be solved, the enemy that she conquered in her usual heroic way. However, whenever Hamer was busy stylizing a portrait of herself, it was important that her condition of need not be linked to the stigma
of nonindustriousness, which has been stereotypically associated with welfare
recipients. This would undercut her role as a celebrated symbol of strength and
hard work. These contradictory versions indicate that Hamer sometimes
masked the truth.

Whatever the impact, financial hardship or personal loss did little to deter
Fannie Lou Hamer from political activism. In fact, she welcomed the challenge
and used it as "fuel," particularly since the stakes included exercising the right
to vote—the key, she believed, to ending her suffering. She once declared,
"They take me from my husband and they take my home from me. But still,
at the next election, I will be there, voting just as much as white folks vote."[81]

By early 1963 Hamer expanded her activities to include a brief stint as a
teacher and supervisor of citizenship classes in a voter education program
administered by SCLC, while continuing to attend various leadership training and voter registration workshops throughout the South. Always mindful
of the plight of the poor, of whom she was clearly representative, Hamer also
worked at gathering the names of needy black families in her community for
a petition to obtain federal commodities.[82]

Although Hamer did a little work with SCLC, an adult-oriented group, she
preferred working alongside the young people in SNCC because they inspired
her the most. As she rose to become one of the organization's leading spokes-
persons, Hamer began traveling across the South, touching many audiences
with her dynamic speaking style and her impassioned descriptions of the tragic
plight of blacks in Mississippi. Her witty, anecdotal speeches combined with

her impromptu singing performances made her an effective fundraiser for the movement in Mississippi.[83] Hamer's main center of activity in the Delta was the SNCC field headquarters, Greenwood, Mississippi.[84] There she acquired a reputation for being hard working and deeply committed. Each and every day one could pass by a church and hear her singing and preaching about the need to join the movement. She was also widely respected for her knowledge of the Bible and her outspokenness. She often challenged pastors in their own churches, calling on them to address the immediate obstacles hampering black life and to embrace the movement in whatever way possible. According to the former SNCC activist and Greenwood native June Johnson, "See [laughter] you really ain't supposed to ask no preacher no questions in the middle of a sermon. But see Mrs. Hamer would get up and disrupt the sermon and want to know certain things that he didn't talk about in terms of how it related to our daily survival."[85]

By 1964 Greenwood had become a hotbed of civil rights activity in the Delta, and Hamer's role in this was certainly not lost on SNCC. As recorded in the minutes of a staff meeting in October, James Jones pointed out, "In G'wood, people are beginning to relate to each other, i.e., to Mrs. Hamer."[86] Greenwood citizens were becoming more active partly as a consequence of Hamer's presence and influence.

Whenever SNCC members addressed Fannie Lou Hamer, they never dreamed of calling her anything other than "Mrs. Hamer," an indication of their deep and abiding veneration. In turn, Hamer had the same admiration and respect for the "foot soldiers," as they were called because of the dangerous nature of their work.[87] She was attracted to their sincerity and to the uncompromising stands that the organization took on a variety of issues. Hamer was skeptical of traditional black leadership, particularly that of the clergy. She believed that they were too quick to "sell out." She often referred to the National Association for the Advancement of Color People (NAACP) as the "National Association for the Advancement of Certain People."[88] Clearly, Hamer and the young SNCC activists stood outside the circle of mainstream black leadership. From the vantage point of more-established activists, Hamer and SNCC represented political outsiders—a category of "other." For Hamer, it was her class that set her apart; for SNCC activists, it was their youth and radical brand of politics. Political style and substance notwithstanding, the mutual attraction between Hamer and SNCC radicals probably had something to do with their perceived status as "others."

SNCC was just where Hamer wanted to be. It was a grass-roots organization that never forgot about the people for whom it was fighting. SNCC's purpose was not to lead the people but to bring out and train the leadership already present in the community. Hamer was such a leader.[89] However, her emergence did not occur until a compatible organizational structure presented itself. Hamer had been a nominal member of the NAACP, which had been on the scene but failed to do the two things that SNCC accomplished: (1) organize and strengthen leadership already present, and (2) articulate realizable and immediate goals (for example, voter registration). Although it had a longtime interest in black suffrage, the NAACP conducted its main battles in the courtroom.[90] This strategy had little mass appeal and was relatively slow and very time-consuming. However, when SNCC hit the scene, it came with a plan of action that produced consequences that were noticeable and appreciated without much delay. Hence, the emergence of Hamer and other leaders of the movement was a matter of both historical circumstance and personal qualities.[91] The nascent civil rights crusade developed a context ripe for unprecedented social progress. As the struggle unfolded, it set the stage for a display of distinctive character and will by individuals soon to be called leaders. And in turn, the emergence of such leadership fueled the movement and kept it alive, generating more and more local leadership.

As Hamer's responsibility and authority increased, she continued to be a popular target for local law enforcement officials. In June 1963, Hamer was returning with seven others from a voter registration workshop in Charleston, South Carolina, when they were arrested in Winona, Mississippi, sixty miles east of Indianola. Hamer and other members of the group were taken to jail, where they were beaten into bloody pulps and detained for four days. Hamer survived to tell this story, and she would tell it repeatedly for the rest of her life.

three

Our big job now is to clean up the state's image, splattered by the rights workers. We'll now have to teach the younger Negroes the Democratic and Christian way of doing things.

—Mayor Charles Dorrough, Ruleville, Mississippi

Winona

In the spring of 1963, thirty-two-year-old Annelle Ponder, a coordinator in SCLC and assistant to Septima Clark on the Dorchester citizenship project in Georgia, came to Greenwood, Mississippi, to teach people about voter registration. Ponder usually worked closely with SNCC in the Delta and the organization was preparing Greenwood for her coming. Widely respected SNCC personalities known collectively as the Big Eight—Bob Moses, Sam Block, James Forman, Willie Peacock, Charles McLaurin, Lawrence Guyot, James Jones, and Lafayette Surney—were already present and holding nightly mass meetings before she arrived.[1]

On Monday, June 3, 1963, a group of Mississippi citizens who had been training with Ponder left Greenwood on a Greyhound bus. Their destination was Charleston, South Carolina, where they planned to conduct teacher-training classes for voter registration work. The civil rights activist Septima Clark had established a number of citizenship schools there that were very successful in teaching people how to pass literacy tests. The Mississippi group was going to learn how to handle this difficult part of the registration process. The group included John Brown, Bernard Washington, Euvester Simpson, June Johnson, Rosemary Freeman, James West, Annelle Ponder, and Fannie Lou Hamer.[2] Some members of the group decided that they would use the trip to test the Interstate Commerce Commission ban on segregated bus terminals.[3] They started in Greenwood, where they met with no significant reaction from white authorities.[4]

The real trouble began for the group in Columbus, Mississippi, during the return journey. Ironically, they had abandoned any plans to integrate bus terminals by the time they reached Columbus. Nevertheless, here the group met with the consequences of earlier actions. When it was time to change buses in Columbus and all of the black people were in line preparing to board the bus, the white driver approached them and started pushing the members of the group, knocking them to the ground. He then told all of the white passengers in line to come get in front of the blacks. As the black passengers were getting up from the ground, Hamer asked the bus driver his name while a few other members of the group took down his badge number.[5] This was one of the lessons they had learned in their leadership training workshops: get an identification of one's assailant and all other necessary information for one's immediate and long-term protection. The bus driver then forced them to sit in the back of the bus. As he was doing so, Hamer said that she was going to report him to the appropriate authorities. Speaking directly to the bus driver, Ponder also added, "You're violating our civil rights." To this the bus driver responded, "Niggers don't have no civil rights."[6]

After everyone was on board (with the civil rights workers in the back), the bus driver drove out of Columbus on Highway 82 and on to the next major layover, which was Winona, Mississippi. But before reaching Winona, the group noticed some very suspicious behavior on the part of the bus driver, which became the cause of great concern. At each little town where the driver made a scheduled stop, he disembarked and made a telephone call.[7]

After a few more suspicious stops, the bus finally pulled into Winona at around a quarter past eleven on Sunday morning, June 9. Since this would be their longest rest stop, five members of the group decided to go inside the terminal to get a hamburger and to use the restroom. Hamer remained on the bus. Those who got off noticed a highway patrolman, a police chief, and a local sheriff watching the terminal as a crowd of white civilians started gathering and staring at the bus. The group ignored this ominous scene and walked into the terminal, where they entered the cafe. Disregarding the custom of segregated seating, they sat down at the lunch counter and waited to be served. Accounts by June Johnson, Fannie Lou Hamer, and Annelle Ponder imply that members of their group actually went in for food, but that they also had social justice on their minds once they sat down. That is, they truly wanted to eat but were intent on getting nondiscriminatory, first-class service at the lunch counter.[8] Two waitresses behind the counter attempted to ignore the members' presence until finally Ponder and a few other riders got one waitress's attention and requested that she wait on them. She replied, "We don't serve niggers." The other waitress balled up her dishcloth and flung it against the wall behind her, sighing and exclaiming, "I can't take no more."[9] Sometimes remaining true to one's individual responsibility to uphold segregation was a disconcerting challenge for the people Jim Crow was intended to protect and privilege.

By this time the police chief and the highway patrolman had entered the cafe from the rear. They walked up to the members of the group, took out their billy clubs, and poked them in the sides, saying, "Naw, niggers eat on the other side. Y'all get out—get out." Ponder attempted to reason with the law enforcement officials by carefully explaining current civil rights laws, but to no avail. One lawman simply replied, "Ain't no damn law, you just get on out of here!"[10] The travelers walked outside the diner, where they continued talking among themselves for the next few minutes. Noticing all of the activity outside the terminal, Hamer left the bus and joined the others. Ponder told her that the police kicked them out of the cafe, to which Hamer said simply, "Well, Annelle, that's Mississippi for you" and returned to the bus to rest.[11] Ponder began considering a collective response. After continuing to talk with some of the other members about what they experienced inside, Ponder went back to the door of the cafe and peered inside to get a good look at the officers. When the officers noticed her looking in, she turned away and returned to the group.

Ponder then suggested that they begin collecting information to make a report on the officers. She started taking down the license number of one of the patrol cars. While she was doing this, a fat white man dressed in overalls rushed back into the bus station and apparently told the two law enforcement officials. The authorities responded with great fury. The patrolman and the chief of police rushed out of the restaurant, one of them declaring, "Y'all are under arrest—you are under arrest—get in that car, there!" The highway patrolman walked up to sixteen-year-old June Johnson, who was also copying down information, and said, "I'll teach you about messing with my car."[12]

Just as the police began rounding up members of the group to take them off to jail, Hamer jumped off the bus again. She asked the others in police custody if they wanted her (as well as the two other members of their delegation still aboard the bus) to go on back to Greenwood. Led by Ponder, all of the group members quickly replied yes. Before leaving South Carolina for Mississippi, the activists had agreed that whatever happened to one would happen to all, especially in the case of arrest. During the time that the bus driver had been making those suspicious stops in the small towns, the group members all reaffirmed their loyalty to one another. Urging Hamer to remain on the bus seemed to go against this agreement. Perhaps the arrested members thought it wise that the older Hamer and the two others return for help.

The thought of blacks standing up for their rights increased the ire of the police with each passing moment, moving them to respond with cruelty. Before Hamer could get back on the bus, the highway patrolman hollered, "Get that black son of a bitch, too! Bring her down in the other car."[13] As Hamer was bending over to get into the second patrol car, the Montgomery County sheriff, Earl Wayne Patridge, kicked her. En route to the jailhouse, the police officer and the sheriff cursed Hamer and asked her questions. Each time she attempted to respond the sheriff hollered, "Shut up!"[14] Two of the original members of the group were not taken off to jail, though the police were sure that they had gotten all of them. The two who returned to Greenwood immediately informed others of what had happened to their six coworkers.

When the activists arrived at the Montgomery County jail, "white folks appeared from everywhere with guns," according to June Johnson's account.[15] None of the officers told any of them why they were being taken into custody, commenting only, "Y'all raising hell all over the place."[16] At each step of the booking process, members were subjected to some degree of physical punishment. Young Euvester Simpson was punched and James West, the only man in the group, was given a swift kick, while an officer jumped on his feet.[17] The interrogation began with a flurry of questions evidently aimed at determining motive and responsibility. "Who is your leader?" "What are you doing [here]?" "Where are you coming from?" The process closed with a threatening statement from one of the interrogators: "We're going to teach you a lesson."[18]

After the general interrogation, the activists were taken to separate cells. As it turned out, they were separated so they could be subjected to individual beatings. Among the first to be taken off by herself was June Johnson, who was placed in a cell where she received what turned out to be the beating of her life. Just before it began, an officer asked her if she was a member of the NAACP, to which Johnson replied yes.[19] The teenager made an unsuccessful appeal to her tormentors as officers of the law by recounting the illegal behavior she witnessed at the cafe, such as the group's being refused service. In the cell with the others, Ponder overheard Johnson's futile efforts, to which one officer coldly replied, "What do you think we are supposed to do about that?" Johnson continued, "You all are supposed to protect us and take care of us."[20] Her faith in the law was slowly waning, but she made one last, futile appeal to whatever sense of fairness and duty the officers might have had.

After this, all Johnson's coworkers could hear in the adjacent room were "screams . . . and sounds of blows" for the next few minutes. A number of white men began striking her in the head and stomach, punctuating each delivery with statements like, "We're going to teach you how to say 'yes, sir' to a Mississippi white man."[21] Johnson began crying and screaming for help. Finally, the men began concentrating most of their blows to her head. In the end she was left with a sizable, permanent knot and a left eye that was irreparably damaged. The attackers then tore off most of her clothes: personal humiliation was just as much their objective as was physical injury and political intimidation. After the beating, the officers left Johnson alone for a time in her bloody and badly torn clothes. They returned and instructed her to get up from the bed immediately and strip in front of them. They insisted that she promptly wash her clothes, which according to Johnson, was an attempt "to get rid of the evidence" of her beating. They also demanded that she wash all of the blood off her body. The highway patrolman said that she had exactly five minutes "to get the blood washed up [off]."[22] They then ordered a jailer to mop up Johnson's blood from the floor. Johnson washed her badly torn dress, but she hid her bra, slip, and panties under the mattress so they would not ask for them. When Johnson's mother came to see her a day or so later, June slipped her the underclothes so that her mother could smuggle them out to keep for evidence. As June later put it, "[I] still had sense enough to keep some evidence."[23] Upon finishing with the young teenager, the officers threw her into a cell with her coworker Rosemary Freeman. As Johnson walked across the large jail room, passing by the cells of other women, the rest of the registration workers started crying as they scanned her bloodied face and tear-filled eyes. They were especially shocked by her badly damaged left eye, which appeared to be bulging from its socket, so much blood was gushing from it.[24]

Next, the Winona law enforcement officials turned to Annelle Ponder. They had warned Ponder, a Georgia native, that she was in line for punishment "because she was an out-of-state agitator and they were going to [also] teach her how to say 'yes, sir' to Mississippi white folks."[25] Ponder was taken away to the same cell where Johnson had been savaged and for a moment was forced to stand in the blood-stained spots that were still visible from Johnson's beating. There are some contradictory accounts of Ponder's experience in the jail. Some versions say that she remained in solitary confinement throughout the group's stay in jail while all the others shared cells.[26] The officers began the same process with Ponder, asking her questions while simultaneously delivering blows: "Can't you say yes suh, nigger? Can't you say yes suh, bitch?" One of her attackers added, "Y'all just stirring up . . . shit and making it stink. . . . Y'all were doing a demonstration." Ponder responded that they were not planning a demonstration at the time, that they only wanted something to eat.[27]

As Ponder was trying to talk, the men kept insisting that she reply by saying "yes, sir." "I want to hear you say, 'Yes, sir,' nigger," one of them demanded.[28] This symbol of their power was of great concern to the officers. When Ponder and the others first entered the jail house, a white man approached her and insisted that she defer to him, which she would not do. He was desperate to know if Ponder had enough respect for him to say "yes, sir" in response to his questions and demands. Ponder replied that she just did not know him well enough to do so.[29] During her beating, this officer and his accomplices continued to hound her about this lack of respect. Three officers and two civilians took turns haranguing her and beating her "with blackjacks, and a belt, fists, and open palms," including a blow delivered to her stomach by the highway patrolman standing nearby. The men repeatedly insisted that she say "yes, sir," and, as Ponder put it later, "that is the one thing I wouldn't say."[30] After ten minutes of being beaten and humiliated, Ponder was placed in a cell by herself. When she fell asleep, she was awakened and made to eat by jail officials, who addressed her as "You black African-looking son-of-a-bitch."[31] Throughout her stay, police officers kept insisting that she say "yes, sir" or "mister." At one point, Ponder asked why this was so important, but her question only resulted in more abuse. Later, after Ida Holland, a SNCC worker, managed to see Ponder on a visit to the jail, she reported back to the SNCC Greenwood field headquarters: "Annelle's face was swollen. . . . She could barely talk. She looked at me and was able to whisper one word: FREEDOM."[32]

After Ponder, officials turned to Fannie Lou Hamer. When Hamer arrived at the jail, she had been placed in a cell with her coworker Euvester Simpson. Immediately, Hamer began to hear hollering and screaming, noise that would remain in her memory forever: "And you know—that screamin' and all of that will always follow me—I will never forget it," she said.[33] After her beating, Ponder passed by Hamer and Simpson's cell, and Hamer noticed "her mouth was bleedin', and her hair was standin' up on her head," while her body was badly bruised and her clothing was torn to shreds from the waist down.[34] When the highway patrolman (whom Hamer later identified as John L. Basinger, from his nameplate) entered Hamer's cell, he asked about her origins and current residence. When Hamer told him she lived in Ruleville and that she had been born in Montgomery County, which was Winona's location, Basinger responded that he needed to verify the information and left the room momentarily.

Verifying her information took no effort on Basinger's part, since his fellow officers had already recognized Hamer by her name.[35]

Nonetheless, because it took him so long to return, Hamer was sure that he verified the information by calling Ruleville's mayor, the infamous Charles Dorrough. Once he did this, she was sure to be in trouble because of the local reputation she had developed as a voter registration worker. Her suspicions proved correct. Upon his return, Basinger announced, "You are from Ruleville alright. You bitch, we going to make you wish you was dead." He continued hitting her with a torrent of obscene names, names that Hamer said she "had never heard . . . called a human in my life . . . all kinds of curse words." Another officer finally ended the barrage of insults by calling her "fatso."[36]

Basinger directed the others to "take her in here," referring to a cell also known as "the bullpen." In that cell stood two young black male prisoners.[37] Along with these young men were the jailer and five officers, whom the victims later identified as Thomas J. Herrod Jr., the Winona police chief; William Surrell, a Winona policeman; John Basinger, a state highway patrolman; Earl Patridge, the Montgomery County sheriff; and Charles Perkins, a former state highway patrolman.[38] Basinger handed one of the black youths a long, wide blackjack, instructing him, "Take this." Apparently in disbelief, the prisoner asked, "This is what you want me to use?" Basinger quickly replied, adding a threat, "You damn right. If you don't you know what I'll do to you."[39] Hamer noticed that this young man was plagued by a badly swollen hip and thought he had already been beaten.

The prisoner then directed Hamer to lie down on a nearby cot, to which Hamer responded by unsuccessfully appealing to the young man's race conscience, "You mean you would do this to your own race?" Giving him little time to reconsider on the basis of Hamer's appeal, the patrolman quickly interjected, "You heard what I said." Hamer would live to tell the rest of this experience, and she would tell it over and over until the day she died.[40]

In an interview given three days after the incident, Hamer recalled that they made her lie "on the bed flat on my stomach, and that man beat me—that man beat me until he give out." She began screaming loudly, when another officer—"plainclothes fellow [Perkins], he didn't have on nothing like a uniform"—walked over and started beating Hamer on the back of her head. Alluding to the sexual aspects of the beating as well as to the man's racist thrill for violence, Hamer recalled that Perkins had gotten "so hot and worked up off" the beating that he could not resist joining in. He began swinging and beating a prostrate, defenseless Hamer. She was terrified. As Perkins and the others battered her head and various parts of her body, Hamer twisted and turned in a futile attempt to protect her polio-weakened left side. "I was trying to guard some of the licks," she remembered. She saw that her bruised and swollen hands were turning blue. Still, a modest and dignified middle-aged woman, Hamer fought to preserve some respectability through the horror and disgrace by holding down her dress. "Quite naturally, being beaten like that, my clothes come up, and I tried to pull them down, you know. It was just pitiful," she reflected. Her brutal assailants allowed her no such momentary release from shame, as "one of the other white fellows just taken my clothes and just snatched them up," said Hamer. As Perkins, the other officers, and the male prisoners continued assaulting Hamer, she continued screaming and writhing in pain, "working my feet 'cause I couldn't help it," she remembered. Perkins ordered one of the "Negro" prisoners to sit on Hamer's feet. The more she screamed, the harder they struck her. Again, she tried whatever she could to bear the torture: "I had to hug around the mattress to keep the sound from coming out." Finally, they stopped and took her back to her cell.[41]

During what Hamer would repeatedly refer to as "the mos' horrifying experience I have ever had in my life," everyone else in the jail could hear her screaming for mercy. It would be nine years before she revealed that one of the state patrolmen "pulled my dress over my head and tried to feel under my clothes in the room with all those men."[42] As the two black prisoners beat Hamer, the officers continued name-calling and taunting her. They derisively asked if she had seen Martin Luther King Jr. that day. The blows became so hard to bear that Hamer began wishing that the two men would strike that "one lick that could have ended [her] misery."[43] After the beating they attempted to force her to back to her cell, but Hamer said she felt "drunk" and could barely walk. In spite of her woozy condition, the jailer refused to believe that she could not stand up and move her legs under her own power. "Hell, you can walk," he snapped as Hamer kept drifting in and out of consciousness. As Hamer struggled to reach her cell, she collapsed before entering, in full view of her coworkers locked up in other cells.[44] The police simply opened up the cell and literally threw her inside, where Johnson said Hamer just "lay there cryin'. All night we could hear her cryin'."[45] Although this would be the only time that Hamer would be beaten, she would have to continue listening to her coworkers getting beaten the same way that night. Each time she would say to herself, "Oh, Lord, somebody else gettin' it, too."[46]

Hamer recalled the only kind gesture that she received from the whites throughout her detention: the jailer's wife and daughter gave the prisoners water whenever the jailer and the other men were not around. (Hamer also received two aspirins for her condition, perhaps from these same two sympathetic individuals.) Hamer thanked them, remarking, "Y'all is nice. You must be Christian people." The jailer's wife assured Hamer that she had done her best to try to live a Christian life. Hamer then instructed the woman to read two Bible verses, Proverbs 26:26 and Acts 7:26.[47] These passages addressed the question of concealing one's wrongdoing and the divinely sanctioned interaction among all human beings. Perhaps Hamer had hoped the women would pass these verses along to the jailer since the verses spoke directly to his cruel behavior as opposed to their good deeds. Hamer saw the women jot down the references, but she never saw them again.

The brutal beating had a devastating and permanent effect on Hamer's physical health. Some three days after the beating, she was still unable to lie on her face while asleep because it felt "hard as bone," as did her entire body, especially her fingers, which she could not bend. She was blinded in her left eye, and her kidneys were permanently damaged. The beating also exacerbated the limp that had plagued Hamer as a result of her childhood bout with polio. Hamer knew she could never really forget this experience if only because the physical reminders were all too prominent. "Every day of my life I pay with the misery of this beatin'," she once observed ruefully.[48] After her beating the police considered beating Hamer's cellmate, the teenaged Euvester Simpson, but there was concern that her bruises would provide unquestionable evidence since she was lighter in complexion than her coworkers.[49] The police were clearly concerned about being investigated, especially by federal authorities, and they did not want to leave any physical evidence of their wrongdoing.

Although unknown to the arrested members at the time, some civil rights workers had come down to the jail that day to inquire about their whereabouts and condition, only to be arrested themselves and subjected to the same degree of mental and physical torture. Among these was Lawrence Guyot, a twenty-three-year-old Mississippi native and Tougaloo College graduate who had built his own impressive record of activism. As Guyot introduced himself to the officers and made it known that he had come to post bond for the group, Sheriff Patridge immediately ordered him "to get out of Winona and stay gone." Just as Guyot was making his way out of the jail, Basinger knocked him down for the same offense as Ponder: failing to say "sir" to Patridge. Soon the others joined in beating Guyot inside the sheriff's office before locking him up in a cell.[50] Guyot's harrowing experience included being transported to nearby Carroll County where he was brutally beaten by a group from the Ku Klux Klan.[51] Afterward he was returned to Winona, where his coworkers were still being detained.

During Guyot's detention at the Winona jail, Hamer and others once caught a glimpse of him when Hamer convinced the jailer to leave open a large door because the heat had become unbearable inside what she later described as a "dungeon." Hamer was particularly disturbed by Guyot's appearance because he lacked his characteristic beaming grin. According to Hamer, "Guyot looked like he was in a bad shape and it was on my nerve, too, because that was the first time I had seen him . . . not smiling."[52] Later, the group would discover the reasons for Guyot's grim look. He had been "forcefully disrobed" before being beaten. But there was more. As Hamer put it in a 1968 interview, his sadistic assailants had also "taken a piece of paper and tried to burn Guyot's private off."[53] He was detained until some time after the larger group was released. When he was reunited with his fellow civil rights activists, the big bruises all across his face and body did more to describe his experiences than could mere words.

During the time the main door remained open, Hamer also overheard the police and jailers openly discuss the charges they needed to trump up for the group. The expectation of legal retaliation continued to weigh on their minds. In their discussion it was also quite clear that one or more of them felt that they had gone overboard in the beatings. According to Hamer, "I heard discussion: 'Now, what is we going to charge them with?' Somebody [else] said something. He said, 'Well, you are going to have to get up something better than that. Man, [this] is the end of the wire.'"[54]

After Sunday evening there were apparently no more beatings. On Monday night the members of the group were notified that their "trial" was to be held on the following day. On Tuesday, Hamer was personally escorted to "court" (an empty building) by one of her tormentors, who was making a halfhearted attempt to conceal his identity, indicating either his stupidity or his underestimation of Hamer. But Hamer was not in the least bit fooled, for this man had played a role in her beating that was etched in her memory. He was the one who pulled her dress up. According to Hamer, "He didn't know I had sense enough to know him."[55]

As with the jailer's wife and daughter, Hamer made an effort to engage him in a discussion about how God would judge his actions the day and night of the beatings. She asked him, "Do you ever think or wonder how you will feel when the time come you have to meet God?" He played ignorant, "Who you talking 'bout?" She shot back, "People who treated us like we was treated in jail." He denied that he was ever on duty that night. Hamer had another motive as well; she had the presence of mind to retrieve information on this man, just she had been trained to do in her voter registration leadership training.

She remembered, "So, I talked so nice, I actually chiseled him out of his name, you know. He was unaware of what I was trying to do, and I acted so dumb, you know, I would get to get their names, and they wouldn't be aware of what was happening."[56]

Significantly, Hamer was able to place the Winona events in perspective after a certain point during her detention. She saw the incident as a part of a much larger struggle, an unfolding civil rights battle in which she could fight back later, on her own terms and under different circumstances. Thus, she got her attacker to reveal his name with the intention of getting some justice, albeit delayed. But, in this regard, she was by no means exceptional. Such was the understanding and approach of many activists.

The trial itself proved to be sheer farce. Hamer and her friends had no legal representative and were just asked a barrage of questions. Wiley Branton, counsel in the 1957 school desegregation case in Little Rock, Arkansas, and director of the Voter Education Project, was supposed to represent the group, but he had spent most of the day and early evening on Monday trying to secure bail bonds. However, bond never materialized, a fact he did not learn until around ten o'clock Monday night. By this time, he could not make the necessary travel arrangements to be in court with the group on Tuesday morning.[57] In addition, there was no one who kept an official record of the court proceedings. Although the police tried to divide and conquer by circulating a rumor that some members of the group had pled guilty, all of the members entered not-guilty pleas. It was just a matter of minutes before they were all convicted of disorderly conduct and resisting arrest, for which each person was fined sixty-five and thirty-five dollars for the respective charges.[58] The officials had plans to release the badly beaten sixteen-year-old June Johnson to her mother, but she insisted that she wanted to wait until the others got out. She was determined to remain true to the vow she had taken with her coworkers: "what happened to one would happen to all." Late Tuesday night, the police held the group at gunpoint and forced them all to sign statements saying that they had beat each other and that the officers had done nothing to harm the badly injured prisoners.[59]

Meanwhile, the condition of the civil rights workers had quickly become the concern of a number of organizations, including SNCC, SCLC, and the NAACP. They had individual organizational as well as collective movement interests. Those arrested were members of the organizations, and their organizations felt an obligation to come to the aid of their members if they found themselves in danger, especially as a consequence of their civil rights work. But more important, those arrested were black citizens who had been taken into custody because of their race and political beliefs. This meant that Winona warranted a collective response. After Ponder failed to appear for a voter registration workshop in Jackson, Mississippi, on Monday, June 10, SCLC got involved. During a meeting on the proposed March on Washington, Andrew Young was slipped a message (some twelve hours after the workers had been taken into custody) that Ponder was being detained in Winona and that the situation did not look good.

On Tuesday, after the trial and apparently as a result of contact with the Justice Department made by Wiley Branton and Julian Bond, the SNCC communications director, the FBI came to the Winona jail and began taking pictures and talking to a few people, including Hamer, Guyot, and Ponder.[60] The Justice Department was planning to bring charges against the officers. But Ponder did not believe that the two FBI officials were really there to help; in fact, she noted that they appeared to be cooperating with the chief of police inside the jail.[61] Hamer shared Ponder's skepticism. An FBI agent came to talk with her, but Hamer found it difficult to trust him in light of the agency's previous unwillingness to investigate the Ruleville shootings after her first registration attempt. Wisely, she suspected friendly cooperation between the Justice Department and local officials, and she was cautious about keeping her silence: "You see, I didn't know whether if I said what had happened to me then he could tell the jailer, and I just couldn't do it—I just couldn't!" When they asked her what she planned to say at the officers' trial, Hamer refused to say. Instead she repeated her request to "get out of here now." She could not face another night in the "death cell." She reminded herself that "God is the only refuge we have because there wasn't nobody there from the Justice Department, nobody there to say nuthin'—just the Negro out by theirself." She wondered "how long will we have to keep on sheddin' blood and [getting] beat."[62]

Hamer and Ponder did not know that Julian Bond had sent a telegraph to Attorney General Robert F. Kennedy at the Justice Department on June 9, the day the workers were taken into custody. Subsequently, Bond sent letters to officials at the United States Commission on Civil Rights and to the Interstate Commerce Commission, asking for an investigation of the arrests.[63]

During the group's imprisonment, some of the local officers could barely hide their desire to get the group out of Winona before word reached the Justice Department. They proved unsuccessful at this and others continued to torture the group. On one occasion a couple of the women were in the bathroom taking showers when one of the prison trustees attempted to scald them by turning the water on as hot as possible. They immediately jumped out and hollered to their cellmates, "Don't get in!" Other abuse came in the form of verbal threats. One policeman threatened, "I can guarantee you these damn bars you won't walk out alive."[64] Hamer also overheard their detainers "plotting to kill the group and maybe throw their bodies in the Big Black River," where, she knew, scores of black bodies had mysteriously surfaced over the years. It looked as if authorities had such a plan in mind when they tried to let the group out, but the civil rights workers refused to leave, believing that law enforcement officials were just trying to establish a pretext for their disappearance and subsequent murder. Hamer believed that the police abandoned these plans thanks in part to the vehement protests of one seemingly sympathetic white male employee in the booking room: "At one time some of them in that booking room[,] . . . they wanted to kill us. . . . But it was one guy there, and I thank God that he was there, and he just rebelled against them killing us." Hamer refused to leave the jail, saying that they would have to "kill me in my cell."[65]

Throughout their detention, group members did whatever it took to keep themselves calm and sane. Sometimes this involved singing songs whose lyrics spoke to their immediate condition. June Johnson recalled Hamer singing "When Paul and Silas Were Bound in Jail."[66] For the most part, it was Hamer who kept the prisoners in good spirits. She drew on her extensive knowledge of the Bible, periodically reciting appropriate verses when it looked as if the group was about to lose faith that it would make it out alive. From time to time, group members tried rebelling in whatever way they could. This involved going on a hunger fast, which ended abruptly when one especially mean black male trustee reported them to jail authorities.[67]

After three days of detention, Hamer and the others were released from jail, thanks to the intensive efforts of many individuals in SNCC and SCLC, including Julian Bond, Dorothy Cotton, Frank Smith Jr., James Bevel, and Andrew Young. Sometime during the group's detention, news of the events at Winona also reached Martin Luther King Jr., who worked to determine the group's status and secure its release.[68] After the group's release, Hamer was immediately rushed to a nearby hospital in Greenwood, Mississippi. However, because her injuries were so severe she was taken to Atlanta for more extensive medical attention, paid for by SCLC. She eventually spent a few weeks there, convalescing with the assistance of movement friends. From Atlanta, she traveled to Washington, D.C., and New York. During this time, Hamer refused visits from her husband and family because she did not want them to see her "in such bad shape."[69] The only person who did get to see her before she healed completely was her sister Laura, who recalled being unable to recognize Hamer because "they had beat her so bad." In thinking about what her own re-action might have been, she thought, "I woulda stopped after that beating, but Fannie Lou just kept right on going. I woulda been scared they'da killed me. But Fannie Lou wasn't scared cause she just kept right on goin'."[70] She was not alone in reaching this conclusion. After the Winona events, many others saw in Hamer the distinctive sign of leadership, and among its central traits were courage and persistence.

On September 9, 1963, the Justice Department filed a suit against five of the officers, charging them with "seven counts of conspiracy to deprive [the] Negroes of their civil rights."[71] Earlier, on June 17, the Justice Department also had filed two other suits, one to overturn the convictions of the voter regis-tration workers and the other to prohibit local Mississippi officials from block-ing racial integration in bus terminals.[72]

Much like the trial of the Winona victims, however, the officers' trial—held in Oxford, Mississippi, site of the Northern District of the United States Court—was a joke. They were tried by an all-white, all-male jury, all of whom were from Mississippi. Repeatedly, Claude F. Clayton, the federal judge hear-ing the case, made little effort to conceal his bias, referring to Hamer and her coworkers as "niggers" and "agitators," while calling the officers "upstanding people" and "law-abiding citizens."[73] During the trial all of the victims were called to testify along with two FBI agents, one of whom showed photographs of some of the detainees. One agent even testified that he had seen the blood-stained clothing that young June Johnson managed to sneak out with the help of her mother. There was also testimony from the doctor who examined Ha-mer and Ponder and from the two black prisoners who were forced to beat the civil rights workers. Both prisoners claimed that they had been "'paid' a pint and a half of corn whiskey" for their contribution.[74] Nonetheless, all the officers were acquitted, prompting Hamer to remark: "I just wonder how many more times is America gonna turn its head and pretend nothin' is happenin'. I used to think the Justice Department was just what it said—justice. I asked one of those men, 'Have y'all got a Justice Department or a Injustice Department?'"[75]

Although Winona represented the most painful tragedy of Hamer's life, it would later serve her well in her efforts to attract attention to the plight of Afro-Mississippians. Nearly all of her many political speeches and public appeals after June 1963 contained a moving, vivid account of that horrifying night. The most notable was her presentation at the 1964 Democratic Party National Convention.

In public accounts, Hamer made sure to highlight the politically inspired racial motives behind the attack. But in private, Hamer (the granddaughter of a woman who stressed the special vulnerability of black women) could not help but speculate on the other very sensitive dimensions of the beating. Jacquelyn Dowd Hall has described the function of violence in the indiscriminate lynching of black men as "ritual [sexual] violence in service of racial control."[76] To be sure, Hamer readily acknowledged that the incident involved racial control, but in private Hamer pondered the degree to which her attackers might have experienced some degree of sexual gratification from the beatings. Among the many images that continued to stand out in her mind were the facial expressions of her white attackers, which she believed displayed pleasure that was sexual in nature. She attributed this to some form of "sexual deviance" on the part of her attackers.[77]

It is difficult to ignore the many sexual elements of the Winona beating: the repeated raising of Hamer's dress and the patrolmen's attempt to feel her body; the forced undressing of young June Johnson; and the egregious example of burning Guyot's penis. One set of questions concerning Winona deals with the meaning these violations held for Hamer's assailants, but there is another that focuses on Hamer herself.

Why weren't these incidents central to Hamer's public retellings of Winona? It is possible that Hamer just forgot these details since her public presentations were almost always delivered extemporaneously. But these do not seem to be the type of minor, insignificant details that come and go from memory. Perhaps it was a question of political serviceability. Hamer used the sacrifices and risks braved by activists like the Winona victims as examples of the extremes to which certain whites would go to prevent blacks from acquiring a political voice. But would not the sexual dimension be even more useful in this case? Perhaps Hamer felt a need to protect the families of the Winona prisoners, her own husband in particular. After all, her personal pain and humiliation were already enough to bear without having to consider that of her husband. Or perhaps Hamer was simply protecting herself against the pain of having to relive that memory and similar ones—the painful memories of a lifetime of sexual vulnerability and humiliation, including her own and that of her mother, her grandmother, and other black women from her childhood.[78] The concern for black women's image, specifically the commonly held negative stereotypes of black women's sexuality, probably had something to do with how Hamer publicly recounted Winona. Like other black women, especially those of her generation, Hamer was inclined to dissemble when it came to sex, race, and violence. Winona seems to be an obvious example of this, if only because Hamer related the incident over and over, using numerous details each time and giving the impression that she told all. But she did not. In any case, it is important to probe behind the fearless public figure to reach her private thoughts and feelings.

Upon her return to her native state, Hamer knew that conditions had gone from bad to worse for black Mississippians. The losses of life continued to mount. On the same evening of the Winona beating, Hamer later discovered, the NAACP field director Medgar Evers had been murdered on his doorstep by a sniper hidden in a nearby clump of bushes.[79] Though this saddened her, it also left her inspired to fight even harder. She returned to her political activities more energized than ever, rising with the sun and going out in the early hours of the morning to canvass among day laborers in the fields, and making evening rounds to small countryside churches where she sang and preached a message of hope to anyone who would listen about the power of the vote.[80]

For months, she tried unsuccessfully to work with the traditional Mississippi Democratic Party by offering to go to work on the precinct level. She had no luck at all. In many cases Hamer and her coworkers were locked out of precinct meetings or the meetings were moved to undisclosed locations without prior notification. Whenever she succeeded in getting into a meeting, economic reprisals were sure to follow. For example, when she attended one precinct meeting in Ruleville, her husband, recently hired on a new job, was fired the following day.[81] Soon Hamer and SNCC activists concluded that the only way to attack the tight Mississippi political machine was to establish a political party of their own. They did, and they named it the Mississippi Freedom Democratic Party (MFDP).

four

I have been so hungry stayin' at a white man's place, that when I did get somethin' to eat, I had to eat it gradually.

—A starving Mississippian, 1964

The best way to stop niggers from votin' is to visit them the night before the election.

—Theodore G. Bilbo, Mississippi senator, 1946

Local Need and Electoral Politics

After Winona, Hamer made repeated attempts to enter national politics. Electoral politics was a means to an end for Hamer. She believed that conscientious use of the vote could be an efficient and near-sure way to meet local needs. Although she valued the symbolic resistance that office seeking represented, ultimately she wanted nothing short of real change. The emphasis on office holding marked a new stage in her young activist career. In 1962 Hamer had envisioned voting as a way to remove wealthy, racist politicians from office. By 1964 she saw the vote not only as a way to depose Mississippi's old guard, but also as a means of installing herself and others as viable alternatives, despite their lack of experience. In issuing her personal challenge to Mississippi's established politicos, Hamer let it be known that the civil rights struggle was as much a battle for black equality as it was a fight to determine the future course of the state. Even though Hamer despised all that was brutal and unjust about Mississippi, she claimed it as "my state," as a birthright and as a product of her physical labor. This was the broader vision of social change that she and SNCC brought to the movement: more than making life better for black people, the civil rights struggle was to save America. While Hamer failed at all of her attempts to win elective office during her career, she did gain national recognition for herself and for her state, primarily because her passionate public presentations showed her to be an authentic representative of those who were seemingly most affected by American racism and poverty.

Ironically, becoming a national figure required that Hamer build a local following. During the first seven months of 1964, she strengthened her grass-roots support by directing a food and clothing drive, encouraging voter registration, running for political office, and serving as a spiritual force for what became known as the Mississippi Freedom Summer campaign of 1964. These contributions were important steps in Hamer's rise to national prominence. She acquired valuable organizing skill for large projects while undergoing on-the-job training in crisis management. In return she taught courage, resilience, and endurance through example. She consequently received unwavering support from her fellow Deltans and other activists. In addition, through it all, the racial inequities of her home state gradually received much-needed federal attention. All of these steps proved necessary before Hamer could play a role in the ill-fated challenge at the 1964 Democratic National Convention in Atlantic City, New Jersey, the event that ultimately gave her a place in history.

For Fannie Lou Hamer, the year 1964 proved to be as politically eventful as 1962 and 1963 were spiritually trying and physically life-threatening. It started with Hamer's local movement work. For COFO and especially SNCC, Hamer was that all-important local leader. She was a key contact person, a source of information on the community. In a January 1964 field report, an unidentified SNCC field secretary ordered someone to "contact Mrs. Hamer . . . and a lady that got fired from a school in Ruleville[.] tell mrs. Hamer and she will tell you the [name] of the other lady (mrs. Clark)."[1] Hamer's pivotal role as a civil rights movement "centerwoman" proved vital to SNCC's local activities.[2] Nowhere is this aspect of Hamer's leadership role more evident than in her food and clothing distribution efforts for SNCC through the Council of Federated Organizations (COFO).

In Mississippi, SNCC's civil rights movement contributions included more than voter registration efforts. There were many aspects to the organization's work, among them its food and clothing distribution to local poor folk. In the Mississippi Delta, Hamer played a central role in this little-known and rarely discussed aspect of movement activity. For Hamer, a movement had little meaning or relevance if it did not address the everyday needs of people. It made little sense to recruit the disfranchised to go into a courthouse and register to vote when they were worried about eating or having shoes to wear.

While most black Deltans were without any political say-so, they were also without the very basic necessities—food and clothing. In comparison to their white farming counterparts, blacks were clearly at a disadvantage. According to a 1964 United States Department of Agriculture report, black Deltan median income was $456 a year, as compared to $968 for whites in the Delta. Black Deltans were poor even in comparison to other blacks statewide. The average black Mississippi income was $606 and the white statewide average was more than three times as much, at $2,030.[3] Infant mortality figures also indicated a struggle for basic necessities. A black baby was twice as likely to die in infancy as was a white infant.[4] Housing conditions also reflected need. In 1965 over 90 percent of black homes in rural Mississippi had no flush toilet, bathtub, or shower.[5]

The practical side of need was hardly ever lost on Hamer. Early in the movement, she embraced a spiritually based political perspective that might be described as "moral pragmatism." The approach of moral pragmatism involved tending to whatever needed to be done wherever it needed to be done because this was only right. If there was a need in a community for food, clothing, or housing, the moral pragmatist in the civil rights movement directly addressed those needs alongside the task of tearing down the walls of Jim Crow. For moral pragmatists like Hamer, the most pressing community needs determined one's political agenda. Hamer addressed this need out of both community allegiance and Christian obligation. Moral pragmatism was politics according to exigent conditions and religious duty—nothing less, nothing more. With need as their guide, moral pragmatists kept their attention focused on conditions in their own communities; they were localistic in orientation. While moral pragmatists were not opposed to organizing around a national agenda, their pragmatism influenced them to take care of business at home first. That is, these activists tended to privilege local matters over a general, less sharply focused national set of goals and strategies. By this definition, the local/ rural scene was the center of attention for such activists, which often led to a clash of views with a more nationally focused leadership.

Beginning in 1964 Hamer's local activities included organizing and overseeing food and clothing distribution for Ruleville as well as surrounding Delta areas. Churches, civic clubs, and trade unions sent food and clothing from as far as New York and Boston. Other movement organizations (for instance, the Southern Conference Educational Fund in New Orleans) solicited donations through their own networks.[6] Sometimes Hamer's home was a terminus for items shipped from the North; donors sent packages to Hamer in care of other Ruleville residents. Sometimes shipments included as much as ten thousand to thirty thousand pounds of food.[7] This work was tiring and often disappointing. Sometimes crowds around a distribution site (usually a home in the neighborhood) grew as large as two hundred, and distributors often ran out of clothing before all needs were met. More than a few SNCC field reports contained messages from Hamer requesting more and more clothing.

While food and clothing distribution showed a genuine concern for destitute Mississippians, Hamer and SNCC also saw this as a way of mobilizing citizens for voter registration. In March 1964, the group known as Boston Friends of SNCC donated ten thousand pounds of food, among other necessities, and sixty people responded by going down to the county courthouse and attempting to register.[8] Shipments of food and voter registration were inextricably linked. The food, which was badly needed, attracted people, who, after hearing a Hamer speech, often felt heartened enough to attempt registration. Hamer's day-to-day field work was a meaningful example to her community. She managed to remain in daily contact with local people, even as she traveled far throughout her tenure in the movement.

At times Hamer had to be blunt about drawing the link between food and voter registration, and she found it necessary to confront her neighbors and peers. On one occasion, Hamer interrupted a freedom school session and demanded that the participants go to Indianola and register.[9] On another occasion, Hamer refused to give clothes and food to women who had lined up in her yard at seven o'clock in the morning to receive commodities. She chided them for being "a pack of them women [who] never even been once to Indianola to try and register to help themselves!"[10] She insisted that no one should receive assistance before one tried to help oneself. In her mind, it was only right and necessary that everyone attempt voter registration before receiving donations. Hamer reassured those women who feared losing their jobs or lives that the movement would take care of them, no matter the consequences. She told them it was important that blacks "keep pounding on that registrar's door." That morning she announced that "no food and no clothes was goin' to be distributed till all the cars come back from Indianola."[11] She borrowed a car and, with help from other drivers, drove the women to Indianola. Hamer made sure that thirty women registered that morning. A little after two o'clock that afternoon, they returned to Ruleville. In a spirited, impromptu speech, Hamer addressed a crowd gathered at her porch. She declared, "These thirty women know that the way we're goin' to change things here in the Delta, here in Mississippi, is by gettin' the vote. Folks up North want to help us free ourselves, and that's why they send these boxes." She then addressed the worries of those who feared near-certain economic reprisal. She had been there; their apprehensions were well founded. She reassured them, "Anybody who loses his job because he tries to register to vote is goin' to be helped."[12]

Hamer felt gratified and uplifted by the women's participation. She needed them and they needed her to achieve social change. Hamer certainly had enormous faith in the vote as an instrument of change, but in her front-porch speech she probably exaggerated the transformative potential of thirty new

Ruleville registrants. However, hyperbolic public appeals by movement activists were not uncommon. A great deal of community mobilizing depended on generating a euphoric sense of power and control over one's destiny.

Just as there were those who attempted registration at the prodding of Hamer, there also were those few who took the food and clothing and, for whatever reason, chose not to make the most of the "opportunity."[13] This small minority aside, most people were beginning to identify with Hamer and her work. While there may have been those who felt some kind of pressure or just obligation to Hamer (or northern donors) to attempt registration, others believed that the food and clothing represented the beginning of even better times and that they should take that additional step and attempt registration. Food and clothing distribution, accompanied by Hamer's message of encouragement, often raised dashed hopes and revived languid spirits.

Sometimes food and clothing distribution got out of hand, and local activists called in Hamer to calm disorder. Mediation was another of her many local leadership roles. On April 22, 1964, Ruleville's mayor instigated a "near mob scene" in Ruleville. A huge shipment of clothing had arrived from Illinois, and organizers stored it at the Irene and Earl Johnson residence, the main Ruleville distribution site. In an effort to undermine the process, Mayor Charles Dorrough announced on the radio where the shipment could be found. He encouraged community folk to go and take whatever they could get. Although organizers planned distribution for later that day, this unauthorized bulletin caught distributors off guard. That afternoon around fifty cars parked outside the Johnson residence, where a crowd of approximately two hundred people quickly formed and began "clamoring for the clothing." The Johnsons immediately called Hamer and asked what to do. Hamer called COFO headquarters in Jackson and officials instructed her to "go over and try to settle things."[14]

Upon her arrival Hamer began one of her patented speeches. Its rhetorical style and tone bore Hamer's unique signature. Her words were pointed and authoritative, as she waxed bold and indignant with the delivery of each sentence. Her objective was clear: restore order, recruit potential registrants, and reclaim what small semblance of self-determination her community had acquired through running its own "relief program." First she needed to set the record straight about the limits of Mayor Dorrough's authority. She told the crowd that the mayor had nothing to do with the operation, nor did he have the right to claim that he knew what was going on. Furthermore, he had no say-so over what black people could or could not do in general. Undaunted by a carload of whites that circled the Johnson house as she spoke, Hamer told the crowd not to be afraid of white people—not those in the car, not the mayor, nor anyone else. By the time she finished, she had effectively served notice that the food and clothing distribution program was not local white folks' business.

Hamer then seized the opportunity to make a pitch for a voter registration attempt. She noted that if the group went down to register to vote and was successful, then mayors like Dorrough would not be in business to create such disturbances and confusion among them. Finally, she addressed the immediate matter—the logistics of clothing distribution for that particular day. She instructed that the clothes be distributed in an "orderly fashion," and the work resumed without incident.[15]

Oftentimes Hamer's own family members relied on the food and clothing drives, for their circumstances were hardly any better than those of their neighbors. For Hamer, it felt good having her own needs met, and there appeared to be little shame in accepting donations. On other occasions, when the drive could not meet her personal needs, Hamer's slight disappointment was eased by the satisfaction she derived from making sure donations reached poor children. During one of her drives, Hamer observed, "The first long coat I ever had in my life came from the clothing drive. It's rather hard to find clothes for me because I wear a size 22½. But the clothing drive is most important for the children. There are children out of school because they have no clothes."[16]

Like her voter registration work, food and clothing distribution had its concomitant dangers. No matter where and how Hamer contributed to the movement, police harassment surely followed. On January 10, 1964, a local police officer approached Hamer and other volunteers. He inquired about the origin of the clothes, their employers, and who gave them "permission" to distribute. Hamer announced to the two officers that she worked for COFO. The officers then took one of the forms that recipients were required to sign and told Hamer that they would return soon.[17] At other times the harassment was anticipated and was suspected at the first sign of anything slightly out of the ordinary. In late June 1964, a field secretary reported, "Packages that have been coming to Mrs. Hamer's place seem to have been opened."[18]

The obsession with Hamer's political activism by law enforcement, plantation owners, and local politicians resulted in a new concern for Hamer by early 1964. While Hamer's 1962 and 1963 acts of resistance were perceived as individual effrontery that warranted individualized persecution, her post-1963 activities were greeted by white supremacists in Ruleville with a seemingly unparalleled urgency and thoroughness that targeted all who associated with

Hamer. This was largely because her sphere of influence was widening locally, presumably beyond realms ever imaginable to her detractors. It was not that her 1964 harassment was any less life-threatening in nature. It was just that by February 1964, not only was Hamer the target of relentless harassment, but those who associated with her were also coming under constant threat and informal surveillance by Mississippi authorities. In a very visible way, Hamer had become larger than her individual challenges and achievement. She was out and about in her community, making bold public appeals, distributing food and clothing, and registering disfranchised citizens. This was a far cry from her relative low-profile days following the first Indianola registration attempt and her subsequent eviction and retreat to Tallahatchie. By early 1964, she was on a conspicuous quest to persuade others to see what she saw in voting and officeholding: an end to injustice—freedom. She tried to make contagious her own burning desire for change. The measure of personal accomplishment for Hamer by this point was the degree to which her individual efforts and collective efforts became one and the same. Their racist assumptions of black inferiority notwithstanding, white supremacists in Ruleville could intuit enough to know that this only spelled trouble for their old way of life, and they responded accordingly.

This new phase of harassment of Hamer and her supporters was focused equally on the food and clothing campaign and Hamer's decision to run for the Second Congressional District House of Representatives seat held by Jamie Whitten in early 1964. Whitten was an influential congressman who had held office since 1941, when, in a special state election, he had been voted into office at the age of thirty-one. On March 19, 1964, the day before Hamer qualified to run against Whitten and launch her COFO-sponsored campaign, she received a threat from her old place of residence, the W. D. Marlow plantation, where she had worked as a timekeeper for eighteen years before her eviction in 1962. The threat was reported by a friend of Hamer's who still worked and resided on the plantation. The source of the threat was Marlow's wife, who felt it necessary to notify Hamer that death was imminent. According to Hamer's friend, Mrs. Marlow warned, "She [Hamer] thinks she's a big woman now, but she'll be killed."[19] On the day after Hamer received her qualification notice, Pap Hamer was fired from yet another job, at the local cotton mill.[20]

Also on March 19, Hamer encountered harassment in her own place of worship. During a mass meeting held at Williams Chapel in Ruleville, Mayor Charles Dorrough interrupted services with an unannounced visit. Some fifteen policemen, two reporters, and a police dog accompanied him. The local activist Charles McLaurin requested that the mayor wait until volunteers had taken up a collection. Ignoring McLaurin, Dorrough pointed out Hamer in the congregation and directed the reporters to take a picture of her. The mayor then exited the church immediately. McLaurin followed Dorrough outside to take his picture, but the mayor grabbed the camera and went back into the church. He told the congregation that no harm would be done to them if they did not try what McLaurin had attempted.[21]

Soon after Hamer qualified to run for office, the telephone company joined in the harassment. In a 1964 public hearing on the persecution of Mississippi citizens, Hamer spoke about this latest invasion of her privacy: "Not only have I been harassed by the police. I had a call from the telephone operator after I qualified to run as congresswoman. She told me, 'Fannie Lou, honey, you are having a lot of different callers on your telephone. I want to know do you have any outsiders in your house? You called somebody today in Texas. Who was you calling, and where are you going? You had a mighty big bill.'" Hamer reminded the operator that her bill was paid, which she implied was the only legitimate concern the phone company should have about her service. The operator repeated her warning about "outsiders," referring, of course, to out-of-state civil rights activists.[22]

Hamer's own response to harassment was to speak out and continue working—to stand her ground. Partly in recognition that violence was a fact of life for the Jim Crow South, and partly in stubborn refusal to display fear, Hamer often observed when questioned about living under the constant threat of death, "I've been in hell for 46 years; it doesn't make any difference"[23] On the possibility of death, Hamer declared that she was fully prepared to fall "five feet four inches forward in the fight for freedom."[24] Fairly or unfairly, Hamer expected the same persistence and boldness from others. Such was the nature of her response to the case of Maggie Spearman of Ruleville.

On February 29, 1964, Hamer came to the aid of Spearman who, like Hamer in 1962, was facing possible eviction if she did not return to the registrar's office and remove her name from the rolls. Spearman was forty-seven years old and the mother of six. She was a worker on a plantation owned by Sidra Livingston, who, upon hearing of her registration attempt, approached Spearman and told her he was "not going to have his people (workers) doing this." He warned her and others about "hanging around" Hamer because she was "nothing but a trouble maker."[25] Upon hearing about Spearman's situation, Hamer sought her out and asked that she not remove her name. She assured Spearman that in the event of eviction she would have a home at the Hamer residence. Spearman agreed, and Hamer then began making arrangements with SNCC to assist Spearman and her family.[26]

■ ■ ■

Hamer's first campaign bid for the Second District congressional seat was characterized by both a hectic pace and incessant violence and intimidation. The campaign was one of six run by local black leadership that, in part, grew out of SNCC's stouthearted voter registration activities in the deep South since 1961.[27] Hamer's decision to run was also the logical outgrowth of a longstanding personal desire to make change. Although she was soon to be disillusioned, Hamer initially believed that electoral politics could be made to work for black people if the process were inclusive, instead of exclusive. To open up the process, she believed that the disfranchised needed only to follow a formula that included lots of hard work, persistence, courage, and a healthy disrespect for injustice. This necessary but idealistic belief would be tested time and again throughout her public life and cause Hamer a great deal of dismay and bitterness by the end of her political career.

Hamer launched her campaign in early spring 1964. She had set her sights on an elective office soon after being notified that she was a registered voter back in January 1963. She announced her decision to run in a speech delivered on March 19, 1964, in Ruleville.[28] Two days later she was in Greenwood addressing a Freedom Day mass meeting. Between March 22 and April 28, Hamer traveled throughout much of the Delta, addressing rallies in Mound Bayou, Shelby, Cleveland, Charleston, Clarksdale, and Marks, Mississippi.[29] At a campaign meeting in Clarksdale on April 1, Hamer told a group of supporters that she wanted to "go to Washington to right the wrongs" committed by the twenty-three-year incumbent, Whitten. Her campaign slogan was "justice today for all Mississippians." In partial reference to her eviction and firing, Hamer also described her run for office as an attempt to regain "what belong[ed] to her." She exhorted all of her supporters to "help fight Jamie Whitten so we can bring democracy to this country."[30]

Not surprisingly, Hamer ran a campaign on a shoestring budget. There were none of the typical campaign paraphernalia of buttons and bumper stickers. Hamer ran for office on mass rally speeches, door-to-door campaigning, and occasional coffee parties. For this reason alone, the *Washington Post* gave little chance of winning to Hamer and Victoria Gray, another Mississippi activist running for a congressional seat in a nearby district. According to the *Post* columnist Sue Cronk, these women would achieve nothing beyond being the first black women ever to run for Congress from their respective districts.[31]

Although Hamer's campaign was run on a tight budget, there was one line item that was an absolute budgetary necessity. As a part of her funding, COFO included a ten-thousand-dollar harassment fund for Hamer's campaign. Based on its 1963 experiences with running black candidates in the Deep South (particularly Mississippi), COFO expected a high number of arrests and increased violence in response to Hamer's bid for public office. As it turned out, the fund was entirely necessary.[32] In a way, the amount of harassment was related to the local focus of SNCC and Hamer. In the Mississippi Delta, they organized in small towns that, individually, had little visibility or significance nationally. These small communities were run by state politicians and local officials who felt no accountability to a disfranchised black electorate or even to white voters who opposed white supremacy. Moreover, often in these small towns, those who were in charge of keeping law and order were the same ones who wreaked havoc on black communities involved in civil rights activities, leaving black citizens nowhere to turn for protection. Thus, along with a vicious racist climate, tyranny and social custom encouraged harassment and reprisals.

Members of Hamer's campaign staff were routinely taken into custody, subjected to abuse, and forced to defend themselves against trumped-up charges. Such was the fate of two young SNCC workers, George Greene and Julius Samstein, as reported in a letter from Julian Bond, SNCC's communications director, to Jamie Whitten, Hamer's opponent.[33] On Friday night, March 20, the two SNCC workers were pulled over by the police. Before taking the two into custody, one policeman struck Greene in the ribs and stomach with a pistol. Upon arriving at the jailhouse, the two were detained without being told of their alleged offense and without being allowed access to a telephone. Authorities fingerprinted them the following morning, and Mayor Dorrough informed them that they were being held as suspects in a number of burglaries that had occurred in the area. He added later that, while they were only suspects in these crimes, they were definitely being charged with "violating the town's curfew law." Greene, who was driving when the two were pulled over, faced the additional charge of "going through a stop sign," which Greene and Samstein denied ever existed. The two were released after paying a ten-dollar fine for their alleged infractions.[34]

Sometimes the harassment prompted by Hamer's bid resulted in mass arrests of voter registration workers, whose efforts were certainly necessary campaign work if Hamer was to have any real chance of winning. The intimidation that accompanied Hamer's campaign was part of a series of incidents associated primarily with SNCC's voter registration work since the organization's initial foray into the Delta. In another letter to Representative Whitten, the SNCC chairman, John Lewis, wrote that a March 31, 1964, Greenwood incident marked an intensification of harassment "since Mrs. Fannie Lou Hamer, a Negro, of Ruleville qualified to run against you in the June 2 primary."[35] In that event, fourteen voter registration workers were arrested as they protested against "the denial of the vote to Negroes." Referring to a United States Department of Justice suit against Greenwood and Leflore County officials that charged them with intimidation and interference with blacks wishing to vote, Lewis wrote that "the arrest of the 14 today compounds . . . further violation of . . . criminal statute [Title 18, Section 594 of the United States Code]." In his letter to Whitten, Lewis mentioned his appeal to President Lyndon Johnson and Attorney General Robert Kennedy "to make voter intimidation and interference with voter registration activity a federal crime."[36]

When the ballots for the Mississippi congressional primary were in and counted, Hamer had lost by a whopping margin, 35,218 to 621 votes. Of the six black candidates running statewide, Hamer received the least number of votes, while the other five (all of whom lost) each received at least 1,000 votes. This outcome is partly attributable to the nature of political repression in the Second District, an all-Delta, predominately rural and black district. It is also attributable to the dire state of political affairs for blacks throughout the entire state. In 1964 only 6.6 percent (25,000) of the state's more than 400,000 eligible black voters were registered.[37] For this reason, none of the candidates, including Hamer, thought they had a real chance of winning in this particular election. Nonetheless, many regarded their campaigns as opportunities to introduce to the state's electorate important political issues that were hitherto unraised, such as poverty, racial discrimination, violence, and disfranchisement. As for the entire nation, theirs were campaigns to expose the "unconstitutional denial of the vote to Mississippi's Negro and lower class whites."[38]

While there was never any expectation of victory, SNCC was pleased about the outcome, especially in light of the opposition's eleventh-hour efforts to ensure that Mississippi blacks would stay away from the polls. On the eve of the election, Federal U.S. District Court Judge Harold Cox had issued a restraining order in a last-ditch effort to circumvent a recently passed Senate bill that banned poll tax requirements in federal elections. Cox's restraining order targeted those election officials dispatched to enforce the bill.[39]

As for the larger meaning of Hamer's election, a few key SNCC members underscored Hamer's local influence as a powerful resource. Among the topics discussed in a SNCC meeting held June 9, 1964, were the significance of Hamer's campaign and the effectiveness of blacks in electoral politics, in particular the Democratic Party. Ivanhoe Donaldson opened the discussion. He asked, "Is it important to run a Mrs. Hamer in the political structure just to be part of the political machine? If we are working in a program which is completely controlled by those working against us what is the point of working within the Democratic Party? It is not a radical tool."[40]

Ruby Doris Smith Robinson, a SNCC administrative assistant and gifted logistician, then spoke to Hamer's special significance as a political candidate: "The candidacy of Mrs. Hamer has value in that she is able to articulate the grievances of Mississippi Negroes. This isn't necessarily true of Mrs. [Amelia] Boynton."[41] Replying to both Donaldson's and Robinson's observations, the revered Bob Moses reassured the others that the young Freedom Democratic Party and SNCC were in no "danger of being sucked into the Democratic Party." Among other reasons, Hamer's authenticity and mass appeal precluded this. He reminded them, "When Mrs. Hamer talks she speaks of her life. She concretizes abstract problems for her peers." He even advised about the emerging class tensions around her involvement. He said, "Note that Jackson Negroes are [embarrassed] that Mrs. Hamer is representing them—she is too much of a representative of the masses. Here the question of human dignity is crucial."[42]

In his customary way, Moses illuminated Hamer's growing importance to local civil rights developments, particularly the emergence of a grass-roots political party, soon to be called the Mississippi Freedom Democratic Party (MFDP). He perceptively located her appeal in her uncanny ability to give collective meaning to her individual struggles. Moreover, he recognized that her popularity was directly related to her ideological and organizational distance from middle-class, established leaders and politicians—that is, her status as "outsider" in relation to out-of-touch mainstream affairs and personalities. In his analysis of Hamer's candidacy, Moses implied that Hamer articulated a perspective and demonstrated a way of being, politically, that presumably safeguarded the Freedom Democrats from "being sucked into the Democratic Party." This was an important consideration for SNCC, which deemed the MFDP a precious component of its overall program in Mississippi. Moses, in his statement, outlined a role for Hamer that was crucial for SNCC's program, MFDP's success, and the liberation of everyday folks in the Delta.

This was probably a much larger role than even Hamer had in mind by spring 1964. In reality, this conferred responsibility was part expectation and part reality. Even the usually level-headed, reserved Bob Moses tended to blur the distinction between what Hamer was actually doing and the immensity of her mobilizing potential. The excitement that SNCC members felt about Hamer's candidacy caused them to define and encourage a role for Hamer that was being shaped as she lived it. It is equally telling that, in defining Hamer's character and political role, Ivanhoe Donaldson referred to "a Mrs. Hamer," as much an allusion to a character-type as it was a sign of respect. For some, Hamer was a category in addition to being a person. Oddly enough, as her charismatic personality was attracting attention, she was simultaneously being made invisible by the categorizing of her persona. This too was an acknowledgment of her powerful character and the degree to which the strength of the movement was measured and judged by the strength of its individual leaders, even for an organization that, in theory, was so vehemently opposed to dominant individual leaders.

The violence and threats of violence in the days following the June 2 election were intense and widespread. In spite of SNCC's commitment to nonviolent resistance, some members found it necessary to keep weapons in the office to protect the lives of those under threat—people like Hamer, Moses, and Aaron Henry, an NAACP activist and local pharmacist. In a June 10, 1964, report filed from the Second Congressional District in Mississippi, James Jones, Charlie Cobb, Charles McLaurin (Hamer's campaign manager and putative "right-hand man"), and Lawrence Guyot all spoke to the issue of weapons in the SNCC office.[43] Jones noted that the organization's concern for safety originated in March 1964: "On March 24 a cross was burned near the office and they received phone threats. The decision was made to protect the people around the office and to prevent people from breaking in and bombing it." According to Cobb, "Concerning guns in the office; they were there for two reasons: (1) people were breaking in for food and clothes. (2) whites are organizing in vigilante groups. A truckload of guns was stopped in Clinton, Illinois, and the feeling is that the truck was originally headed for Mississippi. Amizie [Amzie] Moore was told by a white that he, Mrs. Hamer, Moses, and Aaron Henry was slated to be killed." Charles McLaurin chimed in, "Throughout the second district people are arming themselves." Guyot then added: "Also, the sheriff rides around and asks people not to house summer project [workers] and tells them not to repeat the conversations to Mrs. Hamer."[44] Maintaining weapons for defensive purposes was not uncommon among SNCC workers and within households that sponsored SNCC field-workers and projects. Those devoted to nonviolent direct action understood that their political reality outweighed their stated political strategy. Carrying a gun could mean the difference between life and death in remote communities where protective law enforcement was virtually nonexistent for black citizens and where politically motivated hate crimes (sometimes perpetrated by law enforcement officials themselves) went unchecked.[45]

In late June 1964, the Ruleville community experienced a brief reign of terror when anti–civil rights forces delivered a disturbing message. On June 24, whites rode around the black community throwing bottles at homes and cars. At least seven of these incidents were reported to the local police, who never responded to any of the calls.[46] On June 25, at approximately two o'clock in the morning, someone hurled a Molotov cocktail at the steps of Ruleville's Williams Chapel, Hamer's church and a frequent site of mass meetings and voter registration classes. This prompted a few male activists with shotguns to rush over to Hamer's house to protect her. Hamer, of course, kept her own guns for moments like this. Fortunately for local movement participants and congregants, the damage was minimal, thanks to the quick response from a volunteer firefighting force of black citizens: two of the structure's steps at its front entrance were charred. Apparently, the culprit or culprits intended to blow up the entire building; investigators located eight bags of gasoline around the church.[47] The attack was the fourth of its kind in ten days throughout the state. In late July 1964, a rock was thrown through the car window of Hamer's brother, Joe Townsend. His crime: he too had participated in the movement by opening up his home to movement workers. And it probably did not help matters that he was Fannie Lou's sibling.[48]

While the violence at the end of spring in Mississippi had much to do with the black campaigns in the election, it was also due to the ambitious Mississippi Freedom Summer project, a season-long campaign of voter registration activity, community work, educational programs, and other efforts aimed at making life better for blacks in Mississippi. The summer of 1964 was arguably the most active and attention-getting summer of the civil rights movement.[49]

The most controversial aspect of the Freedom Summer plan was the decision to involve an estimated one thousand volunteers from the North, mainly students, a great many of whom were white.[50] The movement had considered their presence necessary to attract federal attention, especially against harassment. For so long, blacks had been victims of violence yet their experiences were not considered serious enough to warrant federal intervention. Reluctantly, the decision was made to include northern students in spite of the potential dangers, particularly as it concerned white women students and all the southern taboos associated with their presence among black men.

This latter issue had Hamer remarkably flustered at the beginning of Freedom Summer. Hamer's worry about the white women's participation dated back to the Freedom Summer training sessions in Oxford, Ohio, held in June. She wondered about the women's youth as well as their race. One day during that summer, Hamer observed a carload full of white female volunteers circling her neighborhood, and she grew irate. The message had already reached her from an old white associate in town: "Fannie Lou, the town is getting upset. There's going to be real trouble if those girls aren't careful." As she stood on her porch watching the women ride around the neighborhood, she told Pap, "They're goin' past the [Freedom Summer Community] center again . . . that's the third time those white women have passed this house in the last hour."[51]

Hamer was certainly not the only one disturbed by volunteers' irresponsible behavior. A number of individuals in SNCC, black and white, women and men, frequently noted in meetings (and later in personal remembrances) the problems caused by interracial mingling, especially between white women and black men. A few former activists and movement scholars still debate the extent to which this issue was more exaggeration than reality. In a southern context where perception nearly always equaled reality, this debate seems to miss the point. The mere appearance of "impropriety" was enough, and Hamer reacted strongly to this fact of Jim Crow life. She and others feared that clear violation of southern race-sex taboos was just begging for a violent reaction that would stifle the movement. In Hamer's case, elements of her family's sexual history probably spilled over into her understanding and appreciation of such danger. From her grandmother's experience, Hamer knew that the mixing of race and sex in the South was a recipe for many things dangerous and unpleasant. One day Hamer's worry and concern uncharacteristically got to be too much for her. In a conversation with Charles McLaurin, Hamer ranted, "Those cars out there cruisin' up and down, lookin' so hard, is full of women!"[52] She then went into a tirade:

> McLaurin, I spent a whole week with those girls in Ohio. I told them frankly what they had to expect. That just bein' in the Delta was goin' to be a red flag to the whites, let alone livin' here in the quarter [Ruleville's black section]. "When you ain't workin'," I'd say, "stay inside. Don't go wanderin' into town. It's askin' for trouble!" I told 'em and told 'em. "It ain't gonna be like home." They're good kids, and they seemed to understand. But they get down here and nobody's settin' their house on fire, so they act like they're visitin' their boyfriends on college week end [sic]!"[53]

Hamer was especially alarmed at the consequences that these women's behavior would have for black men in Ruleville and the outcome of the movement. "If some whites laid hands on one of those young girls, every Negro man in Ruleville would be in trouble. That kind of trouble kills people in Mississippi. And what would become of the Movement then?"[54] Hamer's special concern for black men reflected her realistic understanding of who was most endangered by interracial liaisons. It was acknowledgment of the racial/sexual hierarchy that determined blame and punishment in cases where sex/race taboos were violated. She knew that white southern men deemed women prized possessions that southern chivalry required them to honor and protect, particularly from the animalistic, rapacious sexual appetites of black men. Her family history told her that the opposite was not true of black female and white male liaisons. Conceivably, this too accounted for her anger.

After Winona, it usually took a great deal to rattle Hamer. Documents and oral histories detailing Hamer's participation in the movement rarely indicate an intense level of panic or nervousness on her part. Even though she exhibited the range of common human emotions from time to time, publicly she usually displayed only anger in extreme form, not worry or fear. Yet, her expressions of concern over white female involvement in Freedom Summer were rare displays of emotion. She watched the women's every move and grew incensed with each violation of taboos: "It's just as if I never said nothin' to them at Oxford! They sit out under trees in the back yard playin' cards with the Negro boys. Why, that back yard faces the hospital! Or they stand around in the front in groups, chattin' and laughin'! Some of them even wave at cars as they drive by! They cut through white property to get to town. And they go to town to buy curlers and cokes!"[55]

In exasperation, Hamer finally admitted to McLaurin that she was "worried sick." She was thoroughly convinced that "all of this [life in the American South] just [wasn't] real for them yet." In a fit of desperation she ended the conversation by declaring, "Then, if they can't obey the rules, call their mothers and tell them to send down their sons instead!"[56] Clearly, the naive conduct of some white women volunteers left her agitated as never before. Ironically, during Freedom Summer, race and sex—the deepest, most personal sources of Hamer's political passion—converged in a way that left her worn, worried, and doubtful, if only temporarily. Violation and injustice around racial and sexual matters usually had the impact of motivating and emboldening Hamer, even as they angered and pained her. But her Freedom Summer experience with some white women left Hamer wavering between disbelief and profound disquietude, and this was not simply in response to the behavior of a group of ingenuous young adults. As Hamer reacted to the women, she was also responding to the weighty and complex place of race and sex in her personal life history, as well as that for all of black Mississippi.

■ ■ ■

Throughout the Freedom Summer campaign, Hamer was a very busy individual; the time she spent at home was brief in comparison to the hours she logged on the road, as she traveled throughout the state and beyond, going as far as New York City and Chicago. She was the quintessential itinerant activist. Her extensive travel was almost always associated with the movement in Mississippi as she spoke to influential northern audiences with an eye toward securing donations.[57] In her public appearances, Hamer displayed a folksy style that was effective; it enthralled. What she symbolized was just as important as the message and the cause, which was true for most of her movement career. Fund raising was not easy work, but Hamer knew its value, and she knew that she had much to offer with her amazing gift of persuasion. But even with her profound commitment to serving the movement in this way, one cannot help but wonder if heavy dependence on her by SNCC and MFDP ever approached exploitation or objectification of her as the grass-roots prototype of deprivation and the will to be free. The evidence available does not indicate that she or anyone else ever felt she was misused or abused. After all, participation in the civil rights movement was voluntary. However, the excitement and enthusiasm that SNCC and MFDP felt about her leadership probably made it tempting to objectify her, as was the case with Ivanhoe Donaldson's categorization of her as "a Mrs. Hamer." The irony of Hamer's leadership was that her very personal, down-home style led some to impersonalize her as a type. Her powerful personal presence probably made it hard for people to see her as a regular human being with regular needs and foibles, like everyone else. This begs the question: did Hamer feel or notice this tendency toward impersonalization? If so, how did this make her feel about being a leader? The historical record reveals little about her subjectivity for this period of her life.

After her long days on the road, Hamer's many homecomings were often news in SNCC's publication the *Student Voice*, as well as a cause for celebration in her hometown of Ruleville. For example, in late July 1964, the paper wrote of one of Hamer's recent returns: "Thirty-three Ruleville Negroes celebrated the return of local leader Mrs. Fannie Lou Hamer from a month long speaking tour by going to the Sunflower County Courthouse to register July 21. All 33 were processed by the registrar."[58]

If there was ever any indication of the "official" response to the ambitious summer project, it was found in the many laws passed or given consideration by the Mississippi state legislature in the wake of the project's training sessions and initial activities. The legislation included a riot control statute that allowed various Mississippi cities to "pool personnel" and share jail space as needed. In addition the legislature passed a law to "boost the state highway patrol," which broadened the powers of the state police beyond traffic law enforcement matters and increased their numbers to 475 from 275. Along with the riot control and state highway patrol measures, the legislature also passed an ordinance that banned picketing in front of "all public buildings, streets and sidewalks and other places belonging to the city, county and state." Anyone violating this law was subject to a maximum penalty of five hundred dollars or a six-month jail term. Other laws passed included a curfew and a measure that forbade the distribution of boycott literature. Among laws considered were bans on freedom schools and community centers, key institutions for the Freedom Summer effort.[59]

Among Hamer's contributions to the movement in 1964, she exposed the ugly side of Mississippi society by calling national attention to her violent personal experiences. This too increased her appeal locally as well as nationally. Characteristically, she did this by offering her personal testimony in official hearings and investigations whenever the movement needed examples of how bad things really were. She seemed to do so without any evident concern for incurring the vicious reprisals that greeted those who simply refused to stay in their place. Almost as if she had never known the horrors of Winona, the Joe Pulliam lynching, or the poisoning of her family's animals—or perhaps because of these tragedies—Hamer eagerly testified about the dire nature of conditions in the Magnolia State whenever called upon after 1963.

On June 8, 1964, Fannie Lou Hamer participated in a public COFO-sponsored hearing held at the National Theater in Washington, D.C. She and twenty-four other Mississippians, including Elizabeth Allen, the wife of the slain federal witness Louis Allen, spoke to a panel of "prominent Americans" about increased violence and intimidation in Mississippi.[60] Panelists included Americans from a number of professions, including a psychiatrist, three writers, and two educators. The original slate included such notables as Lorraine Hansberry, Michael Harrington, and James Baldwin. The final panelists included Robert Coles, Noel Day, Paul Goodman, Joseph Heller, Murray Kempton, Judge Justine Polier, Gresham Sykes, and Harold Taylor. In his opening comments to the panel, the COFO program director, Bob Moses, noted, "The purpose of the meeting is to try to open to the country and the world some of the facts which we who work in Mississippi know only too well. They deal with some of the things which have happened to Negroes across the years and which, for one reason or another, have not been publicly aired and it is very difficult to get across to the country."[61] Among other purposes, the hearing was to make a case for federal protection for civil rights volunteers during the imminent Freedom Summer campaign. The panel issued its recommendations in a document entitled "Summary of Major Points in Testimony by Citizens of Mississippi." According to SNCC's communications director, Julian Bond, such

a hearing was conceived originally with a venue in Mississippi, not Washington, D.C., but the federal government (in the form of the U.S. Civil Rights
Commission) never had held such a forum in Mississippi and there were concerns about holding the hearing in that state.[62]

The hearing marked one of the first significant meetings of local and national interests during the Mississippi civil rights movement. Hamer and other
local activists used the occasion to air their political concerns and experiences
to a distinguished group of outsiders to Mississippi's "closed society." In doing so, they made a dramatic attempt to turn the national spotlight on their
pressing issues. For local activists, capturing national attention seemed to be
based on a rather simple, self-evident premise: Influential outsiders needed
only to hear about the political atrocities endured by honest, freedom-loving
citizens, and instantly they would be moved to help by deploying resources and
soliciting federal pressure. Almost from the outset, with the near-fatal experiences of Bob Moses when he attempted to register Mississippi citizens in Liberty and Amite Counties in 1961, it was apparent to activists that the battle to
enfranchise blacks could not be won without federal intervention. But they
knew that federal attention would not be forthcoming without local efforts.
From the earliest days, therefore, they had planned their local efforts always
with this larger objective in mind.[63] Moreover, recent history proved that reliance on federal intervention was simply necessary for black southerners. The
need for and effectiveness of federal help was demonstrated in the 1940s and
1950s through a series of court cases involving segregated colleges and grade
schools, and in cases involving segregated interstate and city transportation
and related facilities. Such reliance showed the understanding and appreciation of federalism on activists' part. By necessity, activists placed a great deal
of political faith in the role and duty of a higher, central government to which
states like Mississippi would have to answer. The three branches of the United States federal government constituted the last and only resort for those with
virtually no power or influence in their home municipalities.

In her testimony at the hearing, Hamer began with her first voter registration attempt in Indianola and her subsequent eviction. After summarizing
these two experiences and the shooting that occurred soon afterward, she
turned to the Winona experience, emphasizing all of its horrors in great detail, including the humiliating experience of having her dress raised and the
anguish of listening to her coworkers being beaten. This public recounting of
Winona marked one of Hamer's rare public attempts to work through the
private humiliation of the experience, ostensibly for the sake of the movement.
Undoubtedly, with the retelling came the reliving of the horror, which was

hardly an easy act for any of the Winona survivors. But the incident had an important double function. The routinizing of the Winona narrative was probably just as much political strategy (for the movement) as it was personal therapy for Hamer. More than any single incident associated with Hamer, Winona justified federal involvement in the realization of democracy in Mississippi. More important, Winona was a story that apparently Hamer needed to tell in order to live with the experience. One tape recording of her presentation indicates that she was crying as she recounted the event. Through the tears, Hamer spoke in a sad and helpless tone of voice, pausing periodically as she recalled each painful detail of her own beating. In spite of her pain (or maybe because of it), she forged ahead to the end of her story, concluding in the angry tone that typified her public manner.[64]

When asked if she wanted to add anything else to her statement, Hamer addressed Ruleville's curfew, the nighttime visit by Milam and Fleming, and harassment from the telephone company. For a brief moment, Hamer then referred back to the lingering physical disabilities resulting from Winona. She recalled how, on a trip in Boston, her chronic back pain led her friends to call in a doctor because the pain bothered her so. Hamer then went on to offer her forecast of what was to come during Mississippi Summer: "Well, I can say there will be a hot summer in Mississippi, and I don't mean the weather. Because the people are really getting prepared. They have been riding with the guns." Another measure of the increased "temperature" were the actions of her nemesis, Mayor Dorrough, who, she claimed, was going out to individual homes and warning residents about the coming of the civil rights workers, "because after they stay awhile, they would just beat [the residents] up." Reportedly, he also added regarding his visit, "Don't say nothing to old Fannie Lou Hamer about it."[65]

When Dr. Robert Coles, the research psychiatrist on the panel, asked Hamer about the legality of local curfews, she observed quite accurately, "As long as there is a white man says that a Negro violated, it is legal with them. . . . You just get arrested, a Negro, if you are out after 12 o'clock."[66]

Hamer's final statement to the panel was one of her first public statements on the forced sterilizations that rural women faced often: "One of the other things that happened in Sunflower County, the North Sunflower County Hospital, I would say about 6 out of the 10 Negro women that go to the hospital are sterilized with the tubes tied. They are getting up a law [that says] if a woman has an illegitimate baby and then a second one, they could draw time for 6 months or a $500 fine. What they didn't tell is that they are already doing these things, not only to single women but to married women."[67]

Hamer was referring to the controversial 1964 sterilization bill. It provided further evidence that racist politicians would stop at nothing to repress the civil rights movement. In addition to its immediate political purpose, the bill concerned Hamer because it was proof that Mississippi deemed black life worthless and dispensable. Some SNCC members referred to this as the genocide bill and argued that it was clearly aimed at black Mississippians in general and local civil rights participants in particular.[68] The timing of its introduction coincided perfectly with the spring campaign of MFDP candidates. If anyone could speak to the sterilization issue it was Hamer, herself a victim of forced sterilization in 1961.

Although Hamer was toward the end of her reproductive years in 1961, the sterilization still represented a loss. She lost not only her capacity to reproduce, but everything that it symbolized for women, especially black women living in a desperately poor, rural environment and possessing nothing that was truly theirs, save faith and their own bodies. Physically, she had been robbed of an important aspect of her creative capacity, and this must have affected her view of self, especially her gendered, sexual self. The impact of this found its way into her political thoughts. During the hearings Hamer raised this issue as if it were the last point on her mind, as if it were truly an afterthought. However, she may have raised it last because it was something that bothered her most out of all the other horrible experiences that typified her life. Nevertheless, it stands out amidst the rest of her testimony, for not everyone in the movement regarded sterilization as a political concern of their work in Mississippi. Clearly Hamer did, and she spoke about it.

Based on the testimony of Hamer and twenty-four other Mississippians, the panel concluded that there had been a serious travesty of justice in Mississippi. Voter registration attempts were often met with "massive resistance by white officials and citizens" in the form of "technical violations of court orders, threats through publication of registrants, economic reprisal, and violence." There was widespread police brutality directed at civil rights workers in particular, routinely resulting in "false arrest, high bail bonds, unjust fines, and persecution for complaining against violence done to them." These workers had no recourse in the FBI and Justice Department since both regularly "failed to provide protection or support the negro or white american in the struggle for civil rights."[69]

This panel of "citizens concerned with the increasing threat of violence and bloodshed in Mississippi" then appealed to President Lyndon B. Johnson "to prevent the deaths and brutality which are sure to come to Mississippi." The panel urged the president to "make a declaration of intention that the United

States Government will protect the rights and guarantee the personal safety of the people, Negro or white, residents or non-residents, in the State of Mississippi."[70] The panel closed its letter by making three specific requests that, in another form, soon became features of the landmark 1965 Voting Rights Act: (1) "assign a sufficient number of Federal marshals to protect the constitutional rights of the citizens of Mississippi"; (2) "instruct the Department of Justice to take the initiative in enforcing the provisions of the United States Constitution in the State of Mississippi"; and (3) hold hearings "by the Civil Rights Commission . . . at the earliest moment in Mississippi."[71]

Impelled by unabated harassment and state recalcitrance, Hamer and other activists let the momentum and attention from the unprecedented hearings carry them further into the national arena. Political strategy and necessity dictated that they continue their campaign of exposure and redress outside Mississippi's power structure. On June 19, 1964, Hamer filed a complaint in the United States District Court for the Northern District of Mississippi, Greenville Division. She was among three groups of plaintiffs: those who had run for elective office in the past; those individuals who were electors; and those individuals who had attempted to become electors but were not allowed to register. Hamer was listed as a plaintiff who had run for elective office through the Democratic Party.[72] The defendants in the case included state officials who served as members of the State Board of Elections: Governor Paul B. Johnson, Secretary of State Heber A. Ladner, and State Attorney General Joseph T. Patterson. Also defending were circuit clerks and registrars of voters from Mississippi's eighty-two counties. The complaint targeted three areas: (1) the system of unpledged electors for the presidency; (2) the discriminatory practice of determining black registration qualifications; and (3) the voiding of recent precinct elections that excluded blacks.[73]

In their suit, plaintiffs argued that after the 1954 *Brown* decision, there was "an arousal of interest in the rights of citizenship by the Negro people of Mississippi," and that "various members of the executive and legislative branches of government of the State of Mississippi . . . [had] entered into a conspiracy to bar and greatly limit any increase in Negro participation in the political life of Mississippi."[74] The suit noted the difficulties of trying to exercise the vote effectively when the laws governing the registering of political parties and the laws governing primary elections and general elections were, for all intents and purposes, decided by Democratic Party–controlled primary elections, in which all the electors were white. The law regarding political parties interfered with black voting activities because they did not allow for the creation of multiple parties using the words "Democratic Party." This law led to an injunction against those running on a slate or participating in activities sponsored by the Mississippi Freedom Democratic Party, created in the spring of 1964 for the purpose of bringing blacks into electoral politics.[75] In addition, Mississippi law enacted after 1963 provided that unpledged electors could appear on the general election ballot, which was not allowed according to a 1948 law.[76] A slate of unpledged electors, however, could prevent a Democratic presidential candidate from running for office in the state since the names of unpledged electors did not appear under the name of a political party. Thus, theoretically, the Mississippi Democratic Party could go on record as not supportive of the national party, while preventing any group of politically active individuals from forming a Democratic party of its own.

Another source of the conspiracy cited in the 1964 suit was voter registration law dating all the way back to the 1890 Mississippi Constitution and its amendments, which allowed clauses pertaining to literacy requirements, understanding of the law, and "good moral" character; the publication of names of registration applicants for two successive weeks; and the challenge to the moral character of an applicant by a qualified elector.[77] The plaintiffs argued that such legislation was enforced "in a discriminatory manner so as most effectively to deny to Negroes their right to register to vote."[78] In addition, the suit cited the intimidation of "Negroes seeking to register to vote, by arrests, assaults, threats, and continuous legal and extra-legal harassment . . . and of persons seeking to organize and assist the Negro people of Mississippi."[79] All of this, the suit charged, meant that in "approximately fifty per cent of the counties of Mississippi . . . sixty-nine per cent of the white population of voting age was registered to vote, while only one and one-tenth per cent of the Negro population of voting age was so registered."[80] Despite their sound arguments and extensive evidence, the plaintiffs saw their case dismissed with little indication that the situation would change.

On July 10, 1964, Hamer attached her name to another federal suit. This time the target was the state's white supremacy groups. The Jackson COFO office called Hamer, who was visiting family in Chicago, and requested that she be a plaintiff in the case. Hamer gladly agreed, saying that "if she could be used as a plaintiff eight times she would."[81] Along with Hamer and Robert Moses, the other plaintiffs in the suit included Dorie Ladner, a local activist, and Rita Schwerner, wife of Michael "Mickey" Schwerner, one of three missing summer volunteers eventually discovered murdered.[82] The suit asked that civil and voting rights workers in each of the state's eighty-two counties be protected by U.S. commissioners. Filed under an 1866 statute, the suit claimed that Mississippi whites under the auspices of such organizations as the Ku Klux Klan, the White Citizens Council, and Americans for the Preservation of the White Race, had a longstanding tradition of intimidation through "'illegal force, violence and terroristic acts.'"[83] On July 30, U.S. District Judge Sidney Mize dismissed the case as "'one of the worst scatterguns I've ever heard of.'" In part, he claimed that he dismissed the case because Moses, Hamer, and Schwerner failed to appear in court.[84]

What Hamer discovered through these defeats was that as activists broadened their local focus to include federal awareness and action, success was never a foregone conclusion. Obviously, a national civil rights effort for Mississippians entailed more than a shift in strategy or a change in venue, from a small rural southern state to a larger national jurisdiction. Such a transition also required perfecting the far more difficult process of linking the most immediate, daily, and personal experience of harsh racism to the highly impersonal and sometimes formidable institutions of United States law and politics. But sometimes not even this was enough. Hamer learned from her cases against state officials and white supremacists that drawing such a link was futile when those rendering a judgment were guardians of the same system from which activists sought relief. Such was evident when Sidney Mize threw out their case and when the same court dismissed their complaint against state officials for discriminatory voting practices. In both court cases, activists' attempts to gain federal exposure and action had little chance in a United States district court located in Mississippi. The outcome of the second case proved that the court and case were federal in name only.

But for Hamer and her coactivists these small defeats only defined more clearly the ultimate political challenge that they would need to make through their grass-roots organization, the Mississippi Freedom Democratic Party (MFDP). These defeats also provided the evidence for the case they soon made that summer before a stunned national audience at the 1964 Democratic National Convention: Mississippi was not a democratic society and only serious federal intervention would make it so. Some movement activists asked what more effective way to demonstrate this fact than by strategic use of those same structures and rules by which Afro-Mississippians had been excluded. Thus, a challenge was born to break up the lily-white state Democratic Party and replace it with "Freedom Democrats." In the process, the nation witnessed the emergence of what many movement outsiders assumed to be a new leader for the civil rights battle in the person of Fannie Lou Hamer. Little did they know that she had already built an impressive record of struggle in the hinterlands of the Mississippi Delta.

five   If those baboons walk onto the convention
floor, we walk out.

　　—Texas Governor John Connally to President
　　Lyndon Johnson

But we learned the hard way that even though
we had all the law and all the righteousness on
our side—that white man is not going to give
up his power to us.

　　—Fannie Lou Hamer

The National Stage

On April 26, 1964, nearly three hundred disfranchised Mississippians arrived
in Jackson to form the Mississippi Freedom Democratic Party, and among
them was Fannie Lou Hamer.[1] Almost immediately after its founding, the party
opened an office in Washington, D.C., from which Hamer and other representatives worked and traveled around the nation, speaking at forums and conventions about political and socioeconomic conditions in Mississippi. In
haunting, vivid detail, they described a decades-old repressive political state
that, through legal and extralegal means, kept blacks from voting. To the shock
of their audiences, they oftentimes identified the perpetuators of their exclusion as the same individuals responsible for upholding state and federal law.[2]
In many ways, Hamer's role in the MFDP was similar to her role in SNCC,
although now her travels took her beyond the South and to regions where she
had never been. In addition, this new national role led to greater exposure for
her powerful image, making her much more than simply a local icon. As a
consequence, her sense of her own influence must have grown in direct proportion.

Although well known and respected throughout the Mississippi Delta,
Hamer did not gain full national prominence until her memorable stand at
the Democratic National Convention in 1964. At this convention, the grass-
roots Freedom Democratic Party challenged the seating of the all-white Mississippi delegation. Fully active in the MFDP since its formation, Hamer was
elected vice-chairperson of the sixty-eight-member delegation that traveled
to the convention in Atlantic City, New Jersey.

Under the dynamic leadership of their storied woman representative, the Freedom Democrats turned the 1964 Democratic Convention into a political contest that occasioned both defeat and victory for Fannie Lou Hamer and the Mississippi movement. While she won increasing national support for the civil rights cause through the message she carried and delivered so eloquently, Hamer also came away from the convention thoroughly disabused of the idea that federal attention automatically led to liberty and justice for all. In going to Atlantic City that summer, Hamer had traveled a long distance in miles and in experience from the cotton fields of the Mississippi Delta. Her travels taught her a number of important lessons. Indeed, the 1964 Democratic Convention was a watershed moment for Hamer.

■ ■ ■

On Friday, August 21, 1964, most of the Freedom Democrats arrived in Atlantic City by bus—unlike other state delegations—and checked into the rundown, segregated Gem Motel. According to the MFDP chief counsel, Joseph Rauh, "You know that's terrible. We couldn't get them decent accommodations. God, it was hot in that motel."[3] The MFDP was trying to make the Democratic Party more inclusive, and, due both to finances and to the dogged persistence of Jim Crow in the North, the Freedom Democrats had to wage their struggle from a segregated base. Hamer, however, had flown to Atlantic City from New York City, where she had made a speech before the parents of Freedom Summer volunteers a few days before the convention. She joined the MFDP delegates on Saturday morning.[4]

As the MFDP delegates got off the bus in Atlantic City, they made a dynamic statement. Their attendance was its own challenge to convention nonbelievers who had all but dismissed the possibility that a meaningful contest would take place. There was nothing else particularly newsworthy about the convention; everyone predicted that the Democratic Party would nominate Lyndon B. Johnson for president. There was some uncertainty about whether Johnson would nominate Hubert H. Humphrey to be his running mate, but no big developments were expected. With such predictability concerning other matters, the MFDP presence attracted media attention. According to one MFDP staffer, Walter Tillow, "The TV people installed a direct line [to the hotel], all the TV and radio people." The *New York Times, Washington Post,* and *Chicago Tribune* covered the challenge story extensively.[5]

Unknown to the Freedom Democrats, the Johnson administration also kept a close watch on challenge developments. According to the presidential biographer Robert Dallek, Lyndon Johnson had an obsession with the MFDP that kept him "almost hysterical" about tracking the party's every move and spoken word during the convention. Indeed, Dallek argues that "White House pressure on the Credentials Committee not to side with MFDP was much more important in shaping the outcome of the conflict."[6] Johnson did not want any embarrassment, especially not from a walkout by white Southern delegates. To keep tabs on Freedom Democrats, Johnson initiated FBI involvement beginning in mid-July with background searches—"name-checks"—on MFDP delegates. Thirty FBI personnel—twenty-seven agents, two stenographers, and a radio operator—arrived in Atlantic City two days before the Freedom Democrats. FBI surveillance included the use of wiretaps and informants who attended all MFDP meetings. With the cooperation of the National Broadcasting Company, the television network covering the convention, some agents posed as journalists to obtain off-the-record information from Freedom Democrats.[7]

Early in the afternoon on the day of their arrival in Atlantic City, Freedom Party delegates held a rally at the Union Baptist Church, their headquarters for the eventful week. Rauh updated the Freedom Democrats on the challenge and briefed the press on behind-the-scenes developments. The Freedom Democrats were serious about the challenge, and they organized as if they had every intention of winning, although some were not as optimistic as others. Hamer had her doubts but was hopeful.[8] The challenge was more than a symbolic gesture for most of them. That morning, Freedom Democrats completed various tasks as they prepared for evening meetings with credentials committee delegates. One major task involved lobbying different delegations. The MFDP delegates went about this task in a systematic and efficient way. They used "information worksheets," on which they recorded assessments of each state's delegates and of the credentials committee members. Handwritten comments on the sheets noted the extent of a delegate's support: "strong"; "definite"; "sold us out." The party decided that most MFDP staff and volunteers would lobby their own delegates or others specifically assigned to them.[9] Hamer's first assignment was Verna Canson, an influential black member of the California delegation. She was also one of two California members of the credentials committee and one of seven black members.

On the following morning, Saturday, August 22, Fannie Lou Hamer and another MFDP leader, Annie Devine, along with a MFDP staff volunteer, Mendy Samstein, met Verna Canson for breakfast. They needed to know if the MFDP could still count on the California delegation support, which had been promised the week before the convention, as was the support of other states, including Oregon, Michigan, and New York. Through the support of the California Democratic Council, the liberal wing of the California Democratic Party, the California state delegates had already voted to seat the MFDP upon hearing of its formation. Canson was arguably the most prominent black convention delegate from California. Challenge supporters had identified her as a key member of the black "upper crust" and a favorite of Pat Brown, governor of California. Her husband was president of the Sacramento NAACP, and rumors had it he was in line for a federal judgeship.[10]

At the breakfast gathering, Devine and Hamer engaged Canson in a passionate discussion about their MFDP cause. They applied significant "moral pressure" on Canson, and in the end she came away moved by their appeal; she was left without any doubts about the legal and moral correctness of MFDP's case. She proved her support later that day during the credentials committee's hearing when she directed pointed questions at the regular Mississippi delegates. At one point, she even asked whether the delegation chairman was a former Klan member.[11] Canson's questioning did not go over well with some Democrats. Later, during the convention, Senator Hubert Humphrey and the Lyndon Johnson administrative staff put significant pressure on Canson by suggesting that her husband might not be considered for a federal judgeship. (Later that week Governor Pat Brown confirmed, indeed, that her husband was no longer in consideration.) She was torn; on one hand there was the moral issue of support for disfranchised Afro-Mississippians, and on the other there was her husband's aspirations. Eventually she ended up withdrawing her support.[12]

At two o'clock on Saturday afternoon, the MFDP and the "regulars" formally presented their cases to the 110-member credentials committee. The MFDP maintained that the lily-white delegation did not accurately represent the voice of the people of Mississippi. The Freedom Democrats claimed that only it remained true to the principles of the national Democratic Party. The all-white delegation denied black participation, opposed President Lyndon Johnson's domestic agenda, and supported Republican presidential candidate Barry Goldwater.[13] In contrast, the MFDP supported the incumbent president's policies and was open to all Mississippi residents of voting age. Thus, the MFDP concluded that the all-white delegation was not comprised of "true" loyal Democrats; instead, it was a party of traitors. Most significantly, the MFDP charged that the seating of the traditional delegation was illegal and unconstitutional because it excluded blacks. This was in violation of the Fourteenth Amendment.[14] To support its charges, the Freedom Democrats circulated four thousand to five thousand briefs to the credentials committee and other delegates. By contrast, the "regulars" presented around sixty briefs in response. Led by E. K. Collins, Mississippi state senator from Laurel, the regulars claimed that blacks had not been excluded. Moreover, they countered that the regulars deserved to be seated based on their past support of the Democratic Party. In defending the legitimacy of his delegation, Collins found it necessary to question the motives of the MFDP. He dismissed the Freedom delegation as being a group of "dissatisfied, power-hungry soreheads."[15]

The challengers' strategy focused on getting 10 percent of the credentials committee delegates (eleven votes) to file a report supporting the challenge. Once the report reached the floor of the convention, the MFDP would push for a roll call vote by getting the support of eight states, thereby preventing individual delegations from hiding behind a vote by acclamation.[16] The MFDP realized that there were four possible outcomes to its challenge: the traditional delegation could be seated; the MFDP delegation could be seated; both could be seated; or neither could be seated.[17]

That afternoon three national civil rights figures, SCLC's Martin Luther King Jr., CORE's James Farmer, and the NAACP's Roy Wilkins, all made statements on behalf of the Mississippi Freedom Democratic Party to the credentials committee. They were preceded by Rita Schwerner, widow of slain Freedom Summer volunteer Michael Schwerner. Representatives of the National Council of Churches also appeared and offered their support. At the end of the hearing, the MFDP counsel, Joseph Rauh, made the summation.[18]

The main feature of the day's testimony was Hamer's emotional recounting of the Winona jail beating. Walter Tillow described her presentation as the "clincher": "She spoke of her experiences, especially in Winona when she got beat up. . . . Half the committee being women, she had a tremendous impact. Lot of women were crying after she finished."[19] Hamer concluded her remarks by declaring: "If the Freedom Democratic Party is not seated now I question America. Is this America, the land of the free and the home of the brave, where we have to sleep with our telephones off of the hook because our lives be threatened daily, because we want to live as decent human beings in America?"[20] By the end of her allotted eight minutes, Hamer had exposed Mississippi for the sadistic brutality so characteristic of its treatment of blacks. Filled with emotion, Hamer wept. "I felt just like I was telling it from the mountain," she told a *Jet* reporter, Larry Still. "That's why I like that song 'Go Tell It on the Mountain.' I feel like I'm talking to the world."[21]

Although the television network hurriedly cut away from Hamer's testimony to cover a press conference that President Johnson called to lessen the impact of her statement, the MFDP received hundreds of telegrams in support of its efforts. After her testimony, the atmosphere among the Freedom Dem-

ocratic Party members was "jubilant," according to Arthur Waskow, another
MFDP supporter. Later, in a written account of the convention experience,
Waskow noted, "Fannie Lou Hamer was agreed to have been its star." Returning to the Gem Motel, the MFDP delegation was in fact upbeat in mood.[22] The
challengers' case appeared "very, very strong" to them and to a significant
number of delegates from other states. Hamer, however, was a bit peeved with
Rauh, whom she blamed for Johnson's ruse. But her irritation soon subsided
when someone watching the news called out that she had reached a television
audience.[23] A television news program aired her full testimony that evening.

After the first round of hearings, the Freedom Democrats began a discussion about what to do next; the consensus seemed to be that the Freedom Party
should make additional contact with individual delegates on the credentials
committee, but the idea proved unfeasible because of time constraints. During the course of conversation that evening, delegates discussed how to keep
the momentum going and how to use Martin Luther King Jr., who had recently
come to town in support of the cause. The Freedom Democratic Party delegates decided that King along with a credentials committee member and
MFDP supporter, Congressman Robert (Bob) Kastenmeier, a Democrat from
Wisconsin, should make a joint appeal to black and white credentials commit-
teepersons in an attempt to secure eleven signatures for a minority report.

On Sunday, August 23, the MFDP delegates caucused to debate a proposal
introduced by Oregon Congressman Al Ullman. After the MFDP rejected an
earlier Johnson offer that the MFDP be considered "honored guests" of the
convention, Ullman proposed that the MFDP be given two seats on the convention floor. Among those present at the meeting were Martin Luther King
Jr., Bob Kastenmeier, Bob Moses, Aaron Henry, Fannie Lou Hamer, Ed King,
Donna Moses (Bob Moses's wife), and representatives from the National Council of Churches. As the discussion carried on, Kastenmeier began inviting in
more members of the credentials committee. Included were Edith Green of
Oregon (the other leading MFDP supporter on the committee); Charles Diggs,
a black congressman from Michigan; and two well-positioned black women
delegates, Canson of California and Marjorie King of Washington state. After
some discussion, Congresswoman Green introduced the so-called Green Compromise, which proposed "that each individual on both Mississippi delegations
should be offered the chance to sign a loyalty oath, that any member of either
delegation who signed should be seated, all others rejected, and the total number of Mississippi votes split among all those who signed and were seated."[24]

Initially, the majority of the Freedom Democrats seemed in favor of this
compromise. But Fannie Lou Hamer, in an outburst of anguish, expressed her

disgust "with a Democratic Party [that] would even consider seating people who had helped participate in the sterilization of women in Mississippi." This was the second time that Hamer had raised the sterilization issue in a semi-public gathering.[25] In her usual clever way, she seized this particular moment to vent genuine rage as well as to regain the political and moral upper hand in the discussion. Later, as it became increasingly apparent that the MFDP would have to concede something, Hamer agreed to support the Green Compromise. At the heart of her initial rejection of the compromise was the unfairness of the entire affair. She was appalled at the thought of accommodating an all-white delegation that had been chosen illegally and at the exclusion of a huge segment of the Mississippi population. Participants agreed that the Green resolution was worthy of consideration, even though the Freedom Party's full demands were still on the table.

When she was not in group meetings, Fannie Lou Hamer spent much of that Sunday lobbying and making sure that everyone understood the issues— as did Moses, Devine, and a few other COFO and MFDP staffers.[26] Of the crucial meetings that took place that Sunday, one occurred at Martin Luther King Jr.'s suite, where individuals gradually arrived for brunch.[27] Kastenmeier arrived on time but, after waiting a moment, decided to leave. He authorized Edith Green to speak on his behalf. Other members of the credentials committee appeared later. Ed King, Roy Wilkins, and James Farmer were there, as were some individuals from the National Council of Churches.[28] Hamer, Moses, and Ella Baker, however, were still at their headquarters at Union Baptist Church, where the Freedom Democrats had met earlier that Sunday morning in preparation for a rally.

As he waited for the meeting to begin officially, Arthur Waskow had an interesting conversation with Wilkins about the history of the NAACP and the need to have its records microfilmed and distributed to university libraries and historians. Wilkins remarked that this was a good idea, "since the NAACP had not gotten enough credit for the way they carried the Civil Rights fight for the last fifty years, and making this material available to historians would make it much more likely that there would be public understanding of the NAACP's role."[29] This conversation foreshadowed the conflict that Wilkins would have later with Hamer and other Freedom Democrats around what he perceived to be their lack of respect for the NAACP.

Eventually, Rauh and Diggs showed up at King's suite and informal discussion began. The reason for the gathering was to determine what the Freedom Party was willing to give up and what it was willing to accept. Some of the time was spent deciding which individuals to target for lobbying.[30] By this time,

Edith Green had reintroduced her compromise proposal and reported that the Freedom Party had considerably more than the eleven signatures for a roll call vote. However, when pressed by Rauh and Diggs to name these supporters, she declined, perhaps to protect her backers from being lobbied by those favorable to the Johnson compromise.[31] Nevertheless, it was clear to the MFDP at this point that members of the Johnson camp were getting worried. Their official offer on the table was still "that of fraternal seats for the Freedom Party, plus perhaps a few items like the right to read from the platform before the Convention." At a moment of seeming impasse between the Johnson and MFDP supporters, tempers flared. At one point in the discussion on this offer, Diggs indicated that it seemed like a "good deal," to which Edith Green snapped, "if it were a matter of women's rights [I] could never conceive of accepting such a meaningless gesture."[32]

Finally, word reached Bob Moses at the rally to send some Freedom Democrats to the meeting in King's suite so that the MFDP would be represented. Moses replied that he could not go because he still had not yet spoken at the rally. Instead, Hamer, Baker, and Henry left the rally, along with other activists, Hartman Turnbow, Victoria Gray, and Annie Devine.[33] They all then directed other members of the party not to go into individual meetings with the credentials committee delegates in order not to "frighten them politically." Although King's suite was filled to capacity, the MFDP leadership insisted that the other delegates join in by standing outside and listening from the hallway through an open doorway. Hamer and others asserted that all of their delegates had a "right to participate in crucial decisions." For Hamer, mass or collective participation meant simply that: everyone would join in the important decision-making process, no matter how large the group. Feasibility and protocol took a back seat to pure democratic procedure in Hamer's mind and practice. Hamer and the MFDP had come too far and been excluded too long to yield at this particular moment to the custom of representative leadership and decision making. After the MFDP delegates arrived, discussion resumed, but no major decision was reached before adjournment.

That Sunday night the MFDP delegates returned to Union Baptist Church, where they met with their supporters. Afterward Hamer and others went to the boardwalk outside the convention hall, where SNCC and CORE held a vigil throughout the four-day affair. While there, Hamer assumed her usual role of keeping everyone's spirits up.[34]

On Monday, the convention opened with both Mississippi delegations seated in the gallery—a temporary solution. The day before, credentials committee chair David Lawrence had postponed making a report to the convention until Tuesday evening.[35] Also, around mid-morning that Monday, another meeting was held among MFDP leaders and their supporters, credentials committee members, and some national civil rights figures. It took place at the Johnson command post at the Pageant Motel, next door to the convention hall.[36] Many of those attending had participated in the Sunday meeting: Aaron Henry, Ed King, Joseph Rauh, Martin Luther King Jr., Moses, Hamer, Bill Higgs, Green, and Kastenmeier. The only newcomer was Senator Hubert Humphrey, who had called the meeting. If the MFDP delegation needed any further evidence that the Johnson supporters were taking their challenge seriously and becoming alarmed, Humphrey's presence provided it.

During this nearly three-hour meeting, the Freedom Democrats made it clear that they would accept no less than the Green proposal, which was already somewhat of a retreat on the MFDP's part since the Green offer was itself a compromise—one that was far less radical than the MFDP's original demand to be seated unconditionally. During the meeting Moses reminded others that "only Negroes could speak for Negroes in Mississippi," to which Humphrey responded, "that meant only Russians could speak for Russians, French for Frenchmen." He turned to King and added, "Now you can throw your book away." After Rauh got up to speak, Ella Baker responded by adding (according to Rauh's interview), "I don't care about people getting $20,000 a year judgeships"—referring to Verna Canson—"And [I] don't care about some professor losing his job. I don't care about traitors like Humphrey deserting their liberal trend."[37]

As her colleagues Baker and Moses castigated those in favor of additional compromise, charging them with indulging in political self-interest, Hamer again took the moral highroad, this time by invoking religion and God. She singled out an equivocating Humphrey, whom she later described as sitting there with "big crocodile tears in his eyes": "Senator Humphrey, I been praying about you; and I been thinking about you, and you're a good man, and you know what's right. The trouble is you're afraid to do what you know is right. You just want this job, and I know a lot of people have lost their jobs, and God will take care of you, even if you lose this job. But Humphrey, if you take this job, you won't be worth anything. Mr. Humphrey, I'm going to pray for you again."[38] Just as Humphrey had started crying, so did Hamer.

Baker and Hamer were not the only ones moved to anger and disgust by Humphrey's condescension. Earlier Green had stormed out of the meeting when Humphrey remarked, "Well, I don't see what all the people from the Credentials Committee are doing here anyway."[39] Waskow described the meeting at the Pageant Motel as "evidently a most upsetting occasion. Moses came down from it looking like death itself. The minority [the MFDP and its supporters] had proved far stronger, far more numerous, and far more tough minded than the Administration or the Liberal Establishment had expected. . . . In other words, our strength had forced another delay."[40] Significantly, this meeting involved a major confrontation among white liberals, national civil rights leaders, and the Freedom Democrats.

At seven that Monday night the Freedom Democrats held a spirited rally along the boardwalk to show the strength of its support from other state delegations and individual backers who showed up just for the historic occasion. Led by Hamer's singing and spontaneous appeals for support, over three thousand people participated. Waskow noted, "It was exciting, it was heartlifting, and the general jubilation was reinforced."[41] Up to this point the MFDP delegation still had the full support of Martin Luther King Jr., who, nursing a sprained ankle, stood on the boardwalk encouraging delegates to "seat the Freedom Democrats."[42] When the convention session ended that night, the Freedom Party and its supporters had completed extensive lobbying, and the mood of optimism had returned. For the most part, everyone expected a floor fight on Tuesday resulting in a roll call vote that the MFDP would win.[43]

Tuesday morning started with another MFDP caucus at its church headquarters. A hasty meeting was called for the Freedom Party delegation and staff. The discussion topic was the latest Johnson proposal, "two seats for two designated people, Aaron Henry and Ed King," and the two at-large seats that would have no ties to the "regular" Mississippi delegation. Moses was present and he was trying to get the MFDP delegation to decide on the least that could be agreed to. Hamer, Baker, and Rauh were also in attendance.[44]

Although most accounts of Hamer's participation in the convention depict her as resolute and confident about not compromising, this moment was actually not an easy one for her. She found herself indecisive. In fact, she even later described her mood as "desperate." During the course of discussion, she went over to Bob Moses and asked, "What in the world should we do?" She added, "I believe it's wrong for us to accept a compromise. I really believe it's wrong. But do you think we ought to accept?" Moses pointed out that since this was going to affect the people in Mississippi directly, it would only be right that the MFDP delegates come to a decision on their own. Slowly reclaiming her assurance of the correctness of her original position, Hamer replied, "Then I'm going to make it even if it is wrong. I know that [two-seat compromise] don't mean nothing to me."[45] She rejoined the rest of the delegation, and finally they all agreed that the Green proposal was acceptable, but not the Lyndon

Johnson compromise. The MFDP and the SNCC staff found this "back of the bus offer" to be too much of an insult.[46]

On this Tuesday the credentials committee went into a closed executive meeting. Rauh attended the session alone. The committee continued forcing the two-seat compromise. Rauh hesitated and fought for an adjournment so that he could consult with the full delegation. He failed. After the meeting, according to Rauh, the head of the subcommittee rushed up to the first media person in sight and announced, "Here is the majority report. The MFDP accepts it." Rauh was then confronted by a reporter, to whom he responded, "I haven't consulted with the MFDP yet."[47] Rauh later charged that the subcommittee chair had lied. However, the damage had been done, as far as Hamer and the other delegates were concerned. News reports announced that a compromise had been reached. MFDP delegates suspected that Rauh had disobeyed party orders and entered into a deal with the committee that favored his close friend Hubert Humphrey and the rest of the Lyndon Johnson camp. This proved to be the incident that precipitated the eventual rupture between Rauh and a hardline, Hamer-influenced Freedom Democrats faction, which held a majority in the MFDP.

Another meeting took place at the Pageant Motel as Rauh met the credentials committee. Present were Bob Moses, Aaron Henry, Ed King, Bayard Rustin, Martin Luther King Jr., Walter Reuther, and Hubert Humphrey. By most accounts, this closed executive meeting proved to be a no-holds-barred affair that resulted in white liberals and national civil rights leadership agreeing to push full-speed ahead in getting the MFDP to accept the administration's compromise. This was the memorable meeting from which Fannie Lou Hamer was excluded, and for that reason it became well publicized and regarded as nefarious in MFDP circles, despite the presence of Bob Moses.[48] According to Tillow, "The day before, they had Mrs. Hamer in that meeting, and she must have given them hell . . . so they cut her out."[49] Those present returned to consideration of the compromise. When Bayard Rustin asked whether the two-vote compromise might include Hamer for seating, Humphrey added, "The President will not allow that illiterate woman to speak from the floor of the convention."[50]

The entire meeting was devoid of any talk of abstract notions of wrong or right regarding the challenge. The tone and content of discussion grew decidedly political: mincing few words, participants spoke of who was beholden to whom. This was especially true of conversations that the United Auto Workers president Walter Reuther had with Martin Luther King Jr. and Joseph Rauh.

Reportedly, during the course of the meeting, Reuther reminded King that "the labor movement gave King and SCLC $176,000, and they won't give them any more if they [won't] go along." Later, Bob Moses said that Reuther remarked, "Joe Rauh works for me, and he's not going to sign any minority report."[51] Eventually Moses left this meeting before it adjourned.

The Freedom Democrats' suspicion regarding Rauh's role in creating the compromise continued to grow. Furthermore, MFDP leadership concluded that, based on what the party instructed Rauh to do before going into the closed meeting, he should have immediately rejected any and all other compromises presented to him up to that point. Many MFDP delegates concluded that Rauh had been presented this compromise by Humphrey, Reuther, the general "liberal establishment," and the Lyndon Johnson administration in order to get the Freedom Party to accept it. Also enlisted in this compromise effort were Martin Luther King Jr., Farmer, Bayard Rustin, and the MFDP chairman, Aaron Henry. The feeling was that, without question, Rauh and Henry had betrayed the delegation.[52]

At around six that evening, the MFDP delegation caucused at the church and pressed its leadership for official rejection of this new compromise. Edith Green joined the MFDP representatives in being upset; she thought she had been lied to, partly by the MFDP because of Rauh's public blunder, and certainly by the credentials committee itself. Also attending this meeting were the credentials committee supporters and others, including Verna Canson, who were now saying that they could not sign a stronger minority report. Even Martin Luther King Jr. was now suggesting that the Johnson proposal was perhaps the best that the MFDP could get.

By this point the Freedom Party members felt angry and betrayed. Fannie Lou Hamer summed up the group's mood when she observed that "the offer of two votes for two named people was exactly the kind of offer that might be expected from Southern whites, and was exactly the reason the Freedom Party was fighting for justice in Mississippi, and therefore [it] was totally unacceptable."[53] Waskow described the mood as one of "enormous bitterness, obviously resulting from deeply disappointed hopes that the Freedom Party had been about to win when the issue went to the floor." According to Waskow this bitterness was directed at "liberals, Democrats, and the regular political system."[54] As an MFDP delegate, Annie Devine called for a vote, which was taken by a show of hands and resulted in an immediate rejection of the Johnson compromise.[55] The delegation reiterated that it would accept no less than the Green proposal. The MFDP had reason to believe that it would still win a floor fight, if it could just get the opportunity. It continued getting tremendous support from the American public in the many telegrams it received.[56] Also, at the beginning of that afternoon, at least twenty-two committee members were ready to vote in favor of the Green resolution. But this number was quickly reduced to half by the introduction of the two-seat compromise.

The meeting concluded and the MFDP delegation left for the convention hall, where Moses reportedly suggested a sit-in on the convention floor by the Freedom Democrats and their supporters. A group of SNCC and CORE activists made a circle around three MFDP delegates and attempted to push their way into the hall, but with no success. Thanks in part to passes from the Oregon, Michigan, and Colorado delegations, other Freedom Democrats and their staff did succeed in getting on the floor. Instead of sitting with their host delegations, the Freedom Democrats took these invitations and sat at the Mississippi standard. Once in, MFDP delegates then sent their passes back outside to other Freedom Democrats still waiting to enter. Five or six managed to get to the Mississippi spot on the floor. A crowd started forming around the Mississippi standard, and this kept more MFDP delegates and their supporters from being removed. Many Freedom Democrat sympathizers used their bodies as "nonlethal obstacles to police action."[57] Meanwhile, hundreds held a support rally outside of the convention hall. Later that evening there was more talk of a larger civil disobedience protest, but MFDP and COFO leaders rejected this, fearing that such an operation would increase nationwide opposition to the MFDP and the movement.[58] Some kept their attention on whether to reconsider the compromise for at-large seats.

Elsewhere another debate ensued between Freedom Party delegates and staff and the national leadership of the civil rights movement. It took place in King's suite.[59] The debate was initiated by Aaron Henry, who, with prodding from Johnson faithful, was determined to get the Freedom Party to reconsider its rejection of the two-seat offer. He invited Ed King, Farmer, Rustin, and some National Council of Churches representatives to address the delegation. Rustin argued that the administration's compromise solution be turned into a "public image 'victory'" and urged acceptance of the compromise. He insisted on a coalition among blacks, labor, and liberals.

Martin Luther King Jr. did not urge reconsideration, but he did say, upon being questioned by Moses, that he would not have rejected the Johnson proposal in the first place. He stressed that there was a danger involved in labeling supporters of the compromise as "sell-outs." He called on Freedom Democrats and SNCC staff to be more respectful of strategic and tactical differences. However, King, unlike the National Council of Churches representatives, did express his support for a sit-in as a "creative response to the tension and bitterness" that had resulted. He vowed continued support of the MFDP no matter what it finally decided.[60] Like the others, James Farmer also encouraged the Freedom Party to accept the compromise.

A number of Freedom Democrats and their supporters responded to the comments of the national civil rights leaders. One was Rita Schwerner, who condemned the entire proceeding as a "sell-out."[61] She noted that she no longer had any interest in opening up the Democratic Party and thought that reconsideration of the rejection was unnecessary. She even challenged Bayard Rustin's right to speak in light of what little, if anything, he had contributed to the Freedom Summer project. She also voiced her disagreement with a sit-in because it showed an interest in wanting to be a part of the Democratic Party. Waskow stood up and denounced the national civil rights leadership for encouraging the separation of morality and politics. He said further that political success should be determined on moral grounds.[62] Fannie Lou then rose and said in her inimitable style that she was not in the least bit interested in reconsidering any motion. When one of the procompromise participants urged her and the others to "listen to their leaders," Hamer snapped back, "Who [is] the leader? I know you ain't been in Mississippi working with us. Who is he?" When asked later to elaborate on this point and her concept of leadership, Hamer said, "See[,] I can't see a leader leading me nowhere if he's in N.Y. and I'm down here catching hell."[63]

Ella Baker then took up where Hamer left off, adding a few points of her own regarding loyalty and leadership. Baker responded to Rauh's somewhat patronizing appeal to forgive: "The great heart of the Negro people had demonstrated its capacity for forgiveness and understanding, and [I] would hope that in this situation [blacks] would still be able to demonstrate this capacity for understanding." At this point, Rauh asked that they acknowledge that Humphrey's vice-presidency was at stake. Baker remarked that "this was the kind of thing that we had to come to grips with, and those who claimed to be with us would be with us when the going got rough as well as when it was easy. . . . To call upon us to be understanding of Mr. Humphrey's desire to win was saying, 'Forget what you need, you're winning and support his winning.'"[64] Addressing the inherent tension between local need and grass-roots leaders on one hand and a broad, unfocused national civil rights agenda on the other, Moses called on people to remember that the primary allegiance of the Freedom Party belonged to "Mississippi and its own hopes and desires." He added that the Freedom Democrats need be concerned about pleasing not the American liberal establishment but instead their constituents. In doing so he implied rejection.[65]

The sixty-eight Freedom Democratic Party delegates again voted unanimously to reject the Johnson administration's compromise.[66] A question was then raised about an alternative course of action for the evening. This time a sit-in was proposed and finally agreed to. Following the vote, the mood, as described by Waskow, was still one of defeat, but not complete failure or loss of hope of working within the Democratic Party. Waskow said, "Well, we were beaten, but not by too much, and we showed enormous power against the overwhelming efforts of the Administration; we can now see how to carry on within the Democratic Party."[67] According to Waskow's account, in this regard there was some split between Schwerner's complete abandonment and Moses's reserved hope that the civil rights movement demands could be pursued through traditional politics. But other participants were not so sure that there was a clear split. According to Baker, "I would imagine that certainly settled any debate he might have had about the possibility of functioning through the mainstream of the Democratic Party, especially if we were having to have a coalition type relationship. . . . Now, I don't know that Bob really believed that they would be seated. Maybe he did. . . . I haven't talked with Bob about this, but I should imagine it had great impact on him, I don't know."[68] After the discussion, some doubt remained, so deliberations continued, leaving open the possibility of another vote on the matter.

On August 26, the MFDP delegates met and made a final decision not to accept this compromise. They were prepared to deliver the official notification to the credentials committee, or so everyone thought. Aaron Henry, the delegate chairman, was not so sure, however. He insisted on accepting the compromise, with a demand for twenty-four votes instead of just two. Henry sought the approval of the most influential member of the delegation. "Mrs. Hamer," he remarked, "I'm going out and we're going to compromise for 24 votes." Hamer, enraged by the mere thought of compromise, replied to Henry, "Why you going to compromise for twenty-four votes, Dr. Henry? You know good and well that we won't have but two. If you go out there . . . and say that . . . you stay there, don't you come home. You better stay in that convention hall then the balance of your life, 'cause if you come out I'm gon' cut your throat." After entering the hall and taking a seat, the microphone was passed to Henry and he quickly responded, "No compromise." Hamer then followed up with her now oft-repeated declaration, "We didn't come all this way for no two seats."[69]

There were many influential black leaders who disagreed with the MFDP's final decision. Among them was Dr. Martin Luther King Jr., who supported the compromise, arguing that "out of thesis and antithesis should come synthesis." Although he had supported the MFDP's efforts since its beginning, King wanted the delegation to come away with something of political value. However, he also recognized a need for the delegation not to take part in "tokenism."[70] Fannie Lou Hamer came away especially disgusted with the NAACP, particularly Roy Wilkins, who, during the convention, had told Hamer, "You all are just ignorant. You have put your point across. You should just pack your bags up and go home." This infuriated Hamer so that, upon returning home, she immediately stopped paying her two-dollar NAACP annual membership fee. In subsequent interviews, she minced no words when discussing her feelings for the NAACP, often noting, "There ain't nothing that I respect less than the NAACP."[71]

Although Hamer was far more reserved when reflecting on the role of SCLC and Martin Luther King Jr., she made it clear that she was not at all happy with them either. Her criticisms of King often took the form of disagreement with his tactics or unhappiness about the attention and credit his 1965 Selma campaign received for passage of the Voting Rights Act. Keenly aware of King's popularity in life and in death, Hamer was always extremely cautious about publicly criticizing him, in part because he had died such a tragic death while serving the movement and she did not "want [any] strikes against him."[72] Hamer's trouble with King seemed to have to do with his company rather than with his abandonment of principles generally held among movement activists. In fact, Hamer refused to attend King's funeral because she "couldn't remorse around the hypocrits [who] were there."[73]

The MFDP's failure to unseat the all-white delegation led to the disillusionment and radicalization of certain MFDP members, especially Hamer, who, in subsequent lectures, lashed out at "tom teachers and chicken-eating ministers," in reference to those blacks at the convention who claimed to be leaders of the people but who were so ready to accept compromise. She later referred to them as the "black bourgeoisie" and accused them of always "thinking they're white." About them she often remarked, "Give 'em two dollars and a car and they think they're free."[74]

After the convention, Hamer not only became disenchanted with traditional black leadership, but she also became even more disillusioned with the white power structure. In her autobiography she observed, "We followed all the laws that the white people themselves made. . . . But we learned the hard way that even though we had all the laws and all the righteousness on our side—that white man is not going to give up his power to us. . . . We have to take for ourselves."[75]

Whether the final outcome of the challenge was seen as a loss or a victory, the MFDP stand in Atlantic City was undoubtedly historically significant. First, it sent a message to the white bastion of power in the South that black Mississippians would no longer collaborate in their own oppression through passive acceptance of human rights and civil rights violations. The MFDP stand notified southern white supremacists and their sympathizers that they would be challenged by opponents using their own political institutions and legal system if necessary. The stand marked the beginning of the supremacists' demise, in the eyes of many.

Second, the challenge was an important vehicle for exposing the virtual powerlessness of black Mississippians to the nation, thereby sustaining the attention of the federal government first attracted by the three civil rights murders earlier that summer. This challenge had some influence on the passage of the 1965 Voting Rights Act, which provided for the presence of federal marshals in the South to oversee the registering of black voters. Traditional historical accounts attribute the creation and passage of the act to King and SCLC's Selma campaign.[76] However, it is important not to underestimate the embarrassment faced by Lyndon Johnson when the official Mississippi delegation demanded that his party respond to the charges directed at the all-white delegation. The MFDP stand was certainly in the minds of Johnson and civil rights supporters in Congress when the Voting Rights Act was passed.

Third, the MFDP challenge marked Hamer's emergence on the national scene. As a result of Hamer's appearance at the convention, she helped fuel a growing social movement by providing an example of courage and determination. Hamer was an inspirational leader of a movement constantly troubled by disappointment and uncertainty. Her personal tragedies and survival of them gave many black Mississippians hope. In August 1964, the entire nation experienced this sense of possibility. She was a symbol of what could be achieved if it only endured the roughest of times. However, it would be inaccurate to attribute the growth of the movement only to her spiritual nourishment. She also influenced the movement in a very practical and fundamental way. As was evident in her individual contributions to the MFDP's growth, Hamer was an important institution-builder.

Last, the challenge was important for Hamer's evolution as a leader. From her defeat Hamer learned in clear and definite terms that appealing to the federal government within the boundaries of the law did not always bring the immediately desired remedy. In this lesson Hamer got an all too difficult introduction to high-stakes, interest-group politics at the national level. More-

over, as she was introduced to the recalcitrance of the Lyndon Johnson administration, Hamer also encountered her first real debilitating conflict with national middle-class civil rights leaders, especially black clergymen and white
liberals. In the long run, the challenge and its defeat marked a decline in relations between Hamer on the one hand and middle-class movement leaders and
the slow-moving federal government on the other. As a result she became increasingly interested in working to build strong local institutions for the problems that plagued her community. When the challenge was over, Hamer came
away from it quite bitter and disillusioned, but ultimately even more resolved
to press her point: the poor would and should have a voice in their own destiny through meaningful franchise. Ironically, she also came away from this
defeat in a better position to assist the movement financially due to the broader
audience she won with her dramatic testimony about the horrible Winona
beating. Despite (or perhaps because of) the MFDP's defeat and her subsequent bitterness, Hamer continued her grass-roots political work by recruiting prospective voters and preaching about the powers of the ballot and other crucial issues. In 1965 she made yet another challenge to take away the power
of white Mississippi politicians. This time the scene was the United States
Congress.

six   Today I don't have any money, but I'm freer than the average white American 'cause I know who I am.

—Fannie Lou Hamer

Returning Home

In fall 1964 Hamer accompanied a SNCC delegation to West Africa at the invitation of Guinea's president, Sékou Touré. Coming on the heels of the disappointing defeat in Atlantic City, the trip was like a balm to Hamer's wounded and dismayed soul. The visit fed her emotional reserve and deepened her commitment to political change. The visitors stayed a little less than three weeks, but during that brief time Hamer collected a lifetime of experiences that led her to reflect on the meaning of blackness. She discovered her African roots and began to feel a sense of racial pride that seemed to match (if not exceed altogether) the more personal pride instilled in her by a strong mother and an interpretation of Christianity that valorized self-love almost as much as love of God. She observed black people running their own government and businesses. Undoubtedly, this was a dramatic expansion of horizons for a woman born a sharecropper.

As she observed life in Guinea, Hamer—always a quick and intelligent thinker—began analyzing the negative racial stereotypes she had been taught about Africa. In Africa she saw strong, independent black people appearing to lead lives free of white oppression—and largely because of their own efforts. Her impressions of the Guineans made her think of her own family and her own relation to history. Moreover, the trip confirmed the necessity of struggle if oppressed people were to be free. It linked her to a worldwide movement and community, as it did for all members of SNCC's delegation and other African-American leaders, most notably, Malcolm X, whose own internationalization paralleled Hamer's in 1964. She began to make connections and arrive at a deeper understanding of the cultural and psychological consequences of oppression. The trip left Hamer more contemptuous of American racism than ever, yet also more hopeful of her own ability to effect change and to realize a world where blacks would be able to live decent lives. Most significant, the good feelings generated during the Africa trip made victory seem possible again.

The idea of a SNCC trip to West Africa was proposed by the world-famous singer and civil rights supporter Harry Belafonte during one of his visits to Greenwood, Mississippi. Belafonte had received an invitation from Sékou Touré, who wanted a group of black American youth activists to come to his country and share ideas about struggle with young Guineans. Belafonte and other famous personalities secured donations and paid for the trip. Many people wanted to go on this first trip, which became the source of more fighting within SNCC. SNCC staff selected Hamer to go because they wanted to honor her many personal sacrifices made for the movement.[1] Hamer was joined by John Lewis, Dona and Bob Moses, Julian Bond, Ruby Doris Smith Robinson, Donald Harris, William Hansen, Prathia Hall, Matthew Jones, and James Forman. On September 11 the activists left New York City on a Pan American flight to Dakar. Lewis described the long journey as a "family outing, with people roaming the aisles, laughing and eating and drinking. You could feel everyone letting go and relaxing almost immediately."[2] In Senegal, the delegation was met by a small group holding greeting signs: "WELCOME SNCC TO SENEGAL." During a reception, the activists and their Senegalese hosts drank banana juice and honored the moment with a toast; "Uhuru" (freedom), they saluted. From Dakar, the SNCC delegation boarded an Air Guinea plane for southward travel to their final destination.

When the visitors arrived in Guinea, the Touré government placed them in comfortable living quarters and gave them two cars for their own use. James Forman described the group as filled with a profound and very memorable "sense of well-being" throughout its stay.[3] The big thrill for many of them came from giving Hamer a chance to see a world outside her home state. During the visit, President Touré dropped by the group's quarters occasionally to see how the delegation members were faring. Overwhelmed and deeply impressed by his visits, Hamer observed, "Imagine the president coming to see us, when in the United States we couldn't even go to see the president."[4] Long after she left, Hamer talked about the psychological value of such a trip. In his 1972 memoir, James Forman wrote: "Today, Mrs. Hamer still talks about the importance of black people from the United States visiting black countries where blacks run the government, industry, everything."[5]

The impressive nature of the trip had as much to do with Guinea's own history as with the history of the African-American visitors. Guinea was the second African nation to gain independence from a European power, in 1958. It had been a colony of France, and when given the choice of continuing such a relationship or becoming independent, the people of Guinea chose independence. The stories are legendary about the manner in which the French cut ties with their former colony. Tales abound about how the French took everything with them, including the telephones. Guinea literally had to start from scratch as a nation. In doing so it declared itself a socialist nation and its leaders pulled the nation together by espousing the value of a strong sense of African history and culture. Moreover, they stressed realizing independence through sound organization and clear political consciousness at every level in society, from leaders and followers.[6]

As the SNCC delegation visited Guinea, it witnessed a recently liberated black nation in the process of rebuilding itself after years of colonial subjugation. On October 2, Guinea's Independence Day, the group attended the opening of a new stadium. The delegates also visited a match factory and a printing plant named after the assassinated Congo leader Patrice Lumumba. Throughout their stay, they read the newspapers and commented on the impressive amount of detail focused on African news, not French or European affairs.[7] In addition to the Independence Day celebration, the delegation got a feel for interaction between culture and politics through the nationally celebrated cultural competitions that were held during their visit.

When it was not out observing and participating in aspects of Guinean life, the delegation spent time relaxing and reading socialist literature. In addition, members of the delegation had several discussions with President Touré. He imparted a great deal of advice to the group, mostly about leadership and organization. He noted that strong leadership was a must in any effort to liberate a community or nation of people. He talked about the necessity for criticism and self-criticism within organizations. He reminded them, as Forman wrote, of "the need for people to examine the good and bad aspects of not only the party's section leaders but officials all the way to the top. The president, he maintained, must be criticized by the base and the base must have the strength to do it."[8] This was certainly not lost on the forthright Hamer. President Touré also asked the delegation about its struggle back in the United States, continually emphasizing political consciousness, good organization, and correct analysis. Moreover, as he listened to SNCC members, he reminded them that the problem was one of exploitation, especially economic exploitation.

The trip bolstered Hamer's self-concept as a black woman. In her autobiography, she noted, "Being from the South we never was taught much about our African heritage. The way everybody talked to us, everybody in Africa was savages and really stupid people."[9] The power and control that Guineans had over their own destinies astounded Hamer. She observed intently some relatively mundane activities that most Americans might have taken for granted, and her mind was on their larger significance for racial oppression: "I saw black men flying the airplanes, driving buses, sitting behind the big desks in the bank and just doing everything that I was used to seeing white people do." Most uplifting for Hamer was the sight of a black flight attendant: "I saw for the first time in my life a black stewardess walking through the plane and that was quite an inspiration for me."[10]

Hamer linked herself, as a black woman, to the daily lives of the Guinean women: "One thing I looked at so much was the African women. They were so graceful and so poised." She observed carefully their physical presentation and customs, their headdress, and their manner of carrying water. She recognized an immediate connection to the women of the Mississippi Delta, including herself: "It was so similar to my own family because it's very seldom that anybody see me without something tied on my head. Most of the African people wear their heads tied up. My mother would do the same thing. She could put something on her head, [and] have two pails in her hand and a pail on her head and could go for miles and wouldn't drop them."[11]

Her favorite childhood activities also came to mind as she observed the Guineans: "A lot of things they do over there I've done as a child. Little common things, like they boil peanuts with salt when they're real green. It just looked like my life coming [all] over again to me." Similarly, the music resonated with familiarity: "Like some of the songs. I couldn't translate their language, but it was the tune of some old songs I used to hear my grandmother sing. It was just so close to my family that I cried."[12]

Apart from giving meaning to her own cultural work habits and other practices, Hamer's careful observation of African women echoed related themes of womanhood, work, sex, and beauty in her own life. Hamer shared a great deal with the Guinean women: she too was a black woman for whom the definition of womanhood was closely tied to a domestic role, among other things. In addition, Hamer saw something in their physical presentation that she truly admired: they reminded her of her own mother and grandmother. A similar impression was implied in Hamer's recollection of the black stewardesses, in an era when the emphasis was still on their physical presentation. What was it about their walking through the plane that left Hamer inspired? Did Hamer see them as beautiful—as younger and appealing? If this was the case, this is an unusual and particularly noteworthy recollection for Hamer, because sex and beauty appear here unassociated with violence, in contrast to their appearance in other places in Hamer's autobiographical accounts.

Hamer was overwhelmed by the connections she was making to her past and present. Mostly she was touched by her perception of historical disruption: "It got to me. I cried over there. If I'm living here, I just might have some people there. I probably got relatives right now in Africa, but we'll never know each other because we've been separated. . . . I'll never know them and they'll never know me."[13]

Hamer, a noted wordsmith herself, observed, "And they can't say that black people can't be intelligent. . . . I met one child there eleven years old, speaking three languages. He could speak English, French and Malinke. Speaking my language actually better than I could."[14] Even with the differences in time, space, and language, she felt a deep connection with her those she met: "I felt a closeness in Africa. I couldn't speak the French and a lot of them couldn't speak English, but the comparison between my family and them was unbelievable. Two peoples that far apart and have so many things the same way."[15]

But through the joy and sadness, Hamer also found the time and mood to get angry and indignant. As she later recounted:

> I wasn't in Guinea more than a couple of hours before President Touré came to see us. And I just compared my feelings. I've tried so hard so many times to see the president in this country and I wasn't given that chance. But the president over there cared enough to visit us. He invited us to his palace and that was the first time I'd ever had a chance to go in a palace. I just thought it was great to see African people so kind. It was so vice-versa what I'd heard that I couldn't hardly believe it.[16]

The group returned to the United States the first week in October, after receiving an urgent phone call from Ivan Donaldson and Betty Garman in Atlanta. Courtland Cox had called an emergency staff meeting for October 10. It turned out to be a staff meeting that signaled a very painful and confusing transition that SNCC was about to undergo. Meanwhile Hamer began work on another challenge.

■ ■ ■

In January 1965 Fannie Lou Hamer reentered the national political scene in another effort to strip the lily-white, traditional Democratic Party of its power. Initially joining her in a congressional challenge were MFDP candidates Aaron Henry, Annie Devine, Victoria Jackson Gray, and Harold Ruby. Aaron

Henry, former chairman of the MFDP delegation, opposed Senator John Stennis, but he later withdrew. Gray, a MFDP national committeewoman and the
owner of a cosmetics business, opposed Representative William Colmer of the
Fifth Congressional District. Annie Devine challenged Arthur Winstead of the
Fourth District, and Harold Ruby, an active Led County MFDP member, faced
Representative Thomas Abernathy of the First Congressional District. Hamer
continued her bid for the Second Congressional District seat "won" by Representative Jamie Whitten.

Before their congressional challenges, Hamer, Henry, and Devine attempted
to place their names on the November 1964 ballot to run against the regular
Democratic candidates. But the Mississippi State Election Commission refused
to allow them because in the spring they had already participated in the Democratic primary (as regular Democratic Party candidates) and lost. Mississippi required that they now support the Democratic victors of the primary.[17]
Hamer and her MFDP candidates then decided to enter the fall election as
independents (as official candidates for the Mississippi Freedom Democratic
Party), so they began soliciting signatures for a petition drive. They submitted their petitions to Secretary of State Heber Ladner, who directed them to
turn the signatures over for verification by circuit registrars. Even though the
MFDP candidates claimed they collected well over the required number of
signatures for their petition, the state election commission, on the basis of the
circuit registrar's count, argued that they did not have enough.[18] (MFDP discovered later that election officials threw away many of its petitions.) Also, the
election commission charged that the MFDP candidates were ineligible anyway because they had not paid two poll taxes. (This, of course, had been out-
lawed by the Twenty-fourth Amendment to the U.S. Constitution.)[19] The
MFDP then decided to hold a mock election in fall 1964.

The disputed election commission decision and the results of the MFDP
mock election provided the impetus for the 1965 congressional challenge.
Termed the "Freedom Vote," the mock election was statewide for president and
Congress. Unlike the official state elections, it was open to all races. Throughout the South, polling places were set up in places where black people spent
much of their time—in churches and community centers.[20] The Freedom Vote
results were the opposite of the returns from the traditional Democratic party primary held in the spring. The mock election proved overwhelmingly that
white politicians were ignoring the voices of Mississippi's eligible black electorate by not giving them a chance to register. Mississippi politicians had argued that low black registration figures were the result of apathy and ignorance.

Blacks gave unanimous support to the MFDP candidates: Aaron Henry received 61,004 votes to Senator John C. Stennis's 139 votes; Victoria Gray trounced Representative William Colmer by 10,138 votes; Annie Devine was victorious over Arthur Winstead, 6,000 votes to 4; and Hamer easily defeated Representative Jamie Whitten, 33,009 votes to 59.[21] In addition to giving disfranchised people an opportunity to prove their desire to participate in a formal political process, the Freedom Vote provided much grass-roots organizing experience for running political campaigns. According to Betty Garman, an MFDP supporter and SNCC northern coordinator, Freedom Vote participants gained valuable experience, "from [organizing] rallies to writing speeches, from debating political issues to using sound trucks, plastering the community with posters and bumper strips."[22]

The Freedom Vote election results made the congressional challenge of 1965 inevitable. After all, from its inception, Hamer and the MFDP had planned to use the results to further the party's national challenge. Devine, Gray, and Hamer took the lead in issuing the challenge when the Ninety-seventh Congress convened in January 1965. The three women and their counsel attempted to unseat Mississippi representatives to Congress by arguing that the representatives-elect had "won" the elections as a consequence of discriminatory voting practices.[23]

The MFDP began planning the challenge shortly after the Atlantic City Democratic Convention and the 1964 presidential election. On November 28, 1964, the MFDP called a meeting at its Washington, D.C., headquarters for its supporters and any other concerned individuals and organizations.[24] At this meeting, the MFDP decided that the challenge would involve a legal approach and political action. Its political approach involved gaining northern support for the party's "Fairness Resolution," which held that "no person claiming [contested] seats shall be allowed to take the oath until this contest or challenge is decided by the House."[25]

The legal approach involved challenging the results of the November 3 Mississippi congressional election on three grounds. First, the MFDP charged that the elections violated rights guaranteed to blacks in the Fourteenth and Fifteenth Amendments. Second, the party charged that the election violated the constitutional provision (Article 1, section 2) that required that members of the House of Representatives be elected by "all of the people." Third, the MFDP charged that the state violated the provisions of the Compact of 1870, which allowed Mississippi readmission to the Union under several conditions. One condition provided that the "Constitution of Mississippi shall never be so amended or changed as to deprive any citizens or class of citizens of the United States of the right to vote who are entitled to vote by the constitution herein recognized."[26]

Along with the other challengers, Hamer began her work by sending a form letter to "Friends of SNCC" soliciting financial and political support for the challenge. In keeping with her other mobilizing efforts, Hamer used an example of violence against civil rights workers as justification for the urgent need for this latest challenge. She cited the well-publicized murder of three civil rights workers in Mississippi during the summer of 1964. She argued that the killing of Andrew Goodman, Mickey Schwerner, and James Chaney was ample proof of the lawlessness that reigned in Mississippi, especially in response to the movement. She called on the friends of SNCC to recognize the enormous need for justice in her home state and to join her in the challenge to unseat the "racists" who perpetrated and allowed such conditions to exist. She closed with a request for financing of the Freedom Democrats and the challenge. She called on citizens to do "all you can in getting your Congressmen and Congresswoman to support the fairness resolution and having these racists unseated." She signed the letter, "Yours for Freedom, Fannie Lou Hamer, Member of Congress, Second District of Mississippi."[27]

Hamer's work on the challenge began the same way in which she had intensified her voter registration work after the 1963 Winona beating. She went on a whirlwind national tour in pursuit of publicity and financial and moral support. Hamer's forte was raising money for the movement's individual battles, and this required a great deal of travel and speaking, which must have seemed endless in the case of her congressional challenge responsibilities. By December 1964, she set up temporary residence in Washington, D.C., along with her cochallengers Annie Devine and Victoria Gray. The women found it easier to lobby legislators on a daily basis if they lived in the area. So they secured an apartment and returned to D.C. after each fund-raising tour.[28]

On December 4, 1964, the notice of the challenge was served to the Clerk of the House. The Mississippi congressmen who were being challenged did not answer the charges until January 4, 1965, when the Congress decided to vote on whether to seat them while the challenge was being resolved. During the month of December, the MFDP and its attorneys organized support groups, which put pressure on various congressmen and raised funds for the party. The attorneys also used this time for preparing briefs, all of which centered around the notion of illegal representation. For example, Hamer's brief stated that she was the only one who represented the Second Congressional District of Mississippi in the House of Representatives because the Freedom Vote was more representative of the democratic process than was the regular party's election since it was open to all Mississippians of voting age. Because Hamer defeated her opponent decisively in the Freedom Vote, the brief concluded that Hamer deserved the seat of her opponent, Jamie Whitten.

On January 4, 1965, the Mississippi Freedom Democratic Party began collecting evidence for its case. In accordance with federal law, the party had the next forty days in which to accomplish this. The Freedom Democrats enlisted the aid of numerous lawyers from around the country. On this same day, the congressmen on Capitol Hill voted to swear in the white Mississippi representatives-elect and let them take their seats while the challenge was being considered. Meanwhile, approximately six hundred members of the MFDP held a two-hour silent march in front of the House of Representatives. Just as the swearing-in ceremonies were beginning, Devine, Gray, and Hamer made an unsuccessful attempt to enter the floor as election contestants. However, one member of the American Nazi Party did manage to make his way into the House chamber before a policeman escorted him out. He burst into the House chamber in minstrel clothes, his face painted black, shouting, "I wants to see what the Mississippi delegation looks like." Later Hamer observed in disgust, "How could twelve policemen block us but could not see that man in the black face?"[29]

The notification of the challenge sent to the House and the subsequent seating of the five white representatives marked the first stage of the congressional challenge. Despite this first concession to the "challengees," the MFDP remained optimistic about the chances of bringing about justice. In a statement released after the House made its decision, the Mississippi Freedom Democrats claimed that once they presented the evidence of "intimidation, bombings and other forms of terrorism used to keep Negroes in Mississippi from voting," Congress and the entire nation would have no choice but to remove those Mississippi congressmen who were undemocratically elected.[30] As if the experience at the 1964 Democratic convention were forgotten, the MFDP seemed to rediscover its trust in the federal government as ultimate protector and provider of justice. A great deal was required to extinguish its die-hard faith in federal intervention. More than simple political naivete, this hope appeared to be a logical recourse around which to plan civil rights strategies. Hamer, believing that some American legislators would sooner or later stand up for justice, directed the party to continue the challenge before the appropriate committee.

Included in the first-stage challenge activities was an effort to get Mississippi state officials to respond to the MFDP's claims of election discrimination. On January 22, 1965, Hamer and the MFDP ordered Governor Paul Johnson, Attorney General Joe T. Patterson, Colonel T. B. Birdsong (head of the state highway patrol), and Erle Johnston (director of the state sovereignty commission) to be subpoenaed to answer a series of questions in response to the MFDP challenge.[31]

During these initial stages of the challenge, Hamer's health began troubling her. She was extremely fatigued, according to letters written by Betty Garman. In a response to the first request for Hamer to speak, which came from the Davis (California) Friends of SNCC, Garman pointed out that Fannie Lou Hamer was desperately in need of rest: "Part of the problem [in contacting her for a speaking engagement] is that she needs a rest rather badly and some arrangements are being made for her whole family to have some vacation."[32] But before such a vacation could be taken, Hamer had to be hospitalized for exhaustion. In a subsequent letter in response to a second speaking request from the same group in Davis, Garman indicated that "Mrs. Hamer is pretty ill and is resting in a N.Y. hospital til she gets a little better. (Mostly exhaustion). So she can't come to Davis for a talk." No doubt her fatigue was the result of a demanding, hectic schedule, which often had her too busy to answer speaking requests herself.[33]

But less than a month later, Hamer was up and at it again, traveling constantly between Ruleville and Washington, D.C., throughout early 1965. She was hard to keep up with, even for SNCC coordinators like Garman. In a letter responding to another speaking request, this one from the California State Association of Colored Women's Clubs, in San Jose, California, Garman noted, "I have no idea at all what Mrs. Hamer's schedule might be and thus suggest that you write to her directly at the following two addresses (send a letter to each place since she is back and forth between the two cities when she is not speaking in other areas)."[34]

Eventually, Hamer went on to honor her numerous speaking engagements from northern California, and this resulted in an increase to MFDP's coffers, although not a hefty one. On April 3, 1965, Fred Hirsch mailed five hundred dollars to Betty Garman for MFDP because of Hamer's participation in some organized activities in San Jose, California, the nature of which was not stated in the letter. Hirsch noted that Hamer's involvement was key to the success of their program. In a message typed in nearly all upper-case letters, apparently for emphasis, Hirsch wrote, "WE PUT ON A PROGRAM WHICH WOULD NOT HAVE STOOD UP ON ITS OWN UNTIL MRS. HAMER CONSENTED TO COME DOWN HERE AND ADD HER OWN PARTICIPATION. WE WERE ABLE TO MAKE THE THING GO BECAUSE OF HER."[35]

While in California, Hamer also attended an "MFDP Benefit and Hamer Party" sponsored by Marin Friends of SNCC, which brought in only $80.21.[36] It was such hard work for so little return, financially at least.

The second stage of the challenge began with the taking of depositions during the allotted forty-day period. The MFDP collected depositions from over six hundred witnesses. Among those witnesses were several people who had considerable information about Mississippi but who were no longer residents of the state. Despite possible reprisal and violence, many witnesses came forth and told stories about how they were denied an opportunity to register.[37] Also, the MFDP, with the aid of its one hundred lawyers, took information on the state's public officials and other members of the white community. Many of these witnesses were asked general questions about voter registration practices and specific questions about efforts made to prevent blacks from voting.

On February 13, the deposition taking was over and the second stage of the challenge had come to a close. On May 17 the third stage of the congressional challenge began with the filing of the six hundred depositions collected by the MFDP. Party members were steadfastly at work holding a major conference and a series of regional meetings in an effort to plan a Freedom Summer 1965 modeled after the 1964 campaign.

As the House continued the challenge proceedings and the Voting Rights Act worked its way to Lyndon Johnson's desk that spring, Hamer continued her traveling and fund raising. In preparation for the final stage of the congressional challenge, she and the MFDP had set their sights on organizing something like the 1963 March on Washington in August. According to a SNCC letter, Hamer had plans to speak (sometime in August) in Denver on behalf of the MFDP in order "to raise enough money to transport Mississippians to Washington at the end of the month for an all-out lobbying effort."[38] Hamer's efforts took her all over the West, including up and down the coast. In early August, Hamer visited Seattle again. As a result of her efforts, she collected $325 and forwarded it to Washington, D.C., to MFDP headquarters.[39]

The fourth and final stage of the challenge included the filing of briefs by both sides, beginning on July 31, 1965. In their briefs, the white Mississippi congressmen made no effort to respond to specific charges made by the MFDP. Their one basic point was that the challenge should not be discussed since challengers were not official candidates and this made them ineligible contestants. The challenge was not a valid one because it was presented by nonchallengers. In their briefs, they completely disregarded the fact that the MFDP candidates had made several attempts to get on the traditional Democratic party's November ballot months before.

On September 15, 1965, the Subcommittee on Elections and Privileges presented its final report on the challenge to the House Committee on Administration, recommending that the challenge be dismissed. The parent committee lent support to the resolution, which was then sent to the House floor. On September 17, the House acted in accordance with the resolution and, by a 228-to-143 vote, dismissed the challenge.[40] However, before the House could do so, Hamer and her two colleagues placed their imprint on another page of history. As a part of a "sympathetic gesture," the Speaker of the House insisted that the challengers take a seat on the house floor while the vote was taken. This made them the first black women to sit on the floor of Congress, although Hamer, Devine, and Gray were once again disappointed and disillusioned. They found little consolation in this sympathetic gesture. After the challenge, Gray stated: "Until the time comes, that they [House members] are ready to argue the Constitution instead of technicalities, the Constitution will not be real to me or to hundreds of thousands of other people."[41] Hamer responded to the defeat by reaffirming her commitment to making justice a reality for black people someday: "I'm one of the black people of America. My grandmother was a slave. With God's help, without violence, I'll keep on fighting until the Constitution means more than a piece of paper."[42]

■ ■ ■

Throughout her work on the challenge against the racist politicians from Mississippi, Hamer continued battling foes within the civil rights community. Her disagreement with and hostility toward traditional civil rights leaders and organizations grew throughout the spring. In March 1965, bad feelings between the Mississippi-based Council of Federated Organizations (COFO) and the National Association for the Advancement of Colored People (NAACP) came to a head in COFO's convention. Relations between the national NAACP leadership and the Mississippi movement had grown noticeably strained. The friction centered around decision making, funding, and publicized personal insults.

On one side were, for the most part, poor, local Mississippi activists of Hamer's ilk and state, and on the other were national NAACP officials who were financially and educationally middle class and had a reputation for being condescending toward the black poor. Local Mississippi activists wanted to identify their own problems and determine their own solutions without much input from middle-class people, whether they were from Mississippi or elsewhere. Deciding whether a particular community needed more resources devoted to self-help cooperatives or intensive voter registration work, or both, should be left up to the folks most affected by such a decision. Those who held this perspective had a political agenda that placed local need above all else. On the other hand, NAACP activists in the state branch and national office had serious questions about the effectiveness of the "localist" strategy. Doubt centered around capability and experience, and sometimes it surfaced in insulting public statements made by national officials such as Gloster Current and Roy Wilkins. Both factions believed the other to have an attitude problem. Hamer's side felt that the NAACP thought itself superior and better able to determine what was best for Mississippi. However, the NAACP thought Hamer and her supporters were unappreciative and unfair in their criticisms of the NAACP, and that the local people only wanted the NAACP around when local campaigns needed financial or legal support.

Although the convention began with customary prayer and singing, the proceedings soon became contentious when the NAACP state president for Mississippi, Aaron Henry, and Fannie Lou Hamer spoke to the issue of NAACP support for local causes in Mississippi. Both Henry and Hamer wanted clarification on NAACP's role in local civil rights activities. Henry was concerned about the perception and understanding of the NAACP's role. Hamer questioned whether the NAACP was actually committed to involvement in local activities, given recent public statements made by NAACP officials. Specifically, Hamer cited Roy Wilkins's alleged disavowal in the *New York Times* of NAACP support for COFO. Henry responded by pointing out how the NAACP was concerned about not being contacted regarding COFO project plans until people were jailed and "bills came due." He also noted the NAACP branch presidents were turned off by a "takeover" attitude that seemed to characterize COFO summer workers. He also complained about derogatory comments made by these same workers about the NAACP. Henry added that the national NAACP had arranged to monitor COFO speakers working in local areas in order to rethink its participation in COFO. On his point about the "takeover" attitude in COFO, a local activist, Georgiana Dyson of Meridian, Mississippi, disagreed and noted that COFO just wanted to get something done. Dyson continued her defense of local movement activists and their decisions. She even defended COFO "especially on the subject of sex."[43] Clearly, Dyson came down on the side of Hamer and other local action-oriented folk.[44]

Fannie Lou Hamer persisted on the matter of NAACP public statements that she found offensive and, more important, indicative of the underlying perception problem facing COFO and NAACP. Most problematic: NAACP officials thought she and others were inferior and lacked what it took to make good decisions. She noted that in a memo from a national official, Gloster

Current, the NAACP had expressed the opinion that "local people in Miss. needed someone to think for them." Hamer "objected" to the Current statement—a statement that sounded all too similar to Roy Wilkins's comment to the MFDP after its 1964 Democratic National Convention challenge. Mrs. Pigee of Clarksdale (Henry's home) told Hamer, "You can't believe what you read in the papers." Pigee defended the NAACP on all counts and noted that "the NAACP was being put on trial unfairly." In fact, a number of local activists defended the "NAA," as they referred to the organization. One was Mrs. Davidson of Columbus, Mississippi, who decried COFO's "insulting treatment" and "atheism." Not all of the local folk stood with Hamer.[45]

Throughout the convention, Hamer continued to challenge the NAACP role in and perspective on the Mississippi movement. The organization was just not engaged in a way that satisfied her. In fact, for Hamer, the NAACP was looking more like part of the problem. At another point in the convention, she broached the issue of class as a factor in the kinds of leaders and the types of decisions made by the national and state branches of the NAACP. In her typical blunt style, she took on decision making as well as the black middle class and its criticism of people's clothing: "How much have the people with suits done? If they, dressed up, had been here, then the kids in jeans wouldn't be here. Preachers and teachers look down on little people, but now these little people are speaking up now."[46]

Another local activist chimed in, offering support to Hamer's charges and general position. Of particular concern was the NAACP's inefficient, hierarchical structure. Hazel Palmer accused people in Jackson ("NAACPers") of "just play[ing] at freedom." She pointed out the inability of the Jackson folk to do anything without prior approval from the national NAACP headquarters. She noted that, by contrast, she and others were not playing at freedom; instead they were "working for a deeper freedom."[47]

After a ten-minute recess, the COFO meeting reconvened and Hamer reopened the meeting, since Aaron Henry had to leave to attend an NAACP board meeting. She moved to resume the meeting by discussing "next summer, not the past stuff." She urged the group along by reminding them, "The Freedom Democratic Party is made of local people, and it is presently making up its own program for the summer." In clear reference to the privileged, mainstream NAACP leadership, she advised, "We shouldn't let a few people determine what's going to happen in Miss. Everybody, even 'little people' should have a move in deciding what kind of project we're going to have." She called on others to be critical and consistent in their thinking and speeches when invoking words like "equality" and "democracy." She underscored what was truly at stake, in her mind: "Some say that we're fighting for equality, but I don't want to be equal to murderers. We're fighting for democracy. If we had it, the Freedom School in Indianola would not have been burned, or the people put it jail. We want to make Mississippi a democracy, where we make our own decision."[48] The meeting broke into applause.

No sooner had Hamer assumed the role of chairing the meeting than Eddie Thomas of Vicksburg took the floor and announced that Aaron Henry had left him in charge and had asked him to chair the meeting. Hamer seemed to have no problem with this. After all, Thomas was a "localist" who supported her perspective on local folks' running their own show independent of the NAACP. After Hamer's opening remarks, the tone and direction of the meeting turned decidedly radical. Thomas made a statement indicating the general tenor of the second half of the convention proceedings. "They [NAACP] can send carloads from anywhere, but they can't change my mind about working with COFO and the MFDP," he told them. He declared: "If the NAACP has a different plan, I don't know what it will be. If it is different from what we've already laid out, I won't support it." Like Hamer, he drew a line in the sand and issued a stern warning. He added, "We have to be aware of the wolves [black moderates]. When we get this thing moving, then they'll sell you to the white man, and it will be another 100 years before we get something half as good. But, if we beware of the wolves, then they can't change us."[49]

During the second half of the convention, participants began to talk openly about the MFDP and its concerns, whereas before Henry had declared that the convention was not an MFDP meeting. Howard Spencer could not think any less of Henry's declaration: "We want anybody who's here to help us, but we want them to know that they have to come on our terms, not on Roy Wilkins' terms. We have the power to make our own decisions. We have to get involved with the MFDP, which is our organization." On the question of educational background, he added, "COFO is a people's movement, not a group of organizations. We have tremendous power if we get our people together. I'm the son of a Methodist minister, but I know that educated people aren't [any] different or better than ordinary people [applause]." To this Thomas responded, "That pretty well solves *that* problem, what about housing." Thomas also noted with apparent jubilation: "I've been going to meetings for over a year now. At COFO meetings last year we used to hear the workers talk. I just listened. But this year the local people are doing the talking."[50]

While the local folk took over the convention, the NAACP board meeting continued upstairs. Hamer was not finished with the issue of an NAACP presence in rural Mississippi. She continued expressing irritation at indecision on whether to work with COFO on another summer project. She observed, "This is the thing which puzzles me. Why can't they tell us now, if they want to work with us? I don't like to criticize, but a lot of things can happen when money is involved." To illustrate her point, she then recounted the tone and content of a conversation with Charles Evers, brother of the late Medgar Evers, the assassinated state president of the Mississippi NAACP. On a trip to Chicago, according to Hamer, Charles Evers told her "she shouldn't be working for nothing." Hamer indicated that she disagreed with Evers and reiterated to the convention that the movement was larger than what went on in Mississippi: "We're not fighting for Miss., we're fighting for the whole country. I learned that in Washington, D.C. [during the congressional challenge]. I'm not saying the NAACP hasn't done good in its time, but we move in the present, not the past. We poor people will have to move without them." Hamer used this occasion to signal the need and the inevitability of poor people taking over the movement, particularly in areas of decision making.[51]

■ ■ ■

Following the COFO convention, Hamer went on with her congressional challenge duties. The national media tracked Hamer's activities and impact like a hawk. National press coverage had been appearing steadily since her stunning appearance at the 1964 Democratic Convention. Little of this coverage was positive. Most often it depicted her as an unwise, impatient, and irreverent rabble-rouser, especially vis-à-vis her more moderate counterparts in such national organizations as the NAACP.

Among the publications that contributed to Hamer's unflattering press coverage in the spring of 1965 was the weekly magazine *Newsweek*. According to a *Newsweek* article on SNCC, Hamer was receiving her share of criticism from black moderates just as she was doling it out to them. In reference to the outcome of the bitter COFO convention, the article noted: "Other Negro moderates say that Fannie Lou Hamer, the Freedom Democrats' leading mouthpiece, is showing disturbingly demagogic tendencies—attacking middle-class Negroes and whites, American policy in Vietnam, and Martin Luther King."[52]

Some of the press coverage simply signaled Hamer's arrival. In assessing Hamer's significance since the convention challenge, the *New Republic*'s Andrew Kopkind wrote that she embodied a new style of southern black leadership. He observed that Fannie Lou Hamer was representative of a cadre that "has little respect for the traditions of political compromise." According to Kopkind, she was among those MFDP delegates for whom the compromise offer meant that "rights delayed were rights denied." Thus, Kopkind concluded that the MFDP convention challenge defeat marked a new phase inside the Freedom Democratic Party. It was at that point that "Mississippi's older and more respected leaders" started to pull away and the new-style leaders like Hamer started to wield greater influence.[53]

Little did the national press know, however, that Hamer and the MFDP were starting to fall out of favor with their mentor organization, the Student Nonviolent Coordinating Committee. By the spring of 1965, SNCC and the MFDP were becoming estranged from one another in the political sense. The source of the strain was twofold: money and the issue of local autonomy. Interestingly, these were the same issues that were bringing both grass-roots organizations into conflict with the national and state branches of the NAACP. Ironically, through its struggle with the MFDP over money and autonomy, SNCC was discovering how it felt to be a jaded political guardian, for during its year-and-a-half-long relationship with MFDP it had assumed the role of parent organization.[54] Strained relations between the two undoubtedly foreshadowed Hamer's personal split with SNCC. In fact, activities and words between the two organizations might have precipitated and hastened Hamer's eventual move away from SNCC. SNCC was already going through an ideological and structural transition, a transition that the MFDP experienced two years later.

Throughout their troubled times each organization bandied about charges that the other was being too radical or not radical enough. At a SNCC executive committee meeting held April 12–14 in Holly Springs, Mississippi, some SNCC members expressed the feeling that the MFDP "was a radical idea but not a radical party." Other discussions regarding SNCC's relationship with the MFDP indicated that relations were not at all cordial between the two. If the minutes from this meeting paint an accurate picture, relations were indeed uneasy.[55]

As Hamer continued speaking throughout the country, she began hinting at the direction in which she would head in following the challenge. In support of the MFDP in Cleveland, Mississippi, Hamer (along with MFDP leaders Unita Blackwell and Susie Ruffin) spoke at the Community People's Conference. Of the three speeches, a reporter noted: "It was impossible for me to capture the emotions of people, when they listened to Mrs. Fannie Lou Hamer, Mrs. Unita Z. Blackwell, and Mrs. Susie Ruffin of the MFDP."[56] In addition to encouraging more Freedom Party movements throughout America, the three women also addressed topics such as welfare, housing, and education. In large part, this was in response to the purpose of this conference, which was "to try to find ways to solve the problems that confront the poor people of

America." The gathering was described as "not a conference of Negroes and whites, but truly a conference of community people." People in attendance came from California and from states in the Northeast, South, and Midwest. In addition to moving the crowd with her speech, Hamer also sang the gospel song "Go Tell It on the Mountain," the lyrics of which encouraged believers to tell of a new day, a new joy on the horizon.[57] For Hamer this new day was about economic empowerment for black people in Mississippi. She returned to this focus through her work with the Mississippi Freedom Labor Union in spring 1965.

Fannie Lou Hamer represents the Mississippi Freedom Democratic Party at the 1964 Democratic National Convention, Atlantic City. (UPI/Corbis Bettmann)

Mrs. Annie Devine, Fannie Lou Hamer, and Rev. Edwin King (seated, left to right) in the convention hall at the 1964 Democratic National Convention, Atlantic City. (UPI/Corbis Bettmann)

Fannie Lou Hamer addresses a crowd, c. 1965. (Fannie Lou Hamer Papers, Amistad Research Center, Tulane University, New Orleans)

Fannie Lou Hamer (center) surrounded by
family members, c. 1966. (Coleman Library,
Tougaloo College, Tougaloo, Miss.)

Perry "Pap" Hamer, 1985. (Chana Kai Lee)

Fannie Lou Hamer speaks at the 1968 Democratic National Convention, Chicago. (UPI/Corbis Bettmann)

Fannie Lou Hamer receives an honorary doctorate from President George A. Owens, Tougaloo College, 1969. (Coleman Library, Tougaloo College, Tougaloo, Miss.)

Poster, Fannie Lou Hamer's 1971 state senatorial campaign. (Special Collections
Section, Archives and Library Division, Mississippi Department of Archives and
History, Jackson)

A weary campaign worker rests his head on Fannie Lou Hamer's shoulder, 1971. (Special Collections Section, Archives and Library Division, Mississippi Department of Archives and History, Jackson)

seven Wake up and think. We as Negroes should
       want to be equal and get high wages. Please
       join the union because if you are not in a
       union you just aren't anywhere.
       —Nola May Coleman

The Mississippi Freedom
Labor Union

As the 1965 congressional challenge unfolded and intraracial class conflict
moved closer to the surface, Hamer refocused her attention in part on the
struggle for economic justice in the Delta. In spring 1965 she supported various economic self-help organizations and projects. Chief among them was the
Mississippi Freedom Labor Union (MFLU), a union of day laborers, truck drivers, and domestic workers. With its emphasis on home, land, and business
ownership, the MFLU was a self-help effort that reflected the changing focus
of the civil rights movement and the unchanged condition of economic exploitation in Mississippi. It emerged on the eve of what would soon be called
the black power era, a period of resurgent black nationalism in political
thought, practice, and rhetoric, as well as in cultural expressions—from hair-
styles and personal names to dress and art. One tenet of black power was the
principle of self-determination, the notion that an oppressed community
should exercise its collective ability to direct its own destiny. Self-determination was a right and a solution to oppressive circumstances. Consistent with
this principle was the corollary notion of self-reliance or self-sufficiency, as it
concerned a community's educational, economic, political, and social well-
being.

In some ways Hamer was already a convert to some of the principles of black
nationalism. Although the Mississippi Freedom Democratic Party (a reform-
ist party) sought to work basically within the system, it was also something of
a self-help effort born out of necessity, in this case, Jim Crow within party
politics. Unquestionably for Hamer, freedom was pursued and taken, not given;

much of it was self-generated or, as 1960s black nationalists described it, self-determined. She supported the MFLU precisely for this reason, in addition to being motivated by her long and intense personal identification with the plight of southern day laborers. She was moved that others in the Delta were trying to realize a better existence without waiting for those outside their community—just as she had done in her early civil rights days. Both need and a belief in organized activism moved Hamer to support the union. For Hamer the MFLU, albeit short-lived, was living proof of the meaning of work for her home region.

The Mississippi Freedom Labor Union officially formed in the Delta town of Shaw in April 1965, when some forty-five cotton day laborers, domestic servants, and tractor drivers convened in a nearby church and decided to form a union.[1] Much like its political cohort, the Mississippi Freedom Democratic Party, the MFLU organized to address the age-old lack of economic opportunity experienced by black Deltans. It formed to fight against the immediate problem of exploitation of day laborers. Indeed, their plight was one Hamer shared.

The MFLU was directly tied to the civil rights movement in the area. In fact, the first set of organizers for the union included many civil rights veterans.[2] The union actually had origins dating back as early as January 1965 when a group of freedom school participants began discussing their dreadful economic circumstances. The MFDP and SNCC encouraged black farmers to take the initiative and seize greater control over their economic and political destinies, a prospect that seemed possible in 1964 when the federal government began a program to assist farmers. SNCC also encouraged black farmers to become active in the local Agricultural Stabilization and Conservation Service.[3] One of many outgrowths of the civil rights movement in the Delta, the MFLU attracted individuals mobilized during Freedom Summer. In addition to its personnel, the MFLU was rooted in the civil rights movement in its choice of tactics. One SNCC press release on the new organization noted, "[Mississippi Freedom Labor] Union members have pledged to use all forms of direct action including 'strikes, picketing and boycotts,' to win their demands."[4]

As Hamer eventually came to realize, MFLU organizers seemed to understand the many difficult sides to the problem facing impoverished, disfranchised folk in the Delta. Their own circumstances spoke volumes about the necessity of self-generated economic relief. In their organizing and in their demands, Delta farm laborers evidenced a visceral understanding of and belief in the symbiotic, interdependent nature of their many oppressions.[5] As sharecroppers, day laborers, truckers, and domestic workers, they all knew that they were getting almost nothing for their work. In early spring 1965, farm workers and other laborers raised the idea of forming a dues-paying union, an idea that they took to other counties in Mississippi.[6]

Beyond the immediate need of organizing exploited workers, the MFLU was also a social welfare organization of sorts. From its inception, it was an organization of the needy to help the needy. The MFLU offered a broad range of responses to various cries for help. At the time of its formation, the MFLU collected dues, fifty dollars of which went to three needy members. One was a citizen who had used his home as an organizing center and was evicted. Another member was in need of money to repay a man who had threatened her, and the third assisted a member (and family) who was starving. Evidently this personal use of dues was not a one-time event. The MFLU's recruitment article in SNCC's newspaper, the *Student Voice,* implied that this practice was entirely consistent with the organization's purpose.[7] Although MFLU membership dues formed the only source of financial support in the beginning, the union's impressive stands later earned it the attention, respect, and financial support of traditional labor organizations like the AFL-CIO in Wisconsin, which sent five hundred dollars to the MFLU during one of the more active periods in its short history.[8]

Through its civil rights connections, the MFLU made use of the *Student Voice* to recruit new members and to discourage potential strike breakers from working for little or nothing.[9] Organizers urged field laborers in the Delta to go "on strike because you are not getting anything for your work." They sought to instill a vision in prospective union members—a vision of a better life. "Why work and be hungry, when you can gain the union [and] get some support," urged their published appeal. The union aimed at permanent change to break generational cycles of poverty. "Why make your child work for low wages when you all of your life have been working for nothing?" In terms the workers could clearly relate to, the appeal measured the stark inequities between workers and landowners: "Why buy the white man steak [when] you can't hardly eat neckbones? As cheap as chicken is you can't even eat it but once a week on Sunday. Wake up and think," the appeal exhorted. The union represented itself as a sensible alternative: "Please join the union because if you are not in a union you just aren't anywhere."[10]

The first mass organizing effort on the part of the union took place in March 1965 in Shaw, Mississippi, where some ninety individuals canvassed the area in an attempt to get workers to strike for higher wages. Initially the organizers targeted the work conditions of cotton choppers and truck drivers. The immediate goal was to raise their wages to $1.25 an hour.[11] Shaw, located in the heart of the Mississippi Delta, was a small town divided by a bayou and enveloped by endless cotton fields. In 1965 Shaw had a population of 2,700, over 60 percent of which was black. As in many of the small Delta towns, Shaw's cotton industry was the main employer.[12] Shaw was located in Bolivar County, where one of the largest plantations in the world operated, Delta Land and Pine Corporation, an English-controlled enterprise. The plantation occupied over sixty square miles. Those familiar with the workings of the plantation described it as "so completely automated, so efficient, so inhuman that it is a wonder there is any resistance to it at all. . . . Foreign visitors came here to see one of the world's largest plantations. . . . They marvel at how so few men can run so many acres with such cold efficiency."[13] The answer was found in the high level of exploitation of day laborers. These conditions inspired, in part, the creation of the Mississippi Freedom Labor Union in Shaw.

The MFLU also formed in response to patterns developing throughout the South, patterns resulting in huge labor losses and continued exploitation for the remaining sharecroppers and tenant farmers. Beginning as early as the 1920s and increasingly between the 1930s and 1950s, the South was destabilized economically by the mechanization of agriculture. In addition, a number of southern politicians and business people initiated drives to attract capital to the South through such programs as Mississippi's Balance Agriculture with Industry program.[14] Mechanization and industrialization resulted in huge job losses, particularly for the unskilled. Between 1950 and 1960, Sunflower County lost 50 percent of its jobs, leading to an outward migration of 20 percent of the population from the county. Many of these jobs were casualties of innovations in chemical weed killers and flame cultivation.[15] Workers fortunate enough to find jobs often labored under horrible conditions with little reward, as most landowners tried to cut their labor costs to maximize their profits. Many farmers felt they had little recourse to rectify their situation. As farm laborers, the MFLU strikers faced difficult employment circumstances because most legislation affecting workers (e.g., minimum-wage laws) left out farm labor.

The conditions faced by day laborers were among the worst on the plantation, according to the MFLU. Over time, day laborers came to constitute approximately 90 percent of the MFLU's membership. A brief history of the union described the typical day laborer as "without security, without tenure, without [rights] of any kind . . . completely 'proletarianized' without property, without security beyond today's piece of bread and land."[16] In comparing the plight of the day laborer with that of the sharecropper, the account noted: "Although the share-cropper has never been able [to] earn a stable, decent income in the Delta, he at least had some feel for the land. In a sense, the land was his. But for the day laborer this was never true. For him, the corporation is his boss man and he works for him on a day-to-day basis. . . . In this 'Age of Affluence' the forgotten man in Southern agriculture is the Negro day laborer. And with automation he too is rapidly on his way to becoming extinct."[17]

Stirred by the larger forces of history and impelled by the misery of their immediate circumstances, MFLU organizers scoured every store, home, plantation, and church in towns throughout the Delta in search of potential recruits in its early days. By April 1965, they had come up with a name for their group, decided on operating rules, and made plans for a state workshop to facilitate organization and coordination throughout the Delta. The matters of funding and recruitment were stressed with utmost seriousness.[18] In addition to membership dues, much of the group's funding was solicited through a nationwide letter-writing campaign, a fund-raising method used by SNCC and other local civil rights organizations.[19]

Although the bulk of the MFLU membership came from cotton workers, from the very beginning the union had a significant number of domestic workers (maids) and tractor drivers among its rank and file. Eventually the MFLU grew to include "any and everybody associated with fieldwork and with any form of exploitative labor."[20] Less than a week after it was officially formed on April 9, 1965, the MFLU had over five hundred members in six counties in the Mississippi Delta, including Bolivar, Sunflower, Washington, Issaquena, Sharkey, and Holmes.[21]

The matter of wages was a serious one for the labor union members, although not their sole issue. For years, day laborers (pickers and choppers on the plantation) were paid a mere $2.50 to $3.00 for ten or more hours of daily work. At the time of the MFLU's first strike, white plantation owners in Shaw were threatening to drop that wage to $1.75 per day. MFLU members felt they had no choice but to organize and plan mass activity in the same way that they sparked civil rights movement activities in the region. The threat of lower wages—combined with the lack of work during rainy seasons and no unemployment compensation or government protective measures like a minimum wage, Social Security, or guaranteed Farmer's Home Administration (FHA) loans—riled them to act and to do so on a relatively large scale, just as black Deltans had done the previous year during the much-publicized Freedom Summer.[22]

As the ranks of the organization swelled, worker demands increased. By April 1965 when the forty-five original members met officially to form the union, they had the rank and file sign pledge forms calling for a $1.25 hourly minimum wage for work;[23] an eight-hour day with time and a half for overtime; guaranteed sick pay; health and accident insurance; employer commitment to equal employment practices in wages, hiring, and working conditions; and prohibition of child and elder labor.[24]

Hamer's involvement and contribution to the Mississippi Freedom Labor Union were both marginal and essential; she wielded a kind of influence that was alternately direct and indirect. She was among the union's most outspoken supporters. Throughout the hectic waves of MFLU strike activity, she endorsed the union in her speeches, usually during her travels to raise funds and support for the MFDP's concurrent congressional challenge. She inspired union members to aim uninhibitedly for complete freedom with every measure of energy they could muster. On some occasions, she lent her fund-raising influence and skill to the union as well. She became the union's adopted leader and figurehead, for obvious reasons. She was the rank and file's role model; she was a former sharecropper and a political activist.

In a symbolic sense, Hamer was the personification of a kind of historical force that created conditions for the existence of the Mississippi Freedom Labor Union. Her life, work, and suffering constituted a necessary precedent to the MFLU; her publicly lived experience in the civil rights movement inspired a parallel movement among farmers and other exploited laborers. Alongside other stories of legendary figures and inspirational experiences, Hamer's courageous tale was retold throughout the Delta between 1962 and 1964, creating a lush environment of boldness and daring for the growth of independent alternative organizations such as unions and cooperatives.[25] In many ways Hamer had helped establish an inspirational and institutional foundation for the MFLU.

Hamer's first public act of support on behalf of the MFLU occurred a little less than a week after the organization's official formation. On April 14 and 15, Hamer appeared before a crowd of some sixty MFLU protesters picketing the Motor Inn Hotel in Greenville, Mississippi. Inside the hotel, representatives of the U.S. Department of Labor were holding a meeting with members of the Mississippi Delta Council (a group of businessmen landowners) and a number of Mississippi state agencies. The purpose was to address some of the issues and problems of farm labor in the Delta. MFLU members sought entrance to the meeting so that they could voice their concerns and demands directly to labor department officials. As one protester put it, "The conference dealt with the fate of thousands of Negroes and none of us were invited to participate."[26] During the picketing, Fannie Lou Hamer managed to get inside the hotel and read the MFLU demands. Although information is sketchy about the full nature and extent of Hamer's involvement, SNCC's newspaper coverage indicates that she was instrumental in helping more MFLU representatives gain entrance to the meeting largely because of her political stature in Mississippi and across the nation. Even more important, she apparently had a hand in setting the tone for the MFLU's participation once inside. As she spoke to the labor department officials, six more MFLU folk were let in to speak, and they wasted little time as they questioned officials about the state of farm wages.[27]

As Hamer helped the MFLU with its strikes and nonstrike activities, so did the union help Hamer and the Mississippi Freedom Democratic Party. This reflected the interconnectedness of organizations and purposes. The MFLU's support for Hamer's congressional challenge involved a Washington, D.C., trip to lobby in support of the Mississippi challengers and for a minimum-wage bill for farmers.[28] Later in the fall of 1965, the MFLU also collaborated with the Freedom Democrats on "Black Christmas," another project supported by Hamer. This project, begun in October that year, helped needy children and their families. In addition, the project had a long-range, fairly ambitious goal of raising support for black-owned co-ops and other self-sufficiency operations in the Delta by encouraging individuals to buy products from these businesses and donate them to various MFLU locals.[29]

The summer of 1965 proved to be a very active one for the union as Hamer continued providing her support, encouragement, and ideas to the growing movement. The MFLU was involved in a great deal of strike activity, much of it in Hamer's own backyard. After two weeks of organizing, some thousand workers had joined the union and more than two hundred of them had declared themselves on strike. Striking in the Mississippi Delta was akin to voter registration work: it could easily cost you your home, family, and life. It often provoked Klan activity, and most sharecropping or share-renting strikers were eventually thrown off their plantations for striking or for being remotely associated with the MFLU.[30]

In striking, the MFLU positioned itself to battle an array of forces, forces that had an enormous degree of control over African Americans' destiny. Along with opposing planters, merchants, and bankers, the union also battled against the mechanization that, by the 1940s, would displace thousands of laborers and completely change the scale of southern agriculture.[31] Counties that witnessed the most strike activity were among the Delta's poorest. In Bolivar, Issaquena, Panola, Sharkey, Sunflower, and Washington counties, over 88 percent of the families earned less than three thousand dollars a year. Blacks comprised a 61 percent majority in these counties, but the pattern of landownership of the plantations on which they worked gave them little hope that matters would change without a protracted, organized response.[32] A SNCC research report on the union noted that these counties were the sites of property owned by a number of powerful Mississippi representatives to Congress, including Senators James Eastland and John Stennis and Representative Jamie Whitten, Hamer's opponent in the challenge. The report noted that these representatives had very poor voting records on bills aimed at eradicating poverty in the Delta, and that these legislators were the recipients of some of the largest federal subsidies. For example, from 1961 to 1962, Eastland received well over a half million dollars in subsidies. The MFLU had taken on some powerful forces that must have seemed nearly omnipotent.[33]

As a consequence of its strike activities, MFLU members remained forever in need of money, food, and clothing as they suffered abuse at the hands of landowners, who responded to the organization with typical vindictiveness. Similar to the state reaction to Freedom Summer 1964, a campaign of state-sanctioned harassment and repression ensued all across the South in the wake of the MFLU strikes. In response, the MFLU formed a community relief fund to assist those victimized by employer retaliation.[34] At the time of the union's formation, it was anticipated that some people would be displaced by angry landowners. Consequently, a number of original union members agreed to open up their homes to striking members who were evicted or facing eviction from their respective plantations.[35] So much harassment and displacement was anticipated in the wake of the MFLU's formation and initial strike activity that SNCC issued a memorandum warning of an increased need for bail money in anticipation of solicitation from the union. The full text of the memo indicates that organizing in the Delta was still a dangerous pursuit. Though the civil rights movement spawned a great deal of ideological meandering and organizational disunity in the mid-sixties, it was still able to elicit a response of repression from vexed members of the opposition.[36]

Perhaps at no time was Hamer's influence felt more strongly than during the second wave of MFLU strike activity, beginning in late spring 1965 and lasting through the summer. It was an intense period of labor organizing and striking that captured attention in newspapers across the nation, especially the *New York Times*. This second wave of strikes was reminiscent of the early days of civil rights organizing. A cycle of protest and persecution was set in motion.

By June 4, 1965, of the one thousand people on strike in the Delta, four hundred were in Fannie Lou Hamer's home of Sunflower County. Along with Washington and Bolivar counties, Sunflower provided the MFLU with its largest number of supporters.[37] In addition to meeting original union demands, this second wave of activity also sought to fulfill the union's long-term objective of capturing federal attention for relocation and retraining programs.[38] In this respect, the MFLU was in step with President Lyndon Johnson and the federal government's War on Poverty programs. The timing of strike activity made it especially significant and effective. June marked the beginning of the peak season for cotton chopping. A great many women and children worked in fields during this period. In addition, owners were forced to supplement this work force by recruiting day laborers from nearby towns.[39]

By July the number of MFLU strikers in the Delta had doubled. Landowners and other employers escalated their response in kind. A SNCC solicitation letter on behalf of the union noted: "The people have planted freedom gardens so that they might eat; they have set up tent cities in order to have a place to sleep at nights. But each day their conditions become worse and worse. Many men are being forced back to work as their families are starving."[40]

The most publicized of second-wave strikes occurred on the Andrew plantation in Tribbett, Mississippi, in Washington County. On May 31, 1965, eighty black tenant farmers walked off a 1,300-acre cotton plantation owned by a former schoolteacher, A. L. Andrews, and his brother, W. B. Andrews. Twelve of the strikers were tractor drivers seeking more than $6.00 a day for their efforts. Nearly seventy of the strikers were cotton-field workers seeking a minimum wage of $1.25 an hour or a guaranteed daily wage of $9.00. Many of the strikers were ten- to fifteen-year residents on the Andrews plantation.[41] When the strikers and their families (nearly a hundred people) approached A. L. Andrews at 5:30 A.M. on May 31 and indicated they had no intention of going out to the field and were planning to strike, Andrews responded by calling the police and telling the workers they would have to leave the plantation. The male strikers decided to stay on the plantation, while the women and children went over to the National Council of Churches Center at Mount Beulah in Edwards, Mississippi, near Jackson, the state capital. The evicted MFLU members were assisted by a local grocery store owner who offered them land on which they could erect a tent city.[42] On Tuesday, June 1, the MFLU strikers continued picketing the Andrews plantation. On the adjacent Dickens plantation, at approximately 8:00 A.M. that morning, the wife of a plantation agent apparently became so incensed that she loaded up a shotgun and fired at the group of strikers picketing next door. (One man was hit and he later pressed charges.) Nevertheless, the MFLU strikers stayed on and picketed to prevent replacement workers from taking their jobs and thereby weakening their strike effort. Later in the day, the Andrews brothers had their attorney serve the picketers with an injunction, which rendered the strikers ineffective. The injunction ordered them to picket with only four people at a time and mandated a limit on the size of their picket signs. In addition, the Andrews brothers were granted the right to throw the men's possessions off the plantation.[43]

Hamer's personal and political acts were a response to the heightened intensity of MFLU activities. She filled her speeches with calls for retributive violence, which characterized the black nationalist phase of the modern civil rights era. She vented rage at mainstream middle-class folk with a force unequaled since she appeared at the Democratic National Convention the previous year. On June 3, Hamer spoke at a rally in support of the union, especially its much-publicized activities on the Andrews plantation in Tribbett. Some 150 blacks were present at the night gathering, according to a *New York Times* estimate.[44] Also in attendance were three Washington County deputy sheriffs, who listened some fifty yards away on an adjacent road. The site of the rally was the black-owned country grocery store operated by Roosevelt Adam, the man who opened his property to the evicted workers' tent city.

Soaked in perspiration from the summer night's heat, Hamer went before the outdoor gathering and delivered a message that aimed to embolden and inspire. In tone and force, it was not unlike most of her speeches. But for a relatively public statement, her remarks were atypical in one particular set of instructions she imparted to the crowd. On the problems of lack of support for the union and the use of replacement workers, Hamer urged the workers to take matters into their own hands through physical intimidation and punishment: "We got to stop the nervous Nellies and the Toms from going to the Man's place. I don't believe in killing, but a good whipping behind the bushes wouldn't hurt them."[45]

On its face, Hamer's presentation that night seemed to belie the God-fearing, nurturing-mother image she had acquired in the civil rights movement. Through the early stages of her movement years, Hamer had come to be associated with good and protectiveness among the members of her community. Only those who denied her justice were in line to receive her wrath. Publicly expressed calls to do harm to political enemies among her own following were out of character for such a loving, Christian woman. But her statement at the rally should be understood in the complete context of Hamer's life and, more specifically, of the evolution of the movement. The reference to violence should come as no surprise from the woman who half-jokingly threatened to slit Aaron Henry's throat when he raised the possibility of accepting the proffered Democratic Party compromise to the MFDP convention challenge. It should also come as no shock when we consider the language of discipline that her father used to put her in line as a young girl. Hamer lived in a harsh and violent world where threatening, profane utterances were commonplace. Neither was this verbalization considered sacrilegious or hypocritical to one's sanctified beliefs and worldview. This was one of the larger, unremitting paradoxes in the life of a very devout and politically inspired Christian woman. Hamer seemed to be fully at ease with her "bad" self and her divinely inspired self. For Hamer they coexisted, and she embraced and understood their mutuality. To be sure, both were working that night at the MFLU rally near the Andrews plantation.

Perhaps most revealing about the comment was its timing, and slightly less so its indication of a radical or extremist departure from Hamer's already forthright style. This comment was part of her ongoing personal fight with mainstream traditional leaders. The reference to "nervous Nellies" and "Toms" resonates quite strongly when we consider the class tension within the movement, even though Hamer directed those specific remarks at perceived traitors of her own class circumstance—replacement day laborers in the cotton fields. But this use is an indicator of Hamer's political conception of class. On the surface, it appears that Hamer often conflated race and class—and this is entirely understandable given the reality of her life in the Mississippi Delta. But Hamer's political conception of class was more precisely defined. It was based on material circumstances and was also measurable in degrees of racial loyalty, not just race membership. In this regard, Hamer was a racial loyalist at heart. Those she often referred to as "middle-class Negroes," or the pejorative equivalent, "Uncle Tom" or "nervous Nellie," were essentially those who failed her litmus test of racial fealty. In this context her rousing remark at the Andrews plantation rally was another expression of frustration with those who would not step up to the plate like "real" men and women and show their racial allegiances in words and deeds.

In another way, the Tribbett strike speech showed Hamer to be a woman of her time. The civil rights movement began a radical shift toward racial separatism and other extremes after the summer of 1964, a shift that was completely defined during 1966–67.[46] The civil rights movement and its many victories raised expectations for African Americans. But heightened expectations soon turned to bitter disillusionment in the mid-sixties when reality failed to change as the hopeful continued hoping. The statistics bore out an unchanged reality of two Americas in 1965: nonwhites comprised only 11 percent of the labor force but over 21 percent of the unemployed; 37 percent of all black families lived under the poverty line; black teenage unemployment was on the increase at 32 percent while that of white teenagers had dropped to 14 percent;

black children had a life expectancy seven years shorter than that of their white counterparts; segregated, inferior schools persisted in black areas in spite of the 1954 *Brown* decision; and poor health services and deplorable housing abounded in black communities nationwide.[47] In many ways, the period on the horizon, soon to be called the black power era, was a militant response to an ironic circumstance. It was a reaction to a combination of increased hope spawned by some degree of change in a few areas of American life and wrenching anger and despair born of stagnation in others. Consequently, in discourse, thought, and practice, what we once knew as the civil rights movement soon changed in tenor, method, and priorities. To be sure, Hamer's message to the MFLU that summer night reflected this fact.

In few areas of grass-roots political life did this shift manifest itself so clearly as in the speeches and public manner of leaders. The rhetoric of moral suasion and loving togetherness found few expressive vehicles as the civil rights movement waned and gave way to this new phase. The matter of appealing to the hearts and minds of the oppressors now seemed a waste of time. The goal of integration as means to equality was soon publicly abandoned and deemed a futile pursuit by many. There was no more room for "love and suffering" slogans. Instead, there was a great, fiery, no-holds-barred quality about speeches, which Hamer was certainly capable of delivering. Increasingly, blacks began to talk less about rights and more about something called "power." Consequently, the language of black power came to focus on the discourse of empowerment, the oration of self-control and self-initiative. Self-help became the order of the day.[48] Tactically, nonviolent appeals to the law were out of the question. Instead of federal government intervention, many activists of the black nationalist persuasion espoused self-determination and community control. The black supplicant (Hamer's Uncle Tom or nervous Nellie) had no place and deserved no voice. Many black people began to talk about pride and selfhood.[49] The only similarity black power discourse had with the rhetoric of the preceding period was one of purpose: it still sought to mobilize and unify. Hamer and her involvement with the MFLU sat on the cusp of this change. Her speech reflected a new ethos in progress. What's more, it foreshadowed even deeper changes to come.

The Tribbett strike was well publicized and undoubtedly touched off a chain reaction of strikes throughout the Delta. News of Tribbett reached as far away as Harlem. More significant, Tribbett was just one of many areas of contention around MFLU demands. On the same day the Andrews strike began, another one began in Cleveland, Mississippi, in Bolivar County. On May 31 ten MFLU strikers approached a truckload of field-workers and tried to dissuade them from going into the field that morning. Some MFLU strikers even sneaked onto trucks themselves with the intention of persuading those already in the fields to cease working, a practice referred to as "infiltrating the plantations."[50] The next couple of mornings they continued their attempts to prevent replacement workers (most of them under the age of eighteen) from taking their places. On June 3, after a night of speaking in Greenville (site of a tent city of evicted strikers), Hamer delivered a speech in support of workers in Cleveland. In a gesture that was humble and self-effacing (considering the historic importance of her own SNCC and MFDP work), she called their activities "the most important thing that has ever happened to Mississippi." In reference to what the union was accomplishing in the way of organizing and stirring people to action, she noted with great respect and admiration, "It's something that we've all wanted to do for a long time. These are the first people that have had the guts to do it."[51]

To halt the efforts of the Cleveland MFLU, the police were called in by a "nervous Nellie"—to use Hamer's characterization—a black woman grocery store owner who relied heavily on the business of the replacement workers. When the police arrived they intervened by trying to "persuade" the replacement workers to get on their respective trucks and go out to the field. Many were arrested as a consequence of activities in Cleveland, and most of them were children and teenagers under eighteen.[52] But the MFLU still proved to be especially effective at organizing workers and keeping laborers out of the fields. Less than a week later, some six hundred workers were out on strike, and the attendance at business and planning meetings sometimes included more than a hundred participants.[53] Other hot areas of MFLU activity in Bolivar County included Rosedale and, obviously, Shaw, where the union originated.[54] To assist and encourage organizing in new areas, there was a fair amount of coordination and cooperation between locals, particularly those in the same county. For example, Cleveland became the center of additional controversy when county law enforcement officials focused on it as the site where allegedly the MFLU was "housing three union officials wanted by the police in Shaw."[55]

An interesting aspect of the Cleveland activities was the direct link between MFDP people and MFLU activists. Among those taken into police custody as a result of the day's activities was the Reverend Leroy Johnson, chair of the local Cleveland Freedom Democratic Party. Although they did not have any formal ties or relationship, the MFDP and the MFLU in many cases relied on the same pool of local activists.

As noted earlier, another site of strike activity and union organizing was Hamer's own Sunflower County, where some four hundred workers went out on strike that spring. The MFLU hit places like Doddsville, Indianola (the county seat), and Ruleville, Hamer's home town. However, the SNCC WATS Reports, press releases, and field notes are silent about Hamer's speaking or working on behalf of the union in her home area, which is not surprising given her other major commitment in 1965. Significant in light of Hamer's political challenge on Capitol Hill, the Doddsville plantation was owned by Hamer's nemesis and political opponent in the challenge, Senator James O. Eastland, one of the biggest landowners in the Delta. The Doddsville plantation drew attention to MFLU organizing, among other reasons, because Eastland's plantation was the source of replacement workers for strikers on plantations throughout the Delta.

Perhaps one of the most impressive consequences of the MFLU effort was the chain reaction it set off among other nonplantation workers throughout the state during the summer and fall months of the same year. Restaurant cooks, hotel maids, domestic servants, and custodians all went out on strike for better pay and work conditions.[56] One of the more heartening stories came from McComb, Mississippi, where nine maids at the Holiday Inn, inspired by MFLU activities in the Delta, walked off their jobs. They struck for $1.25 an hour, instead of the measly thirty-nine cents they were being paid. The women walked out and picketed the hotel. They later received support from northern unions representing steelworkers and longshoremen.[57] Perhaps an equally impressive result of the MFLU effort was the formation of other locals in other states, such as the Tennessee Freedom Labor Union, which was in constant and very close contact with the MFLU. Several states entered the planning stages of an FLU, including Arkansas, North Carolina, Alabama, and Louisiana.[58]

Other MFLU-inspired efforts included a selective buying campaign, an effort that Hamer also backed and joined. The campaign originated in the wave of formation of cooperatives in the fall of 1965. It began with a boycott of white businesses in Natchez, Mississippi. The boycott grew in intensity when white city officials responded by firing all black city employees, thereby creating an enormous need for food, clothing, and money.[59] Toward the end of 1965 and the beginning of 1966, Ruleville was the site of an effective selective buying campaign. Others campaigns took place in Fayette, Moss Point, Greenwood, Rosedale, Canton, and Columbia. The motto and premise of a selective buying campaign was, "If you can't get to his heart, talk to his pocketbook," no doubt a reference to the exasperation felt when the strategy of answering racism with moral suasion was exhausted. Citizens were resolute about "refusing to spend their money in places which practice discrimination in serving, hiring or buying." And boycotters not only stayed away from the small neighborhood stores and businesses. They hit the big retailers as well: J. C. Penney, Sears Roebuck, and all others that refused to hire black clerks.[60]

In Ruleville, the selective buying boycott began when Hamer accompanied a group of blacks to the mayor's office to request the firing of a policeman who shot a young black man, Paul Jackson, for no apparent reason. According to an account by the Delta Ministry, an interracial civil rights organization of clergy, it was at that point that an incensed Hamer and other citizens decided to quit buying in Ruleville stores. During the campaign, Hamer noted that the boycott had been "98 percent effective." With indignation, she observed in her signature style: "Some of the storekeepers complain they may go out of business; well, we've been out of business all the time! And everybody has quit [buying]. They go to Drew or Cleveland, but they won't buy here. The white man around here don't realize how good it would be to let us up out of the ditch. He can't keep us in the ditch without standing on us, and he can't get out of the ditch without letting us out."[61]

In addition to the firing, the group demanded desegregation of public accommodations in Ruleville, especially the Delta Theater. They demanded an end to unfair hiring practices, police brutality, and "discourteous treatment."[62] Protesting in the holiday spirit, Hamer and her coworkers distributed leaflets that read "Black Christmas for White Man Means White Christmas for Negroes." The message was clear: continued black support of white racist businesses would only prolong oppressive conditions for black people. The leaflet was also an endorsement and call for redirecting energies and resources to the concurrent Black Christmas campaign being cosponsored by the MFLU, MFDP, and the Poor People's Cooperative.[63]

As was soon to be the case for the Student Nonviolent Coordinating Committee, the MFLU fell apart during the winter months. Some accounts attribute its quick demise to the weather and to workers' need to survive the winter by returning to the plantations. Other accounts highlight the significance of internal squabbling and disunity that had begun to plague the organization with the coming of winter.[64] And then there was the longtime problem of funding for the group. Money was just not forthcoming toward the end of 1965.[65] Soon, however, Hamer had in mind another project for the poor. She called it the Freedom Farm.

eight

You can make it pretty good, until last month,
this month, and next month; cause by that
time, you owe everybody.

—Mississippi farmer

If we have that land, can't anybody starve us
out.

—Fannie Lou Hamer

Poverty Politics
and the Freedom Farm

Between 1966 and 1968, political disappointment, fights over poverty programs, and personal tragedy derailed Hamer's plans to retool the local movement for an attack on poverty. She split with SNCC, and her daughter died tragically. Hamer eventually resumed her work but with a heavy heart and a little doubt. Nonetheless, she maintained enough resolve to realize her proudest accomplishment, the Freedom Farm.

Hamer's deteriorating relations with SNCC coincided with SNCC's ideological and organizational disintegration after 1964. As much as the Democratic Convention challenge resulted in the radicalization of Hamer, the MFDP, and some elements in SNCC, it also led to some unforeseen and ultimately destructive consequences for one of the most militant and respected organizations in the civil rights movement. The 1964 defeat and the relative failure of Freedom Summer to sustain itself left many SNCC leaders wondering if the organization could continue to be effective with its strategy of guerrilla-style mobilizing of severely repressed and disfranchised communities. SNCC veterans such as James Forman and Bob Moses persuaded SNCC to pull back and reflect on how to proceed. It was a question of method and goal, means and end. Yet with this determination to reevaluate's SNCC tactics and mission came a more pronounced fractionalization of the organization.

At a November 1964 retreat in Waveland, Mississippi, SNCC addressed its own future. Staff members tackled a number of charged issues all for the purpose of getting SNCC back on the road to effectiveness. Among the issues raised was the subject of whites in the organization, a concern that had resulted in

Courtland Cox's calling the SNCC delegation back from Africa earlier than planned. The specific concern was the increase in white membership in the organization as a result of Freedom Summer. Before the summer ended, young white activists, many of whom were college educated and middle class, moved into the ranks of the organization. They became full-time SNCC members; they were no longer just volunteers. This led to a significant change in SNCC's racial and class composition, thereby unleashing a panic among some of the organization's faithful. This change took place against the larger changes of that turbulent summer: calls for black pride and self-determination gained increased acceptance throughout SNCC and other segments of the civil rights movement.

In addition to these internal matters, SNCC was also experiencing a deterioration in its relations with black middle-class leaders and organizations. SCLC and the NAACP both perceived that SNCC had steered the MFDP wrong in not accepting Lyndon Johnson's compromise. SNCC was also getting more than its usual share of bad press during and after the summer campaign, much of it filled with red-baiting charges of Communist infiltration. In addition, the lack of personal discipline in the organization was hurting its own cause. According to the SNCC historian Clayborne Carson, marijuana use and absenteeism among project workers, as well as other forms of irresponsible behavior, hurt the organization's public image.[1] The cost of SNCC's difficulties in financial resources was significant; this transition period for the organization led to an erosion of its liberal support base in the North. Another issue, although minor, was the role played in the organization by individuals with little formal education, and this included Fannie Lou Hamer.

In February 1965, SNCC held an important executive committee meeting to discuss additional support for poor people and to elect new committee members. Hamer was present at this meeting. Unexpectedly, the selection of the new committee caused her both confusion and dismay. In a patronizing way, a SNCC member proposed that education be used as a criterion for selecting committee members. He suggested that no one with more than a twelfth-grade education be put on the new committee. Hamer, formally educated to the sixth grade, was not amused or flattered. Instead, she wasted little time expressing her confusion and disagreement. She demanded that the staff take her name out of consideration because she wanted no part of such a process. Although the motion never passed, the selection process turned up a number of individuals who fit the education criterion. A sizable majority of the new executive committee members had less than a twelfth-grade education.

Hamer did not read this as an honor. She was hurt and embarrassed. Although she often reminded people that it was no fault of hers or her parents that she had little more than six years of schooling, Hamer was not comfortable when others called attention to her lack of formal education in demeaning ways. This issue and that meeting left Hamer disaffected, and she had little reason to be hopeful about the organization's future, given SNCC's other problems, including its growing rift with the MFDP. Although her name appears on lists of the 1965 SNCC executive committee and although Carson notes that she became a member despite her disaffection, the attendance records for executive committee members indicate little if any involvement on her part. In fact, one scribbled note in the SNCC Papers Collection indicates that other members of the executive committee tried to contact her repeatedly to inquire about her nonparticipation, but to no avail.[2]

By 1966 it appeared that Hamer and SNCC were on a collision course. The clash of perspectives was caused by a number of factors, but the main catalyst appears to have been the issue of white involvement in SNCC. By spring 1966, SNCC was controlled by a faction of black separatists from Atlanta, where SNCC had been involved in some controversial and violent acts of resistance. As a result of their daring campaigns in the city, the Atlanta separatists attracted young people who soon injected new blood into the organization, locally and nationally. They planned a meeting for the end of the year to resolve finally the matter of whites in SNCC and to deal with other issues related to the meaning of black power.[3]

That meeting took place on December 1, 1966, in upstate New York at the home of the black entertainer "Peg Leg" Bates. The meeting lasted several days, much of it taken up by the subject of whites. Beginning at Waveland, Hamer had opposed the move to expel whites from SNCC. She believed that they had been there from the very beginning and that it made little sense, nor was it fair, to jettison them now. She was certainly not alone in taking this position. There were a number of whites in attendance at the New York meeting as well as black SNCC members who shared Hamer's position. After days of debate, a motion called for a vote on the matter. In a very close balloting, SNCC voted to expel whites from the organization. Nineteen decided in favor of expulsion, while eighteen voted against, with twenty-four individuals abstaining (a noteworthy and telling outcome in and of itself).[4]

The expulsion did not come without scorn and dismissal for Hamer. During the course of heated discussion, a few of the black separatists rose and denounced Hamer for being "no longer relevant." They chided her for not being at their "level of development." This shocked and pained some of those who witnessed the incident.[5] One can only imagine the suffering it must have caused the object of such derision. Hamer never talked publicly about what happened at the retreat, nor did she ever make any negative observations about SNCC, black separatism, or the black power movement. In fact, with the exception of the issue of racial separatism, she remained devoted to black nationalism and its various cultural, psychological, and institutional manifestations. But she remained opposed to judging people on the basis of their race. She believed that this only defeated the purpose of the movement. Although she subscribed wholeheartedly to the principle of black control over black lives, Hamer maintained that white participation in a movement for racial justice was not at odds with the intentions and achievement of black self-determination.

After 1966, Hamer's name appeared less frequently in SNCC field reports, letters, meeting minutes, and other documents. The outcome of the Peg Leg Bates retreat did complete Hamer's disaffection with the changing organization, but the break was not a clean one. Hamer did not halt communication with the new SNCC. Post-1966 records indicate that she still occasionally reported to the organization on matters in her home county. However, the historical record, or perhaps the lack of such, does generally suggest an abrupt and difficult change in relations between the two, a change that affected Hamer deeply.

SNCC was the organization that had given her a chance to move beyond the Delta and to begin dreaming about another life, one free of racial oppression. She often remarked in appreciation of the group's presence and work, "If there hadn't been a SNCC, there would be no Fannie Lou Hamer." Hamer felt so strongly about her historic encounter with SNCC that she once remarked, "To me, if I had to choose today between church—and I'm not against the church—I'd choose these young people. They did something in Mississippi that gave us the hope that we had prayed for so many years."[6] The loss was painful, no doubt, not simply because she was losing her first political family, but also because of the way it happened. But Hamer did not manifest this pain in any direct way until her bout with depression six years later. Perhaps for the first time Hamer now tasted what it was like to be scorned and criticized by those whose cause she still basically believed in. It was one thing to have national NAACP leaders like Roy Wilkins tell you that you had no place, but it was another to be told that by those whose opinions once mattered.

■ ■ ■

Hamer contacted SNCC sparingly during 1967. By then she deeply invested her efforts in special elections called for the towns of Moorhead and Sunflower. SNCC still had some interest in developments there too, and she still had some friends in the organization with whom she wanted to work. She reported back to the organization about local affairs and national travels in preparation for the elections. Earlier in the year, she had gone on a torrid fund-raising campaign for the MFDP candidates running in the elections. National fund raising continued to be her strength, even as she pulled away from nationally recognized civil rights organizations.

The origins of the special elections extended back to 1963, when the U.S. Justice Department filed suit against Sunflower County. In April 1965, a federal district court ruled that Cecil Campbell, Sunflower County's registrar, had denied blacks the right to register. Two weeks after this decision, Hamer and four others sued the county to get changes in elector qualification rules and new municipal elections. (The case was known as *Hamer v. Campbell*).[7] Specifically, they requested that the poll tax be suspended and that the upcoming municipal elections be delayed until more blacks had a chance to register.

On April 29, 1965, Hamer testified before Claude F. Clayton, the judge who had presided over the federal Winona case. She spoke of the many blacks in Sunflower County who wanted to register but were intimidated. Hamer was her usual sharp-witted self. When Mississippi's assistant attorney general questioned her qualifications, she rejoined that she was prepared to serve every citizen in the state: "I told him that I wouldn't only represent the Negroes, I would represent him, too, if he was in my municipal election district." Unpersuaded by the plaintiffs' claims, Judge Clayton denied the requests made in *Hamer v. Campbell*. Hamer then appealed. In March 1966, the Fifth Circuit Court of Appeals overturned Clayton's decision. The state appealed that decision, but its appeal was denied by the U.S. Supreme Court in October 1966. Clayton then ordered new elections in the towns of Moorhead and Sunflower. They were scheduled for May 2, 1967.

Hamer worked hard on the 1967 election. She regarded *Hamer v. Campbell* as a big victory for Sunflower County and the state of Mississippi. She appreciated the historical significance of the moment and was hopeful: "We have enough people to do this. For peoples to win this election, it would set a precedent for other counties in the state. Peoples need a victory so bad. We've been working here since '62 and we haven't got nothing, except a helluva lot of heartaches."[8]

More than anyone, Hamer knew that setting such a precedent required enormous effort. Accordingly, she spent most of her time on the road raising money, from fall 1966 to early spring 1967. As usual, her Northeast-Midwest connection was key. She spent a good bit of time in Manhattan, site of the headquarters for the National Committee for Free Elections in Sunflower. In

March, one ten-day trip to New York and Connecticut netted seven thousand dollars.

Hamer's travels were hard on mind, body, and soul. She missed her family very much. She worried about her relationship with Pap, who was not always pleased about the time she spent away from home, especially during this period of her career. Hamer also worried unceasingly about the direction of the civil rights movement, or what remained of it. Even as she poured everything into the historic special elections, she had genuine doubt about her own direction. Emotional depression was not far away; fortunately, her work activities kept her afloat. She moved at a furious pace between her final SNCC meeting and the Sunflower elections. But the pain was still there, and she spoke about it to close friends every now and then.

When it came to delivering speeches to raise money, Hamer's genius was not unlike that of Martin Luther King Jr. She was keenly aware of audience, and this showed in the rhetoric and content of her stirring speeches. In the North, she consistently couched the meaning of Mississippi's struggle in national terms. Many times, she noted that racism "is not Mississippi's problem. This is America's problem." She often used the familiar refrain, "America is on the critical list." Unendingly, she noted her many personal experiences with racism in the North and the South. But even as she noted the similarities between the regions, she set aside a special moment for detailing the persistence of racial violence in the South. For example, when she spoke before a Norwalk, Connecticut, crowd in March 1967, she mentioned the murder of Natchez leader Wharlest Jackson and the burning of a Grenada, Mississippi, church whose congregation had invited her to speak.[9] She also made sure to criticize the federal government's refusal to send registrars to Sunflower County until three days before the special elections. In asking for donations from the audience, she pointed out that the issue was about freedom for America and for the sake of humanity. At the end of one speech, she closed, "Whatever you give, it's not only to free me in Mississippi, but it's also to help to free yourselves because no man is an island to himself. And until I'm free in Mississippi, let's not kid ourselves, you're not free in Connecticut."[10]

Working the large crowds was probably Hamer's strength during her speaking tours. But during her 1967 tour, she also made appearances on radio and television shows, and at press conferences, receptions, and parties planned by local leaders and organizations in support of her cause.

When Hamer was not traveling, she was in her home county helping to register, educate, and mobilize voters in Moorhead and Sunflower. The atmosphere was as tense as earlier times in the Delta. Intimidation and threats set the tone, but there was work to do. Of the 13,524 eligible black voters in Sunflower County, only 1.1 percent were registered. There were 8,785 white residents in Sunflower County, and 80 percent of them were registered. In the town of Sunflower, blacks comprised 70 percent of the town's 800 residents but had been effectively excluded from voting: only 24 percent of black eligible voters were registered, while 85 percent of eligible whites were registered.[11]

On the morning of the elections, Hamer, still upbeat and hopeful, stood outside the Sunflower town hall and observed the scene. She had good reason to be optimistic. This was perhaps the most well-organized registration campaign she had orchestrated in her home county. The Mississippi Freedom Democratic Party candidates had money, the law, national attention, and enormous moral support on their side. Yet, they still lost. The MFDP's mayoral candidate, the twenty-one-year-old, unemployed Otis Brown, lost to the incumbent, W. L. Patterson, 190-121. Hamer had been especially vocal in her support of Brown, who had promised to bring jobs, poverty programs, and medical care to his town. The MFDP also lost the Moorhead mayoral contest and the aldermanic races in both communities. Once again, political defeat hit Hamer hard, as it did many other MFDP activists, some of whom cried and cursed in frustration. In searching for some consolation, Hamer found none and remarked, "There was nothing symbolic about this election. I'm sick of symbolic things. We are fighting for our lives."[12]

The MFDP and Hamer immediately charged interference and intimidation and filed suit. Again Hamer was the lead plaintiff in a suit against Sunflower County's registrar, a slot now filled by Sam J. Ely.[13] Some historians and political scientists have noted that cheating accounted for the losses, in part. Also determinant in the MFDP losses was a series of laws passed by the state legislature in 1966. The laws effectively diluted Mississippi's black vote after the passage of the 1965 Voting Rights Act.[14]

Between December 1966 and the end of spring 1967, it appeared that loss shadowed Hamer at every turn. First it was the split with SNCC, then MFDP's most disappointing defeat since 1964, and finally the biggest loss of all: the death of her beloved twenty-two-year-old daughter, Dorothy. Throughout her short life, Dorothy was sick and in need of nursing, which Hamer constantly provided when she was home. The biggest and longest battle was with Dorothy's malnutrition. A few weeks after the special election, the Hamers and Dorothy lost the battle. On the last day of her young life, Dorothy was so ill that Hamer sought medical help. She carried young Dorothy to the car and drove her to a nearby hospital, which refused them medical attention because they were black. Hamer drove to another hospital, which also refused to admit the dying young woman. Hamer continued driving until she located a hospital that would admit Dorothy. Hamer found herself in Memphis, 119 miles away from home. As Hamer approached the hospital entrance, Dorothy died in her mother's arms, leaving two baby girls behind in addition to a loving mother, father, and sister. The cause of death was a cerebral hemorrhage. The blow was a crushing one for the family.[15] Hamer's grief was enormous. For healing and solace, she turned to a few close friends and her church.

Hamer spent the next few months on the road, making speeches and thinking about her fall political work. She had hoped to run for the Mississippi state senate in the November 1967 election, but legally she was prevented from running, so she had to wait for 1971. She did spend the time working on the campaigns of other MFDP activists. Finally, the party achieved a victory: Holmes County elected Robert Clark the first black legislator in Mississippi since the end of Reconstruction. Hamer was proud. The achievement of Clark and other MFDP candidates was rightly credited to her efforts and those of others. After being sworn in, Clark received a call from Hamer, who reminded him what it was all about: "Young man, I called those white folks. We got you there now. And if you don't do right, then I'm going to march down on you just as hard as I would those white folk."[16]

■ ■ ■

From 1965 to 1969, Hamer appeared to be in a transition to full-scale antipoverty work. The journey was a rocky and unsettling one, if only because she found herself at odds with some grass-roots poor people to whom she devoted her life's work.

In 1965, a statewide poverty organization formed, calling itself the Child Development Group of Mississippi (CDGM). Included among its founding members were Tom Levin, a New York psychoanalyst and Freedom Summer worker; Art Thomas of the Delta Ministry; Polly Greenberg; and Jeannine Herron, a journalist. They wrote a proposal for a seven-week preschool program and submitted it to the Office of Economic Opportunity (OEO), the administrative agency for Lyndon Johnson's War on Poverty. Initially, the OEO granted CDGM nearly $1.5 million to serve over 6,000 youngsters in 84 centers and 24 counties. CDGM founders knew that local leaders would be central to the success of the programs; there were no programs without them. In Sunflower County, Cora Flemming, Alice Giles, Thelma May, and Annie Mae King had run their own preschool program for a time without any government or agency funding. After they attended a statewide CDGM organizational meeting in Jackson, they sought support to expand their own program. In

October 1966, they opened four centers in Indianola, all in private homes. CDGM Head Start provided children with preschool training, medical care, and hot meals. It was also an important source of income for teachers, drivers, and other workers. In February 1966, CDGM received another federal grant, for $5.6 million.[17]

Conservatives and moderates alike found it hard to resist not going after federal grants. Jealousy, political fear, and an unabashed arrogance combined to create a sense of entitlement. They wanted in on the receiving end. They would create their own poverty programs and show the ignorant poor how to administer social services. During the winter of 1965/66, Sunflower County Progress, Inc. (SCPI), formed as a community action program. It was officially launched on February 2, 1966, when it received its first grant ($27,000) from OEO. On its board were white business people and middle-class blacks, who were appointed by a county board of supervisors, various city councils, civic, ministerial, and teacher organizations and by "target area" groups.[18]

From the outset, SCPI faced opposition from the CDGM, which already had numerous Head Start Centers in the county. The SCPI was, of course, equally critical of CDGM administrators, who were often accused of financial mismanagement and general incompetence. In addition, the SCPI had no love for those with a history of civil rights activism, which many CDGM participants had. Among the most vocal critics of the SCPI was Hamer, who accused it of not representing poor folk. She demanded that the SCPI reorganize its board of directors under countywide elections.[19] After her individual protest, SCPI's leadership appointed her to the board of directors. But Hamer refused to attended any board meetings. Publicly she claimed that the meetings were closed to her. Board members denied this.

In the beginning, Hamer seemed uncertain about how to define her relationship to SCPI. It disturbed her that SCPI ignored the voice of local poor folk. She found herself in an awkward position that would become more uncomfortable as the local struggle for poverty funds intensified in the Delta. Moreover, Hamer, like some SNCC and MFDP activists, was not thrilled about the creation of yet another organization. She was concerned about focus and spreading thin; the movement could not lose the little momentum that remained.[20] A year later, she did run for a place on the SCPI board. Process was important to her. She decided to involve herself with SCPI on her own terms. In addition, she believed by this point, perhaps remembering the 1964 challenge nearby, that some compromise was important so that poor folks could get funding. In the April 1967 SCPI board election, Fannie Lou Hamer was defeated by Miles Foster, who had received significant white support.

Hamer's ambivalence about joining SCPI's administration was linked to another conflict of interest and perspective. She had her own poverty organization, the Associated Communities of Sunflower County (ACSC), which had been operating six months prior to SCPI's creation. The concept of ACSC originated with the Associated Community of Bolivar County, a poverty outfit begun by a local activist, Ramsey Moore. Charles McLaurin, Hamer's close associate in Ruleville, approached her about starting a similar antipoverty organization for Sunflower County. She agreed and began organizing local support. The ACSC targeted young and poor blacks opposed to the funding of SCPI. Hamer and ACSC fought hard to become an OEO-recognized antipoverty program so that it could get funding to operate its own Head Start Centers, which Hamer claimed were serving a thousand children. Finally, by 1967, ACSC succeeded. It convinced OEO that it was a grass-roots organization and received a grant to run a six-month Head Start program, from July to December.[21] ACSC became an associated agency under the SCPI. The support would not last long, however. By August 1968, the SCPI cut off ACSC amid charges of civil rights activism and financial irregularities. In quick response, Hamer led a demonstration on the SCPI's county offices in Indianola. Inside she spelled out the scope of her frustration to reporters, protesters, and all others who listened: "We seen [Head Start] was something could lift people up by their bootstraps. The boot is being taken away from us and the strap, too."[22]

In fall 1966, Mississippi Action for Progress (MAP) formed as a rival to the CDGM. Like CDGM, MAP was a biracial coalition, but its majority was white and it had no board involvement by women or by poor people of either sex. Its leadership came together at the urging of Sargent Shriver, director of OEO. MAP was the moderate counter to the CDGM and the ACSC. Most significant to the demise of the MFDP in the area, John Dittmer notes that MAP leaders were the same individuals who had worked to subvert the Freedom Democrats and move the "regular" state party back to the center. Millions of dollars in poverty monies could only help their pursuit of more leverage, political and financial.[23] In the fall of 1966, the OEO cut off the CDGM's money, claiming to be concerned about financial irregularities.

The existence of such organizations, all vying for OEO War on Poverty funds, made for an intense, sometimes violent rivalry among antipoverty activists. The war of words was just as intense. Hamer spared no criticism of MAP or SCPI. When thirty-five hundred people met in Jackson to protest the OEO decision not to refund CDGM, Hamer appeared and spoke. She zoomed in on her nemesis group—the sell-out bourgeoisie: "we aren't ready to be sold out by a few middle-class bourgeoisie and some of the Uncle Toms who couldn't care less."[24]

No amount of tough talk, however, could have fended off attempts to weaken or do away with Head Start in Sunflower County. The local conflicts and competition, among other factors, eventually forced the issue of realignment. In early 1971, OEO mandated that there be a single Head Start program for Sunflower County. Hamer and other poverty activists (including Cora Flemming of CDGM Head Start) requested a hearing to appeal the decision. In the meantime, Hamer removed over six hundred ACSC children from the county Head Start program. The OEO granted the hearing. In June 1971, Hamer traveled to the OEO regional office in Atlanta to make the appeal. The stress was high, and many were angry. Once again, Hamer had to weigh the value of compromise and symbolic victory. The odds were against her. After speaking her mind about local control and the needs of poor people, she had to face her allies and convince them of the inevitable: a merger of poverty programs.

The objections and ill will generated in response were overwhelming. Hamer had badly underestimated her influence. Flemming, a hardworking woman and respected grass-roots leader in her own right, was outraged—and deeply hurt. She felt betrayed. Although Hamer demanded an administrative position for Flemming and others as part of the merger arrangement, Flemming was not the least bit mollified. She rejected what she regarded as tokenism, much like Hamer did back at Atlantic City in 1964. Most serious, she believed that Hamer had made a deal with OEO and SCPI behind her back. She recalled: "[Hamer and others] had joined forces behind our backs. They just sold out. It was the most horrible thing I ever saw. I hope I never go through anything like it again." Flemming viewed Hamer as abusive and antagonistic: "When I got to the meeting, she said the meanest things to me. She called me everything but a child of God. She was just as vicious on me as she was on those chicken-eating preachers she was always after. . . . She knew better."[25] Others witnessed the two having differences. Indeed, Hamer arrived at the meeting quite defensive and worried that there were enemies in her ACSC camp. In her mind, she had just cause to be on guard. Six months earlier, on January 28, 1971, someone had tried to kill her and her family by throwing a Molotov cocktail into their house. (The device failed to ignite.)[26] Flemming and Hamer continued having a very difficult relationship after the Atlanta hearing. The bitterness was wrenching for both of them. Forgiveness would not come until Hamer was on her deathbed six years later.

Even though Hamer wanted in on Johnson's War on Poverty, she really was more comfortable with running her own antipoverty operation independent of local, state, and federal government. She kept her mind and hopes on such a plan, even as she fought it out with SCPI.

■ ■ ■

In 1969 Hamer laid the groundwork for an elaborate project to make poor folks economically self-sufficient. That project became the Freedom Farm Corporation. Through her work with the farm, Hamer broadened the meaning of civil rights activism to include addressing the economic needs of black poor folks. Her focus on poverty did not mark a major turning point in Hamer's agenda. She had always, since her first official civil rights activity in 1962, envisioned her activism in this broad sense. She was obsessed with ending human suffering around her, and this included suffering caused by decades of racism and poverty.

Food, clothing, and shelter were natural concerns for the civil rights movement in the Mississippi Delta, an area with a majority population that was black and poor. According to the 1960 census report, some 5,000 families in Sunflower County lived below the poverty line, earning less than $2,000 a year. Seven hundred of those families were white and 4,300 were black. Sixty-eight percent of Sunflower County residents lived on $1,000 a year or less. Many relied on meager assistance provided by welfare and charitable contributions.[27] Land ownership was extremely rare among black residents. Only 71 of the 31,000 black residents in black Sunflower County owned any land. The median annual income for all black Deltans was $456. In 1967 a Senate subcommittee "found extensive starvation and malnutrition" when it visited Sunflower County.[28] By 1969, 32 percent of blacks were on public assistance; 12.6 percent were unemployed; families averaged 5.69 members; residents received on average a sixth-grade education; 70 percent of homes were deteriorating or dilapidated, and 60 percent lacked plumbing.[29]

Sometime in 1969 Hamer began thinking further about an intensive effort to address the extreme need in her home county of Sunflower. She wrote a letter about her plans for a "Freedom Farm," detailing the plight of a hungry neighbor's son to underscore the urgency of such a project: "A friend walked into my house in Ruleville, Mississippi. She had lost her son a day or two before. He was 18 years old, but was never able to walk because he never had bones strong enough to walk on. My own daughter is 16 years old. She was in the hospital a few years ago. They fed her glucose because she was suffering from malnutrition."[30]

Hamer began the farm with a small project known as the "pig bank." At Hamer's request, the Sunflower County section of the National Council of

Negro Women (NCNW) donated fifty pigs to the Freedom Farm. Any family that had the requisite facilities could receive from the "bank" a female pig (a pregnant gilt), who eventually would have anywhere from nine to twenty baby pigs. The mother pig (the principal) was then returned to the general bank. When two female pigs from the litter became pregnant, the family then had to donate them to the next needy family. The initial objective was to breed as many pigs as possible before slaughter. In the first year and a half of the pig banks, approximately 135 families received pigs.[31] According to Franklynn Peterson, "By [the third year of operation] the bank had benefitted at least 300 families with a yield of between 2,000 and 3,000 new pigs." By May 1973, close to nine hundred families had participated in the program.[32]

The second component of the Freedom Farm was the acquisition of land for raising vegetables. In 1969 Hamer purchased a forty-acre plot of land—located just northwest of Drew, Mississippi—for $20,000 (with an $8,000 down payment). This initial acquisition was used for the pig bank. On January 15, 1971, Hamer made an $85,000 down payment on 640 additional acres of land. (The total cost was $288,000, with a $19,000 yearly obligation for the farm.) As of June 1971, Hamer had nearly seven hundred acres of land that were seriously underdeveloped because they lacked irrigation. This prevented Freedom Farm from developing a cash crop early on that would have helped the corporation become self-sustaining.[33] Farming operations greatly expanded in 1971, and new equipment was needed to farm newly acquired land. A significant portion of Freedom Farm's initial donations and revenue went toward the purchase of new equipment to make use of the land. A 1975 proposal noted that the Freedom Farm owned "$65,480.35 worth of mechanized farming equipment, free and clear." An earlier progress report, in March 1973, said that the farm had begun replacing vegetable production with an expanded cotton crop in order to generate a profit that could be applied toward the annual land payment.[34]

Land payments were always the single largest expenditure for the farm each year. Other needs of the farm included irrigation pipe and pumps, buildings to store the equipment, cotton trailers, seed, fertilizer, hand tools, ladders, and boxes.[35] In 1971, there were 33 plots of land totaling 1,940 acres owned by blacks in North Sunflower County. This meant that Freedom Farm comprised almost 33 percent of the land owned by blacks in the area.[36]

The land was used to raise fresh vegetables (soybeans, greens, corn, sweet potatoes) and small amounts of cotton. Some of the vegetables were harvested and given to needy families in Sunflower County, and the rest were canned and preserved. As members of the corporation or other local organizations encountered needy families, they would take a representative from that family to the vegetable project, where they would help the family collect fresh produce.[37] An estimated 250 families benefited from the first crop. This was significant, since in Sunflower at the time, no food stamps were available and surplus commodities were distributed only during three months of the year. (Interestingly, in 1970 Freedom Farm donated some of its surplus vegetables to needy folks in Chicago.) Between 1972 and 1973, Freedom Farm harvested seventy acres of "nutritional foods . . . for member families."[38]

The cotton was picked, taken through the other necessary processes, and sold. Proceeds from the cotton were used to defray administrative costs and to purchase seed for new crops.[39] For example, the profits from the cotton and soybeans met the 1970 land payment of a thousand dollars.

The third project associated with the farm involved housing; it was also conceived in 1969. Hamer recalled, "We decided to organize everybody who lived in a shack—which was most of us . . . and teach them how to take advantage of low cost FHA and farm mortgages. Once we got started, we found that so many people wanted to take part that we didn't have time to give the organization a name. We just sort of call it 'The Co-op.' "[40]

With crop revenues and small loans from compliant local banks, the Freedom Farm Corporation helped provide thirty-five families with down payments on FHA-financed, two- to four-bedroom homes in and around Ruleville.[41] For ten thousand dollars the Freedom Farm also purchased three houses and two lots in Ruleville and planned to resell them to the families who were living there. The amount they previously paid for rent now started going toward purchase of their homes.

Aided by local contractors, black and white, the Freedom Farm had built seventy affordable homes by 1972. For many inhabitants it was the first time they had lived in anything but a shack. The mortgage on a "comfortable two-bedroom" ran as low as $38 a month for a couple on Social Security. The most expensive mortgage was around $100 a month. This was for a family in which both mother and father worked, usually at some occupation like teaching. Freedom Farm's housing development program was quite extensive, providing for the construction of streets and alleys, the laying of water and sewage pipes, and the securing of electrical and gas services.[42]

No doubt, Hamer was proud of the housing component of Freedom Farm. She recalled one of the most memorable responses to the farm: "The one kind of remark which really means the most to me is one that I hear frequently outside on really cold mornings. You'll see two men walking out their front doors. One will kind of stop, look around and say, 'Phew I didn't realize how cold it was outside!' Every place they ever lived in before, it was always just as cold inside as it was outside."[43] Hamer and her family also enjoyed a new home. They moved into a yellow-brick dwelling, where Hamer spent the rest of her life. In total, the Freedom Farm secured more than $800,000 in FHA loans for the housing project.[44]

The fourth project focused on education, providing grants to several students from the area so that they could complete or further their schooling. Between 1973 and 1974, Freedom Farm targeted three high schools in Sunflower County (specifically Indianola, Ruleville, and Drew) to receive two scholarships of three hundred dollars each.[45] According to the March 1973 status report, twenty-five students were granted scholarships and grants to pursue a college education or vocational training. The Freedom Farm board of directors had hoped to establish trust funds for future scholarships.[46]

The fifth project envisioned by the Freedom Farm was a business development plan. The Freedom Farm lent its support to an "African Fashion Shop," which had its home branch in Drew, Mississippi. The shop sold clothing sewn by local women, and the proceeds from sales went toward the purchase of more material and toward income for the seamstresses who made the garments. The Freedom Farm also provided loans or grants to others for establishing or improving a local business. According to a 1969 annual report, Freedom Farm purchased buildings in Doddsville and Drew for a sewing co-op or laundromat. There were also plans for a clothing cooperative and community center in Ruleville. Eventually, with the help of the National Council of Negro Women, the farm started a sewing factory in Doddsville. It operated for a year before "marketing problems" forced it to close. In Drew, Freedom Farm began an African garment operation called "Afro-Botique." This same report noted that the farm contributed $500 to rebuild O'Neal Chapel church in Sunflower. The farm also made loans of up to $2,000 to establish new black businesses in the area.[47] Seasonal farm labor usually provided work for at least twenty-five individuals, who were selected according to need. Some of them were young students needing work to support their families. The farm also served as a sort of referral service. Through its referrals and recommendations from 1969 to 1972, some fifty individuals found employment. Between 1969 and 1972, the payroll averaged a little more than $43,000 annually.[48]

One of the more successful businesses that the Freedom Farm helped start was a plumbing operation run by Jimmy Douglas of Moorhead, Mississippi. The farm loaned Douglas money to purchase a used backhoe for laying pipe for sewers and water lines and then helped him get contracts through its low-income-housing construction project.[49]

The Freedom Farm also acted as a social service agency for folks in crisis. On August 23, 1971, Hamer wrote a letter to the Black Economic Research Center requesting help with the family of Mary Lou Taylor, a deceased mother of nineteen:

> Mrs. Mary Lou Taylor [w]as the mother of (20) twenty children in Ruleville, miss. Throught [sic] the years Mrs. Taylor was able to scratch, fight and earn enough to enable herself and family to survive. Her children range from ages 4 years to ages 20 years. Last Saturday Mrs. Taylor died, leaving her 19 [living] children without support. In order for this family to survive, we desire to establish a fund as we created for the family of Miss Jo Etha Collier, so that this family can stay together. We need funds to feed, clothe and house the Taylors who still live in a plantation shack house. We are hoping to get them any source [with] $10,000 to keep the Taylors family alive and together.[50]

Hamer often used her influence to help folks outside of Sunflower County. She developed a strong Northeast and Midwest connection among nonprofit churches and associations that were interested in social uplift projects. In late 1971, she used her connection with the American Freedom from Hunger Foundation to assist friends in surrounding Bolivar County.[51]

The Freedom Farm threw its resources behind disaster relief efforts in Sunflower County in 1971. In February of that year, a series of tornadoes swept through the county (particularly the town of Inverness), leaving some three hundred families homeless amidst death and destruction caused in just two hours. The farm provided relief in the form of money, food, clothing, housing, transportation, and access to medical facilities. In the months after the disaster, Freedom Farm continued using resources to provide clothing and financial assistance.[52] The farm commended Hamer for her tireless work in response to the disaster: "This dedication and selfless action by Mrs. Hamer in the name of the Corporation has made a reputation for Freedom Farm. Mrs. Hamer has always believed in helping a family today instead of making promises for tomorrow."[53]

Between 1970 and 1972, the farm helped hundreds of families to purchase food stamps. (The food stamp program was introduced in the county in 1970.) During such time, the farm also made outright "grants to hundreds of families needing medical care or clothing for children." In addition, the farm provided "transportation to and from medical facilities" and carried out "picket lines and boycotts of local merchants that abused Black customers."[54] The social service component of the farm also dealt with employment. According to the 1975 proposal: "At a time when unemployment is wide spread this worker will be assisting rural based families in finding employment and better jobs for the qualified, underemployed. At times, direct intervention and representation may be necessary as well as referrals."[55]

On an application for funding to the Minority Group Self-Determination Fund of the Commission on Religion and Race of the United Methodist Church, it was noted that the Freedom Farm served approximately 650 families a year. The average age of people served by the program was forty-five and the educational background was the sixth grade. For this group the main source of income was public assistance.[56] According to a 1975 proposal for funding, the annual income of folks served by Freedom Farm projects ranged from $0 to $5,000, with the average per year at roughly $1,800. Those served included infants and adults as old as seventy; the total number of people served was over a thousand.[57]

In the 1975 funding proposal, the Freedom Farm emphasized the need to target women. According to this proposal, "The primary target segment will be women heads of the households along with farm laborers." The proposal went on to note, "There is a tremendous number of families residing in Sunflower County that presently receive public assistance and/or are headed by women."[58]

Hamer's targeting of women may have been a function of her involvement in gender-based politics, although she felt ambivalent about this. It may also have been a reflection of changing demographics or of Freedom Farm's perception of demographic factors, such as more women starting to head their own households. This new emphasis reflected a change in the farm's direction. Another change was the absence of white farmers as a target, which probably had been just political in the beginning anyway.

The farm was run as a cooperative. There was a one-dollar monthly membership fee, but few folks could afford that. Yet, no one was ever denied participation for this reason. The primary members of the Freedom Farm were residents who had lost their farm jobs to mechanization. According to Lester Salamon, a Harvard teaching fellow and organizer of a Harvard-based emergency fund drive for the Freedom Farm Corporation, in 1966 approximately 30,000 farm laborers lost jobs to mechanization. In 1967 the number was 100,000. During this time, only 100 new jobs were created statewide in Mississippi.[59]

The Freedom Farm was a multifaceted program of economic self-sufficiency and community development. Hamer envisioned it as freedom on another level—freedom "from hunger, poverty, and homes that did not adequately protect needy families from the cold winds of 'Old Man Winter.'"[60] In the sense that the farm was another way to reach freedom, it was a continuation of Hamer's civil rights work, not a departure from it. According to a November 1971 memorandum on Hamer's underlying philosophy for the farm: "Mrs. Hamer envisions Freedom Farms as a[n] agricultural mecca for blacks and a possible housing development." The document then quoted some of Hamer's thoughts about self-sufficiency: "We must feed people for hunger is the enemy. Land is food and food feeds people. . . . The condition is crucial. . . . Most people have nothing to live on, nothing to eat, no jobs, no place to stay. . . . Our place has kept many of these kids alive."[61]

The guiding philosophy of the Freedom Farm was empowerment of a long-term nature. Hamer argued that giving food or food stamps or cash to the poor addressed a fundamental problem with only a short-term solution. This idea was expressed fully in a brief history of the Freedom Farm: "Feeding the hungry and giving aid to the poor usually meant giving cash for food, purchasing food stamps, etc. to individuals and/or families who usually find themselves in the same destitute condition after several days when the money was no longer there." The farm was necessary, therefore, so families could "provide food for themselves on a continuous basis."[62]

This too was a reflection of Hamer's beliefs and experiences. She saw during the summer of 1964 how people would sometimes take food without registering to vote, and how, despite these donations, the hunger continued. She realized that money and food were needed in order to gain the freedom she envisioned. Hamer was also influenced by her trip to Africa, during which she witnessed black folks running their own businesses. Also, the context for the farm—the black power era—influenced its philosophy about the possibilities and necessities for long-term improvement and empowerment. The Freedom Farm was a self-help institution that paralleled those founded by other civil rights and black power organizations.

Although the farm was not closed to poor whites, there was little doubt that Hamer intended the farm to be a black-run operation. According to a 1973 Freedom Farm status report, Hamer "wanted to develop a Black controlled institution that would have its strengths in the land and would be able to support the indigent Blacks and Whites of the Sunflower County area that are being displaced by increased mechanization of agricultural production."[63]

In 1975 the Freedom Farm unabashedly espoused a self-help philosophy that described the "need for an organization which allows people to work and reap the benefits of their labor" as a "paramount priority." The proposal goes on to note: "Freedom Farm Corporation is that kind of organization. It has been proven time and again that handouts do not work. The only way for a family to break out of the bondage of the Welfare rolls is the SELF-HELP method.

SELF-HELP provides an incentive, a motivation, an achievement—in essence—a reason for being."[64]

In this respect Freedom Farm came close to sounding conservative (an institution in the Booker T. Washington tradition)—or contradictory. After all, part of its social service agenda did entail helping people to secure food stamps. However, there was probably more consistency than contradiction and ambivalence, for Hamer believed that welfare was an entitlement, albeit one that offered a double-edged sword.

Hamer selected a business partner to help the Freedom Farm get off the ground. He was Joseph Harris, a young, local activist who had worked as the chairman of Mississippians to Elect Negro Candidates, from 1967 to 1970. He had also been a SNCC organizer during 1963–64. Harris came to the Freedom Farm Corporation with a wide range of experiences in citizenship education. As a participant in the Delta Ministry and the Southern Regional Council, he directed numerous voter registration drives and performed citizenship education work in Sunflower, Moorhead, Indianola, and Ruleville. Harris also came with broad experience in welfare and relief work involving food and clothing distribution to over 967 families; food stamp purchasing; welfare public hearing assistance; assistance in applying for federal emergency food stamp provisions; and food purchase for emergency relief.[65]

The Freedom Farm was run by a board of directors, which included eleven members, all from Sunflower County. Staff personnel included a director, assistant director, secretary, secretary-bookkeeper, farm manager, fund-raiser, vegetable bank worker, and more than a dozen farm laborers. The positions of director, secretary, and secretary-bookkeeper had formal education requirements. These were also the highest-paid positions, along with that of the fund-raiser, who was Hamer.[66]

Besides being the founder of the farm, Hamer also served as assistant director. But her primary and most important duty was fund-raising. Hamer's influence often surpassed her official Freedom Farm titles, however, and she and Harris made most major decisions.[67] Harris was the business manager and director of the farm. Hamer was responsible for writing proposals and program development. Specifically her responsibilities were described as: "To seek out new sources of funding and technical assistance for Freedom Farm Corp."[68]

Hamer's work for the Freedom Farm consisted of a great deal of traveling and speaking. Fund-raising was exhausting work, and the most important for the farm. Through her travels, Hamer's constant refrain was "Give us food and it will be gone tomorrow. Give us land and the tools to work it and we will feed ourselves forever."

Hamer brought her movement skills and reputation to bear on Freedom Farm fund-raising. For the most part, she drew on her civil rights networks for funding and apparently recognized this as her strength. She appeared to have great confidence in her ability to raise money, a clear sense that she could almost single-handedly provide for the enterprise. In this regard, she was empowered in the same ways she had been as a timekeeper and civil rights voter registration worker. Although wary of outside help and the obligations that come with it, Hamer realized that Freedom Farm could not get off the ground on its own. She thus targeted a list of old civil rights allies. From this group came more ideas for other funding sources.

In describing Hamer's Freedom Farm work, someone dubbed her a "latter-day, female Gandhi."[69] The residents and officers of Freedom Farm held Hamer and her work in high esteem. A 1973 progress report described her value to the organization: "The inspiration that Mrs. Hamer has given the downtrodden and poor people of Sunflower County and the surrounding Delta area is almost impossible to measure. Her personal example of fearless leadership and honesty in the face of personal injury and abuse has given strength to the people she serves best, [the] displaced and poor."[70]

Hamer began traveling and soliciting monies for the farm as early as the fall of 1969. She drew on her personal power and tragic personal history, making an impact in places as far away as Seattle. On January 30, 1969, Hamer appealed to residents of that city for help for Sunflower County. She told her audience: "Today I'm suffering from a blood clot that almost cut off the vision in my left eye and a damaged kidney for the balance of my life."[71] In this speech, as in so many others, she referred to the 1963 Winona beating that law enforcement officials gave her in punishment for her voter registration activities. One newspaper described Winona as Hamer's "battle ribbon." Hamer made numerous trips to Seattle, where she spoke on a number of issues related to black power, black pride, black separatism, and poverty. As a consequence of her January 1969 appeal, a movement of blacks and whites formed to "adopt the poor people of Sunflower County, Miss." The plan was devised by Lloyd Jackson, chairman of the Negro Voters League. King County agreed to "donate food, money . . . clothes, building materials and agricultural supplies." The drive began at Seattle University and spread to other universities, high schools, church groups, corporations, and individual contributors.[72]

Hamer also took her cause to Cambridge, Massachusetts, where she spoke at Harvard. In January 1969, she got a group of Harvard teaching fellows to organize an emergency fund-raising drive for the Freedom Farm. The group opened a bank account in Cambridge under the name "Freedom Farm Co-op." It planned to raise the money by placing collectors in campus dining halls. From the Harvard group, Hamer was seeking the $1,300 down payment to hold Freedom Farm's option on forty acres of land, the final purchase price for which was $22,000.[73]

Hamer's travels also took her to Omaha, Nebraska, in November 1969, where she succeeded in getting pledges for the Freedom Farm from those who planned to tap other donors, including college students and business people throughout the state. Hamer's Northwest-Midwest connection extended to Wisconsin as well.[74] Most of Freedom Farm's funding came from a Wisconsin organization known as Measure for Measure, the National Council of Negro Women, individual donations, and college organizations such as Young People of Harvard University. This kind of support was crucial since membership fees were not enough to keep the operation going. Freedom Farm had 500 paying and 1,250 nonpaying members.

Among important individual donors, Harry Belafonte worked tirelessly for the farm. He lent his name and reputation to a number of solicitation letters and helped raise funds through his Belafonte Enterprises.[75] But Hamer received numerous letters and donations from individuals far less famous and well off. Many of these individuals were barely surviving themselves. Such was the case for Frederick W. Bassett ("Jim"), a retired San Francisco longshoreman living on a pension and Social Security. He identified himself as white and concerned about "the fight for all the human values because without this we are living in a jungle." Bassett closed his letter by pledging five dollars monthly and asking for a monthly report of the Farm's progress. He also asked for six envelopes.[76]

Hamer received numerous letters from white leftists, such as Kelly James of Massachusetts. James identified himself as a "former socialist, now a Democrat, a member of the United Church of Christ, and a poet married to a poet."[77] He noted a special appreciation for Hamer because she was a woman undertaking such a cause. On November 3, 1972, an attorney from Berkeley contacted the Freedom Farm about making it a beneficiary in the will of one of his clients.[78]

Hamer also took the Freedom Farm cause to television. In early fall 1969, she made an appearance on the "David Frost Show." A number of viewers wrote to her directly after the show, offering donations to the Freedom Farm. Grace Mitchell, director of a summer day camp in Waltham, Massachusetts, sent a check to Hamer (in care of the show) and wrote: "The enclosed check is for Fanny (I didn't hear her other name) from Missippi [sic]. I wish it was ten time[s] greater. She [is] obviously great in many ways. Her sincerity, and courage, leave us embarrassed. I hope she has her $24,000 plus by now."[79] In

July 1973, Hamer made an appearance on Phil Donahue's show, where she showed off a garment bag from a Freedom Farm business. In response, one viewer, Marguerite Rabbitt of Perrysburg, Ohio, sent Hamer a check for fifteen dollars. Rabbit wrote: "I saw you on the Phil Donahue show, and I'm writing this note to let you know that I think you're a wonderful person. I admire your courage greatly, and I wish you continued success in all you're doing to make better lives for the black people of this country."[80]

As with SNCC, youth organizations proved to be especially helpful to the impoverished Delta. A coalition organization known as Young World Development organized a series of "walks against hunger," which netted $120,000 from places throughout the country for Sunflower and other poor areas. After receiving a portion of the proceeds, Freedom Farm was able to purchase 640 acres of rich Delta land.

Among other young people who reached out to help Hamer were entire classrooms of small children, such as a fourth-grade class in Cambridge, Massachusetts. In October 1970, a group of Milwaukee youth raised $40,000 and donated it to the farm through Measure for Measure. The city of Madison added another $3,000 and sent Freedom Farm a check for a total of $43,000.[81] The huge donation from the Milwaukee youth helped the farm make its 1970 land payment. In January 1971, Measure for Measure gave Hamer and Freedom Farm another $30,000. In the same month a Milwaukee youth group held a fund-raising walk marathon.[82]

Wisconsin's Measure for Measure provided the most funding during the farm's first two years of operation. The group also donated much-needed farming equipment, such as tractors.[83] Measure for Measure had been organized in 1965 to alleviate hunger in Mississippi, and then began raising funds specifically for Freedom Farm Co-op in Sunflower County, Mississippi. In July 1971, Measure for Measure sent money to Hamer for farm equipment. It came in the form of several checks—one for $12,750 (from the Milwaukee Hunger Hike) and another for $27,250, which included money collected from Walks for Development in Minneapolis, Minnesota ($19,000); Winston Salem, North Carolina ($3,000); East Windsor, Connecticut ($500); Green Bay, Wisconsin ($2,000); Brycus, Ohio ($1,100); Indianapolis, Indiana ($600); and Madison, Wisconsin ($900).[84] One of the Measure for Measure sponsors was Representative Robert Kastenmeier, a leading supporter of the MFDP challenge in 1964. Most of the others were academics and clergy.

Besides Measure for Measure, the American Freedom from Hunger Foundation also gave Hamer and the farm significant sums of money. In September 1970, this foundation gave a check for over $21,000 to Freedom Farm.[85] On

August 3, 1971, David M. Landry, Domestic Projects Coordinator, American Freedom from Hunger Foundation, wrote to Hamer, informing her of a speakers program at St. Edward's University (Austin, Texas), which had expressed interest in having her come to speak at the school for an honorarium of between $1,000 and $1,500. Landry noted that Hamer's name came to the school and its speakers committee on the strength of her "reputation and by [the] support of your work."[86]

In August 1971, the American Freedom from Hunger Foundation mailed Hamer and Freedom Farm a check for almost $300, proceeds from the Barrington, Rhode Island, Walk for Development, and another $1,000 from the Green Bay, Wisconsin, Walk for Development. The foundation sent Hamer another check for $7,500 from a similar walk in Eugene, Oregon. Money continued to pour in from this foundation, raised in places like Chenoa, Illinois; Ashland, Wisconsin; Buffalo, New York; and Tampa, Florida. The foundation also asked Hamer to endorse other walks for other hunger projects, such as the one in 1972 in Atlanta.[87]

The year 1971 was actually a slow fund-raising year for Freedom Farm. The American Freedom from Hunger Foundation was late in getting out information to its many sponsors. By the time it sent out solicitations, many of its sponsors had already committed funds to other projects. Thus Hamer continued to seek assistance elsewhere, most notably from Catholic churches and organizations. Hamer wrote many letters to church officials. She also made phone calls and negotiated loans from these organizations.[88]

On November 16, 1971, Hamer appealed to the Field Foundation in New York City for money. Attached to the grant proposal was a letter that was uncharacteristic in tone. In the letter, Hamer sounded a bit short and got right to the point. There was a tinge of frustration in her tone, perhaps having to do with Freedom Farm's difficulties and maybe even with the nonpoor who help and discuss the poor—including philanthropists. This was not the typical Hamer solicitation. She wrote:

> Perhaps the major problem of Freedom Farm Corporation is simply that it is not [generating] its own capital. The only thing Freedom Farm is generating is food—and lots of it. It is feeding people who previously starved in one of the richest agricultural [areas] in the world. It is building pride[,] concern and all the other superlatives professionals use to describe hard-working folk. But much more important[,] Freedom Farm Corporation is working. Its purpose of feeding people on [one] hand is the essence of humanitarianism; but at the same time it allows the sick one a chance for healing, the silent ones a chance to speak[,] the unlearned ones a chance to learn, and the dying ones a chance to live.[89]

Freedom Farm did not have tax-exempt status. Therefore it had to receive contributions through foundations such as the Madison Measure for Measure if donors wanted their contributions to be tax deductible. Freedom Farm did not explore the possibility of becoming tax exempt until late 1972, when the organization retained a lawyer. By 1973, the Freedom Farm was soliciting funds from the Ford Foundation, the Oscar Meyer Foundation, the Stein Family Fund, and the Rockefeller Foundation.[90]

Donations also came from individuals. In July 1973, Hamer acknowledged receipt of clothing and money from Leah Carver Toabe of Brookline, Massachusetts: "This is to acknowledge receipt of the box containing linens and clothes and your contribution in the amount of $15.00. The bed sheets came in handy because I have been unable to purchase any in quiet [sic] sometime. It is contributions and gifts such as yours that make me feel good deep within my heart."[91] In general, however, Hamer kept hardly any donations of clothing for herself.

On May 29, 1974, Harris sent out a letter announcing the Fannie Lou Hamer Anniversary Committee, a special project of Freedom Farm. The idea was to honor Hamer on July 12, 1974, her thirtieth wedding anniversary. The letter noted: "The ANNIVERSARY Affair will also be an appreciation day for the 12 years Mrs. Fannie Lou has been fighting for social, political and economic change for poor people in Mississippi and across the country." In October 1974 there was interest in setting up a Fannie Lou Hamer Foundation, but by 1974 the farm had failed.[92]

The Freedom Farm failed in part because of poor management. Individuals were often loaned money and could not pay it back. For example, sometime in early 1972, George Jordan requested that Freedom Farm co-sign a bank note. His property was in foreclosure. He also already owed the farm some money. Hamer intervened in the discussion among board members about this. She noted that she would "call the bank and ask for an extension of his loan and would make every effort to make other contacts to secure funds for him."[93]

The case of Freedom Farm's secretary-bookkeeper, Nora L. Campbell, was an interesting example of some of the farm's internal problems, though not necessarily representative. On May 10, 1973, Harris notified Campbell of her termination, effective May 31, 1973. Harris terminated her with Freedom Farm owing her salary with "a net balance of $938.06 as of May 31, 1973." Reasons for her dismissal included "failure to report to work on time" and "inefficiency and failure to do Freedom Farm work when [she did] report to work." According Harris, Campbell had personal problems as well that led to her termination: her "failure to stop drinking in the office and during [her] working hours." Not the least of the reasons was "the financial situation of Freedom Farm Corporation is presently experiencing," although Harris mentioned it as an afterthought.[94]

On May 11, 1973, Campbell responded to Harris's letter by first stating that she accepted his request for her resignation. However, she went on to "[set] the record straight" and to list some of her personal losses as a result of working for the Freedom Farm. She noted that she was sometimes not paid and therefore her car had been repossessed, which caused her great difficulty getting to and from work. She also pointed out that she had "given many hours of [her] own time to Freedom Farm Corporation without asking or even expecting any compensation." Finally, she noted that performing her job effectively had been made increasingly difficult by the "taking away of the most important business machines (typewriter and xerox) in the office and the disconnection of the telephone." She went on to say that she had stuck with the Freedom Farm because she "wanted to see it develop into the kind of business that would be truly representative of what it should be." Campbell said she "wanted to be a part of this development, else why would I work day after day for months without receiving one cent for my time." On the cause for her dismissal, she noted that the real reason was "that Freedom Farm Corporation no longer [had] funds to pay a secretary and bookkeeper or even to maintain office equipment." She rebuked Harris for not being honest about this: "You know as well as I do this is the truth of matter." In closing, Campbell again summarized her personal sacrifices as a result of sticking with the Freedom Farm Corporation: repossessed furniture and car and a foreclosed house, which she called "everything I have worked for all my life." She urged Harris to reassess the reasons for her dismissal.[95]

Another problem for the farm was the matter of keeping funds separate, given Hamer's multiple activities. Around 1973 the farm undertook a reorganization. The report on this plan carefully noted that the reorganization was not to interfere with Hamer's other activities, namely, her regular political activities. According to the report, "Mrs. Hamer will continue to assist in Voter Education Projects, independent political campaigns and demonstration[s] in the name of social justice." The report clearly indicated, however, that these activities were to be supported by funds "separate from the farming operation profits until such [funding] . . . is self-sustaining."[96]

The move to reorganize resulted from the 1972 financial difficulties, which were only made worse by poor crop yields due to bad weather. Profit from the 1972 crop was predicted to be $21,750, but the weather was so terrible that "40% of a record crop was left in the fields during the harvest season due to early rains that have continued through the winter months of 1973. Freedom Farm suffered with the rest of the Delta farmers and the anticipated profit turned into bank debts that couldn't be paid." Among the losses was a 150-acre cotton crop. Freedom Farm also owed taxes, and land payments were always delinquent. In a 1973 progress report, farm officials described the farm as a "dream struggling to survive."[97]

New officers were elected and special meetings were called during the period of reorganization. Organizational self-criticism was directed at "the informal operation that has dominated the Corporation since its formation [in] 1969."[98] One idea growing out of the reorganization effort was to work more closely with a professional management team "that will set up the means for recording and controlling the financial business of the Corporation." As a result, Freedom Farm contacted several auditors and consulting firms to audit the organization and "set up the bookkeeping and management programs that will record and control the future activities of the Corporation." Freedom Farm finally decided to work with "a minority business concern from Memphis, Tennessee," Otha L. Brandon, pending funding for 1973.[99]

Despite the efforts at reorganization, a significant development contributed to the demise of the farm. Hamer's health was declining, and it continued to deteriorate in 1973 when she was plagued by both a nervous breakdown and stubborn exhaustion. Joe Harris wrote in a letter on May 29, 1974, "Mrs. Hamer has been ill for the past 18 months and have not accepted any speaking invitations since October 1973. Perry, her husband, only works nine (9) months as a transporter for Head Start." He requested that the Fannie Lou Hamer anniversary committee "give the Hamers a cashier check for their 30th ANNIVERSARY GIFT."[100]

Then, in April 1973, Harris confronted a crisis of his own. Although a young man, he had a heart attack.[101] He continued having problems, and on August 5, 1974, he died.

■ ■ ■

The Freedom Farm was not unique in its focus on the poor. There had been many organized efforts to bring economic well-being to black Deltans. It also was not unique in terms of the type of institution it was—a cooperative, or co-op. There were others that preceded and succeeded it. The farm was among a number of self-help cooperative efforts throughout the South during the civil rights movement. Many of these grew out of evictions and displacements that took place as a result of movement activities. And they were not all in Mississippi. One effort was a home industries project set up by the Haywood County Civic and Welfare League in Haywood County, Tennessee. There was also the Poor People's Land Corporation. Sometime after a group of federal registrars started showing up in parts of Alabama, white plantation owners began retaliating through mass evictions. This resulted in dozens of families being thrown off plantations. Beginning in December 1965, some of the displaced farmers took up residence in tent cities in Lowndes County and Greene County, Alabama. The Poor People's Land Corporation apparently grew out of this effort to acquire land for these displaced families and was funded initially by contributions from the Atlanta SNCC, Alabama SNCC, and a Chicago-area radio station. These contributions were put toward the purchase of land.[102]

The North Bolivar County Farm Cooperative was formed just before Freedom Farm. North Bolivar was incorporated in December 1969. It too had various components: a community center, sewing and clothing cooperatives, and a housing development.[103] At the time that Freedom Farm began, a number of similar co-ops had already been set up in the Delta, five of which were producing cash crops (e.g., cucumbers and beans) for market.

Initially Freedom Farm distinguished itself from these others in two ways. First, it started not from pooling black land already held by blacks, but by trying to "start from scratch by buying land from white men." Second, the Freedom Farm made a deliberate attempt to avoid relying on federal funds by seeking private financing instead. According to Hamer, "If the black communities are going to move economically and politically, they must have non-federal [support]." A white Harvard student and farm supporter, Harrison Wellford, said that Freedom Farm was also concerned about local white control: "They want to by-pass federal programs because of all the strings attached—they don't want the local white power structure taking over."[104]

The Freedom Farm marked a culmination of sorts for Hamer's career. It was an achievement made possible by local activists' persistence in response to stubborn deprivation. More than anything else, the farm was an extension of Hamer's legacy of institution building. But even as Hamer poured everything she had into the farm project, she continued her political activities with her 1971 run for the Mississippi State Senate and her large-scale voter registration efforts.

nine

I tried to warn my wife, I told her, "You can't do everything." But they still called on her. . . . They wore her down.

—Pap Hamer

The pain was like nothing I had ever imagined before, it was as if it defined pain itself; all other pain was only a reference to it, an imitation of it, an aspiration to it.

—Xuela, *The Autobiography of My Mother*

Last Days

The last six years of Hamer's life were among the saddest. Through these years she maintained a steady but ineffectual presence in national politics. But events around her continued to change in ways that made Hamer an increasingly difficult fit for the mainstream. Still there were the exceptional occasions that carried her back onto the national stage, if only momentarily. There were national conventions, state elections, school desegregation contests, and a passing but significant alliance with white feminists. For the most part, however, victory remained out of reach. More wrenching than her continued political defeats were her battles with disease. Depression, hypertension, diabetes, and heart disease left her periodically exhausted and immobilized by 1972, and four years later, breast cancer had begun accelerating her decline.

■ ■ ■

In 1968 Hamer appeared at the Democratic National Convention as a delegate with the Loyalist Democrats, a coalition of representatives from the NAACP, Mississippi Young Democrats, AFL-CIO, Prince Hall Masons, the black Mississippi Teachers Association, and the MFDP. This 1968 delegation bore little resemblance to the one in 1964. The majority of the most vocal and influential Loyalist Democrats were representatives from the NAACP–Young Democrats faction, comprised mainly of black and white professionals. Among the state NAACP activists in the coalition were Charles Young, a well-heeled businessman, and two familiar civil rights personalities, Aaron Henry, the chairman of the Loyalist delegation, and Charles Evers. A leading figure among the

Young Democrats was moderate Hodding Carter III, editor of the *Delta-Democrat Times* out of Greenville, Mississippi.[1] Although the Loyalist Democrats were committed to integrating the party, the coalition's overall objective was to move the party back toward the center. This was hardly a grass-roots effort, Hamer's brief participation notwithstanding.

To be sure, Hamer was troubled by the Loyalist alliance's proximity to the political center and its disregard for Mississippi's grass-roots poor. Additionally, Hamer was not pleased about the participation of black Loyalist Democrats who had no personal history of service in Mississippi's movement. The Masons and the black teachers had no "civil rights credentials." After all, neither contingent supported the 1964 challenge. Nevertheless, under the MFDP banner, Hamer reluctantly joined the Loyalist delegation, partly because she wanted in on another organized challenge to the regular state delegation. She still had something to contribute on this front, so she planned to be in Chicago that summer. Her principles would not let her stay in Ruleville, thereby allowing others to build on her legacy of challenge. Just before heading off to Chicago, she indicated that she was attending the convention to keep others honest: "Whole lot of us they are not representing, and we have to be there to say they ain't representing us; we are here to represent ourselves."[2] She openly questioned the motives and objectives of moderate white Loyalists. In her estimation, some of these individuals just plain resented "too much recognition for a bunch of niggers" fighting to make a change in Mississippi. Furthermore, she knew that the MFDP was hardly in a position to mount a challenge on its own. Owing in large measure to reductions in staff and monies, the MFDP's statewide influence had waned shortly after the 1967 special election, and the party lacked the muscle needed to resist cooptation of movement momentum by moderate forces.[3] However, it was also obvious that the Loyalists needed the grass-roots folks to legitimate their challenge. Hamer's participation, then, was crucial. Nonetheless, the MFDP's decision to join the Loyalist Democrats was an agonizing one. It was certainly not well received by Hamer, who noted about some Loyalists: "these same folks in 1964 were willing to sell us down the drain and tried to do it."[4] Hamer continued to rail against this group at the 1969 MFDP state convention, where she was elected vice-chair of the party: "We knowed when we left Mississippi, we had some house niggers with us. As soon as the FDP walked through the valley of the shadow of death, they hopped on the bandwagon."[5]

In late July 1968, Hamer was elected as a delegate in Loyalist precinct and county conventions held in Sunflower County. She was the first choice among those selected. She still had considerable popular support in some circles, especially among MFDP activists. The 1968 challengers had a distinct advantage over the 1964 contestants: the national Democratic Party had already promised to refuse seating to any delegation that had excluded blacks from participating in any stage of the political process—a concession from the 1964 convention. The credentials committee voted to seat the Loyalist group and to expel the regular delegation. The "victory" was bittersweet for Hamer. She knew that others had come in and realized a victory on the backs of the poor. Still, she maintained her focus and used her stature to help other convention challenges directed at the Georgia and Alabama delegations. Earlier that year, she had already visited Atlanta, where she endorsed the Georgia challenge and denounced the Vietnam War. Once seated at the Chicago convention, she voted to unseat the Georgia regulars. The Georgia challengers won half the seats given to its state delegation. The Alabama challenge, however, went down in defeat.

Naturally, Hamer felt a responsibility to other challenges that summer. She had full appreciation for the long-range impact of the 1964 effort, even as bitterness and disappointment endured. Indeed, her deep dissatisfaction kept pushing her to be a voice of the marginalized despite the slow onset of debilitating fatigue and physical pain. She was not the least bit flattered about the token acceptance she received from middle-class Mississippi moderates or the national Democratic Party. To the contrary, she was indignant and refused to play along just to get along. Her sole allegiance was to those *not* in Chicago with her that summer, and she did not leave the convention without serving their needs.

Just before the convention began, Hamer and Lawrence Guyot (chairman of the MFDP's executive committee) spoke before the platform committee. They wanted consideration of the MFDP's platform. Hamer hit the committee with the problem of rural poverty. She called on the Democratic Party to support land grants and low-interest loans for cooperatives. She added that there must be guaranteed annual income, extended day care, comprehensive medical care, increased federal provisions for food programs, and free higher education. Turning to the MFDP's platform items on current affairs, Hamer called for an end to the Vietnam War and compulsory military service and for renewed diplomatic ties with Cuba and China, an arms embargo of South Africa, and an end to Middle East arms shipments.[6] Amid these concerns, Hamer also made a point of protesting the gender inequities within the delegation and the entire convention. A couple of Loyalist delegates later said they were convinced that her extemporaneous diatribes in private caucus to the 1968 delegation went a long way toward opening up positions for women in the 1972 convention.[7]

Hamer was just as outspoken and involved in convention discussions about the next Democratic candidate for the presidency. None of the leading figures really appealed to her. Hubert Humphrey was not someone she supported. She just did not think too highly of him. Not only were there lingering feelings from their interactions during the 1964 convention, but he was a supporter of Johnson's Vietnam War policy, which she vehemently opposed. (She had voiced her opposition in a telegram she sent Johnson after the 1964 convention. She urged him to "please bring those troops out of Vietnam where they have no business anyhow, and bring them to Mississippi and Louisiana, because if this is a Great Society, I'd hate to see a bad one.")[8] Hamer did raise the possibility of nominating Edward Kennedy from the podium, but others advised her against doing so.[9]

Outside the convention hall in 1968, Hamer and other MFDP members took in the historic clashes between police and antiwar protesters. She and other delegates observed the police brutality with outrage.

Hamer, generally a good-natured person, even among those with whom she held serious disagreements, did socialize with the other delegates throughout the convention. She could laugh at herself as easily as she laughed at her detractors. Laughter was healing for her. By nature, she was a person who loved people and loved having a good time, even at high-stakes affairs. Her light-heartedness was the flip side of her rage and indignation: she was passionate in the fullest sense. At some point during the convention, she noticed that she was under surveillance, so she decided to play a little game: "I watched this guy while he be watching me and . . . I put this dodge to him. They must have told him, 'You better not let her get out of your sight,' because this little man had some of the saddest little blue eyes. He'd be ducking through that convention and I'd be standing off laughing, and after I would let him go through total hell, I would stop where I could see him and you could just see him relieved."[10]

Following the convention, Hamer resumed her national and local travels. She mobilized local registration drives and election campaigns and organized antipoverty work. In mid-fall she was back in the Delta campaigning for candidates running for election commissioner and the board of education. On October 20, 1968, she spoke at the Bolton Community Center, where she continued hammering away at her essential message: justice is needed now; get out and vote.[11]

In late fall 1968, she visited Harvard University, where she spoke to an American history seminar about her firsthand experiences in the civil rights movement. The seminar had been organized in response to black student protests calling for more African-American history and culture courses. Hamer was one of many visitors to the seminar. Reforming American education, especially redesigning curriculum, was especially close to Hamer's heart. She had a keen interest in black history. She read about it whenever she created time for herself, and she recalled how important the subject matter was to Freedom Summer students and teachers. Although a strange contrast to her usual surroundings, Harvard's pompous atmosphere seemed to amuse Hamer more than anything. She mingled with her company and joked about the food and overall formality of the place. Surely she was struck by the world of privilege around her. But she changed nothing in her own manner of presentation. When it came time to go to work, she delivered a speech similar in tone and content to earlier speeches made for far less stodgy audiences. Her remarks at Lowell Lecture Hall contained the familiar refrains, metaphors, personal anecdotes, and clever quips. She spoke about racism as a stubborn illness that had the nation "on the critical list." She condemned conservative cries of "law and order" in reaction to urban uprising and other expressions of race rage. There was no substitute for "plain respect for blacks as blacks." No one individual or institution got off her hook, certainly not the church, the house for hypocrites, according to Hamer. About her own politics, she admitted representing the Left—the *left out*—"I've been left [for] four hundred years."[12]

Hamer continued touring schools in 1969, as she launched the Freedom Farm. She spoke at Seattle University in January; Duke in February; Minnesota's Carleton College in March; and Tougaloo and Ole Miss in April. Local student protests easily won her respect and support. Few things could change that, not even her painful memories of breaking with the SNCC students she loved so much. In the same year, she appeared in Leland, Mississippi, where she reminded students that a new day was upon them—a day that afforded them more opportunity to finish waging a successful battle. As was her practice with everyone, she warned them about the "chicken-eaters"—the preachers and teachers with no loyalty to anything or anybody beyond their individual selves.[13]

At Mississippi Valley State College in Itta Bena, a small Delta town, Hamer appeared and again offered support to students protesting against complacent, self-interested administrators. Hamer had personal ties with many of these students. Some had worked on her voter registration drives and walked picket lines with her. She applauded their courage in confronting those in power (such as J. H. White, the college president) and their demanding that they have a say in shaping their college experience. Among other demands, they wanted to be citizens in the fullest sense of the term without fearing some reprisal from their college if they engaged in community activism. The Itta Bena student protest evolved to include specific demands about life on campus. Students wanted black studies courses and less administrative control over dress code, speakers, and relations between the sexes. They also called for an end to remedial education. Hamer underscored this concern in public remarks. She cautioned that higher education in Mississippi was still inferior to that offered by many colleges and universities she had visited. Hamer put much time into the demonstrations. She spent hours talking to students and their parents. The administration knew she was a force it had to reckon with. Eventually, the Mississippi Valley State boycott ended in victory for the students. Most of their demands were met.[14]

Hamer opened the new decade by continuing her battle against unequal education. She filed a class-action suit in May 1970 against Sunflower County's school officials, whom she charged with failing to desegregate schools and protect the jobs of black teachers and principals. Her own experiences were proof enough that Sunflower was still failing to comply with *Brown v. Board of Education.* In fall 1968, Hamer took her own daughter, Virgie, to an all-white Ruleville school, an action that was not easy, despite Hamer's many individual experiences going up against Jim Crow. She recalled that as they approached the door, her daughter noticed Hamer's slight hesitation. "Come on, Mama," Virgie insisted. With a mixture of shame and pride, Hamer remembered, "That's hard when it's your child. But she's not afraid."[15]

Out of the new *Hamer et al. v. Sunflower County* case, a biracial committee on desegregation was formed and Hamer was appointed its head. The decision rendered in June 1970 was a victory for Hamer and all who supported integrated schooling and equal protection for black teachers and principals. The black and white public schools merged into one system, and the court ordered the implementation of a fair policy for filling teacher and principal vacancies by race. In essence, the court order followed the recommendations of the Hamer-led biracial committee.[16]

■ ■ ■

School desegregation, campus protests, and an ambitious farm cooperative did not stop Hamer from making one more run for office. In 1971 she ran for the Mississippi state senate as an independent, and she remained true to her own brand of inclusive grass-roots politics. For the aborted 1967 campaign, she had drawn up a detailed platform, portions of which she articulated in her 1971 campaign. The platform addressed the core concerns she had held since her earliest movement days. The poor and disfranchised held center stage:

I, Mrs. Fannie Lou Hamer, representing ALL people of Sunflower County, am running for state senate. If I am elected, I will do my uttermost to carry out my duties as State Senator.

My platform consist[s] of the following:

WELFARE

1) Welfare legislation is necessary to provide 100 per cent of need rather than 27% and to require that Black Workers are hired in policy making positions.

2) Legislation to change law which prohibits counties from recieving [sic] Federal Funds to set up housing for poor and elderly.

3) Erect legislation for State Medical Aid program for poor of all ages under Federal law which provides for Medical program.

VOTER REGISTRATION AND ELECTION LAW

4) Mobile Voter Registration

5) Change law to permit registration after 6 months residence and to permit registration up to one month before election

6) Support MFDP court action to change election law:

    a) Independent[s] qualify one month before general election

    b) Voting in party primary shouldn't disqualify an Independent Candidate.

    c) Lower voting age to 18.[17]

Throughout the campaign, Hamer continued focusing on local causes dear to her political heart. One such cause was the murder of Jo Etha Collier. Collier was an eighteen-year-old Drew High School graduate who was shot in the neck while standing in front of a grocery store. She had just left her graduation ceremonies, where she was honored for her achievements in the classroom and on the track field. Authorities charged three drunken white men with the killing.[18]

In Drew and Ruleville, town demonstrations followed, and Hamer stepped forward to comfort Collier's mother, Gussie Mae Love, and to condemn the reactions of the mayor and others. When Hamer met with W. O. Williford, mayor of Drew, she discovered that the two had opposing purposes, which did not surprise her. Williford had hoped to get Hamer to stop some of the demonstrations. Instead, to his frustration, she promised more demonstrations. While consoling young Collier's mother, Hamer expressed outrage at this killing and other recent killings: "How much longer are things like this going to be allowed to happen?"[19] She had one more meeting with Mayor Williford, to negotiate the release of thirty-one people arrested in Ruleville demonstrations the Thursday following Jo Etha's murder. At the Sunday funeral, Hamer was the first speaker. She cried as she urged others to help buy the Colliers a new home. Toward this end, she set up the Jo Etha Collier Building Fund in Ruleville.[20] This death pained Hamer, and she made herself emotionally available to the Collier family for quite some time after the murder. Less than three years earlier, she had lost her daughter Dorothy, who was Jo Etha's age. For many blacks, Jo Etha's killing was politically motivated because it was one of two during an intense week of voter-registration campaigning. For Hamer, it was political in a broader, transhistorical sense: "Jo Etha was smart and she was black. That was too much for the whites."[21]

■ ■ ■

In early summer 1971, Hamer focused her sights on what some probably regarded as a natural constituency for her leadership: white liberal feminists. The relationship was not an easy one, but it was certainly a political one. The alliance included many common causes and engendered genuine mutual respect and admiration. But the association was clearly a pragmatic one. When Hamer appeared at the founding conference for the National Women's Political Caucus (NWPC) on July 10, she went seeking financial support and national exposure for her state senate campaign. In turn, mainstream feminists needed legitimacy through association with a black female icon of the civil rights movement. Some younger black women felt that Hamer let herself be used by the NWPC; they believed that Hamer's symbolism served white women better than the NWPC could ever serve Hamer's causes. But Hamer knew that her symbolism was currency, and the exchange seemed to make sense, at least in the short run. Besides, she had a more substantive role to play in the NWPC's founding, and this certainly surprised many white women, and a few black women as well.[22]

At its inaugural gathering, the NWPC articulated its central aim of greater government representation for all women. Specifically it set a goal of putting women in half of all local, state, and federal government jobs. The black women present at the gathering represented just less than 10 percent of the registrants. Hamer and Shirley Chisholm were among the most well known representatives of the NWPC's black caucus, which fought for passage of an antiracism resolution, the NWPC's first official action. Passed by unanimous vote, the resolution held that the NWPC disclaimed all racist candidates, be they women or men. Chisholm remembered, many years later, that she and Hamer worked like a tag team in challenging white women on their limited understanding of the term "sisters." For Hamer and Chisholm, there was no "sisterhood" without an expressed commitment to end all forms of discrimination and suffering for all women. Chisholm recalled: "What Fannie did on the other hand— she was trying in her own inimitable way to caution these women that black women would never join their organization unless they understood the particular depth of our concerns. It was kind of harsh. I remember it was a hot meeting. Fannie 'told them off,' and I put that in quotes. We were both quite militant in our different ways. A lot of women could not understand what is Fannie Lou Hamer railing about?"[23]

In principle, of course, the black women of the NWPC favored the general goal of more government representation for women. But some black caucus members believed that there was some insensitivity and some discriminatory attitudes within the caucus that required immediate attention. Chisholm told the committee that black women decided on a formal resolution (the antiracism resolution) in response to comments heard earlier in the day, and out of concern for the direction of the NWPC. Hamer, Chisholm, and others worried that the NWPC might feel inclined to support a woman candidate over a male candidate, regardless of her race politics. Chisholm told the caucus, "Black women want to be part of the women's movement but we are also part of another movement—the liberation of our own people."[24] Vivian Mason of Norfolk, Virginia, added: "[Black women] would not like to leave you but [we] are prepared to leave you if you cannot say to us 'We will have no part of racism in any of its forms.'" Mason then asked for a "public and irrevocable commitment."[25]

After the antiracism resolution was passed, Hamer decided it was time to make her announcement. She told the caucus that she was running for the Mississippi state senate later that fall, and that she would run the following year for the U.S. Senate seat of James Eastland. The audience cheered loudly. She reminded the caucus that her battle was "for the liberation of all people, because nobody's free until everybody's free." She added, "I've passed equal rights. I'm fighting for human rights."[26]

Hamer was her usual honest self at the caucus, even if this meant taking public positions that left her among a minority. When the child-rearing specialist and best-selling author Dr. Benjamin Spock spoke to the caucus, the women jeered, a reaction to Spock's writings about women's place in the home. Hamer wasted little time in standing up and chastising the women, "I'm ashamed of you. I know what it is to be harassed."[27]

On the question of sex discrimination, Hamer noted what she perceived to be a difference in outlook: "I'm not fighting to liberate myself from the black man in the South because he's been stripped of being a citizen." Later she added, "I got a black husband, six feet three, 240 pounds, with a 14 shoe, that I don't want to be liberated from. But we are here to work side by side with this black man in trying to bring liberation to all people."[28] She did claim that she had recently experienced sex discrimination, when the insurance on her house had been canceled. She believed this happened, not because of her ten years of civil rights or race activism, but because she had recently started speaking out more and more against involuntary sterilizations.

Hamer also held some definite views on other "women's issues," such as abortion, contraception, and out-of-wedlock births, opinions she expressed many times in speeches in 1971. She argued that contraceptives and abortion equaled genocide and sin. Both amounted to interfering with God's will, and thus history. She believed that all conceived life should be allowed to develop, "because if you give them a chance, they might grow up to be Fannie Lou Hamer or something else," a pointed reference to a sense of her own historical importance.[29] By any ethical measure, she was hardly prudish or conservative about sex and reproduction. She was a Christian, and certainly morality had its place in her political belief system. But often what figured larger in influence were her individual and family histories. To be sure, abortion and contraception were issues of morality, but morality situated in a history of limited (sometimes nonexistent) reproductive autonomy for black women. The meaning of choice or reproductive freedom was relative and subjective for Hamer, but in different ways.

Clearly, Hamer did not regard herself as a feminist, not by anybody's definition, even if her own accomplishments and stature translated into greater influence and other positive results for other women. She was a "nonfeminist" whose life and powerful presence had undeniably feminist consequences. In this sense, she was like many other black women of her generation and of other historical periods and places.

On July 12, the NWPC met and decided on guidelines for supporting candidates and selected a policy council. The caucus decided to support candidates who advocated ending the Vietnam War and "the elimination of sexism, racism, violence and poverty." The policy council included a number of high-profile women with established records in various activist communities. Hamer was one of seven black members, including Chisholm, Mason, Myrlie Evers (then a California legislator), and Dorothy Height, president of the National Council of Negro Women.[30] On November 9, 1971, Hamer, along with Liz Carpenter, Bella Abzug, and Mildred Jeffrey, signed a letter addressed to the chairmen of the Democratic and Republican parties. The letter called for equal representation of women (50 percent) at both presidential nominating conventions for 1972.[31]

Some weeks after the caucus, Hamer called on the NWPC to help with her senate campaign. She wrote a letter to the NWPC's Washington office requesting help with monitoring the climate for about two weeks, including watching the polls on election day. Betty Friedan answered the call for help and arrived in Mississippi the Wednesday before election day. As election day approached, Hamer put out another call for outside help. Liz Carpenter, former press secretary to Lady Bird Johnson, arrived with Xandra Kayden, a graduate student. Carpenter and Kayden drove Hamer around to do some last-minute canvassing. They spent over six hours riding around, making stops. This was vintage Hamer, the grass-roots activist. Every single vote, every single opinion in her community mattered and was necessary for victory. By this time, drawing on significant past losses, such as the 1967 special elections defeat, Hamer was not taking anything for granted. Besides visiting individuals, Hamer, carrying nearly two thousand dollars wrapped in a handkerchief, stopped to make announcements at several radio and television stations in her district. She used the cash to buy airtime.[32]

Hamer received over 7,200 votes, but this was not enough to win against the incumbent, Robert Crook, who received 11,770. Hamer even lost the battle in Ruleville, 720 to 434. She wasted little time in complaining about irregularities and intimidation. In her estimation, the election had been stolen. In December 1971, appearing before an NAACP hearing, Hamer spoke of witnessing a guard keeping voters away from one precinct. Others told similar stories immediately after the election and for some years to come. Hamer ran on a slate known as Concerned Citizens of Sunflower County to Elect Black Officials. None of these candidates won election. Perhaps most devastating were the statewide results: of the 309 black candidates, 259 went down in defeat. As with the special elections defeat of 1967, many reflected on other reasons for the latest loss. Some explained Hamer's defeat in part by citing the controversies and divisiveness that grew out of the Head Start battles. This made sense, although she never acknowledged as much. Others suspected that some white candidates had effectively split black votes. Still others surmised that a sizable number of black voters simply had no confidence in folks who ran on good intentions and the strength of some impressive work in the civil rights movement. All of these factors accounted for the tough defeat.[33]

■ ■ ■

Hamer was an extremely sick woman as she made her way through the 1970s. She was sick during the state senate race. She was sick during the spring and early summer, when she mobilized folks in protest of the Jo Etha Collier murder and when she made her presence felt at the NWPC's founding. Finally in

January 1972, she suffered a nervous breakdown. She collapsed while protesting outside a Ruleville grocery store, where the white owner had kicked a black female teenager. Hamer had joined in the picket and two-week-old boycott of the business after returning from traveling and speaking. After collapsing, she was taken to a Mound Bayou hospital. She desperately needed rest. Public concern about Hamer's health grew among the locals. Many flooded her hospital room, making it impossible for her to rest. Eventually she moved farther away, to a hospital in Nashville. After her release, she continued worrying about the Freedom Farm. She needed to be out raising funds, but her body would not let her. Frustration and impatience got the best of her during this period. She wrote to friends about her inability to do basic activities like cooking and cleaning her house. She became depressed and began to cry periodically. Physical suffering left her feeling defeated and overwhelmed.[34]

After the 1972 breakdown, Hamer missed many engagements, often without notifying the organizers of various events. Sometimes this led to bitter, embarrassing miscommunication with her supporters. On July 24, 1972, Louise Mitchell, the president of the Selma Alumnae Chapter of Delta Sigma Theta sorority, wrote a pointed letter to Hamer requesting that she pay back two hundred dollars she had received for a scheduled appearance at a Founders Day program. Clearly displeased with Hamer, Mitchell wrote: "I have called and written you many times without any communication from you. Each time that I have called or written, I have given you my address and telephone number with instructions that you could call me collect. I suppose that I would not feel so let down except for the fact that I continue to read and see pictures of you appearing in other places. But I suppose that we here in Selma are a bit small and should not have dreamed that you could find time to come here."[35]

Hamer was too sick to reply. Instead, a little over a month later, Joseph Harris answered Mitchell's letter: "We regret that your Founders Day Program was a disappointment: however, we hope that you understand Mrs. Hamer was in the hospital at that time. Our office was unaware of the engagement because we cancelled all of her engagements that we were aware of from January 6, 1972 to July 31, 1972." Harris reassured Mitchell that Hamer had not become too important for Selma, Alabama: "I would like to assure you that Selma is not too small for Mrs. Hamer. She has spoken in towns much smaller than Selma. She would like very much to come to Selma, and certianly [sic] hope that your Sorority will invite her again."[36] Harris went on to note that Hamer had improved, but that she had attended only two engagements since her release from the hospital: she appeared at Howard University to take an honorary degree, and she attended part of the National Democratic Party convention in July.

Prior to the 1972 convention, Hamer found herself at the center of another Loyalist controversy around representation. Weak and pained, she struggled to attend the Loyalist Party meetings in Jackson, where delegates met to select a committeeperson for the Democratic National Committee. The Loyalists had a policy that required that there be biracial leadership among party officials. Additionally, there had to be gender balance. If a black man was chosen as one leader, than a white woman had to be the other choice. Some old SNCC-MFDP faithful wanted Hamer as Mississippi's national committeewoman at the 1972 convention. For some, it was another struggle for a militant grass-roots voice within the Loyalist party. Reluctantly (and against her better judgment), Hamer ran against Pat Derian, a white woman Loyalist from Jackson. Hamer lost, but she won a delegate seat. Her supporters and rivals both charged that she was being used and needed to be home in bed. On one occasion, short of breath and drenched in perspiration, she spoke to the other delegates about the need to stay unified, especially along racial lines. She noted that much work remained.[37]

Although her health remained unstable, Hamer did make it to Miami Beach. She was one of few from the original 1964 MFDP delegation, and she remained bitter about this. In interviews after the Miami convention, she waxed passionate about her "disgust" because "the Loyal Democrats didn't know what suffering [was]."[38] Still, she could not resist the symbolic honor of making history at the convention: she seconded the vice-presidential nomination for Frances "Sissy" Farenthold, a Texas state legislator. Hamer struggled against physical pain and fatigue to reach the podium, where she added, referring to Farenthold, "If she was good enough for Shirley Chisholm, then she is good enough for Fannie Lou Hamer. Thank you."[39]

On February 20, 1973, Hamer made good on an invitation to lecture before students at Ohio State University. However, because of her deteriorating health, she now required a traveling companion. On February 22, 1973, she wrote a letter requesting compensation for travel expenses: "Prior to the date of February 20th I had been hospitalized, therefore, being advised by my doctor it was necessary for me to have a traveling companion. The expense was 250.00 (includeing [sic] the traveling companion). Enclosed please find two (2) airline ticket stubs."[40]

Along with serious illness, Hamer faced dire financial hardship. The disability income she finally received on appeal in 1974 was not nearly enough. Friends and family continued donating food and clothing to her, Pap, and their granddaughters, Jacqueline and Lenora. Her family and close associates wrote to numerous individuals and organizations seeking assistance for family. On

March 1, 1977, two weeks before Hamer's death, Eleanor Holmes Norton, a close friend who then chaired the New York City Commission on Human Rights, wrote to Perry Hamer informing him of attempts to claim royalties that June Jordan had promised Fannie Lou after publishing a short young-adult biography of the leader: "We have finally been successful in getting the publisher to set up a system for paying the royalties. Ms. Jordan promised Ms. Hamer the next $2,500 in royalties from book sales. Unfortunately, royalties accumulate very slowly. . . . This coming April we are told Ms. Hamer can expect only about $65 to be turned over to her. It is unfortunate that the entire $2,500 cannot be paid immediately." She also informed Mr. Hamer about an $8,000 fund-raising effort for the family organized by Bayard Rustin and others. She closed by reminding Pap that Fannie Lou remained very close to many people's hearts: "All of us feel great concern for Ms. Hamer's comfort and peace at this time. She is one of the great American women."[41]

In late fall 1976, Hamer received numerous honors, including another commemorative Fannie Lou Hamer Day in Ruleville, on October 31. To add to her honorary doctorates, she was given humanitarian and other service awards by Alpha Phi Alpha fraternity and the Congressional Black Caucus. Of course, she deserved and enjoyed such recognition. Such honors did her spirit good. Still, she struggled emotionally.

By January 1977, Hamer was in a deep depression, a paralyzing gloom that occasionally left her listless. She knew that she was dying from breast cancer. She had had a mastectomy the previous spring and could not afford to buy a prosthesis. Instead she stuffed socks into her clothing where her left breast used to be. On one of her last trips to New York, she confided in Eleanor Holmes, who took Hamer to buy a prosthesis.

When Hamer was not in the hospital, she sat at home, rocking in a chair, crying and pulling at her hair, trying her best to comb it. After Hamer endured a series of hospital stays, her niece moved in to help with the girls, and her movement protégé, June Johnson, stopped by often to provide companionship and perspective. Hamer was frustrated because friends were not responding to calls for help, and Pap was spending time away from home. Hamer would ask Johnson to brush her hair, just in case someone else dropped by to see her. Johnson recalled that Hamer was quite vain about her hair; it was her "pride and joy."[42]

Numerous letters in her collected papers document the extent of her sadness and the tremendous outpouring of concern about her mental and physical state. A person named Vickie sent Hamer a long, handwritten letter, in which she expressed empathy and offered perspective. She opened:

Dear Fannie Lou,
   I've just heard by way of the grapevine that you're feeling very depressed and out of sorts. Having recently overcome a very bad siege of depression myself, I have some appreciation of what you're going through. I hope that yours is not as bad as mine was, at times it was so bad I couldn't function.

Vickie suggested that she call a help line: "Fannie Lou, call this number and tell whoever answers your call what your problem is, no matter what it is. You can tell them and I promise you that you will be comforted and moreover your problem may be removed." After going on at some length about her own family, Vickie turned to contemporary politics: "What do you think about our new President? I'd be interested in hearing your position."[43] Undoubtedly, Hamer's political opinion still mattered to some people right up till the very end.

Hamer sometimes tried not to alarm close friends and family members, although they knew something was wrong. On January 1, 1976, Hamer's stepdaughter Linnie Smoote wrote: "I could tell the last time I talked to you [you] didn't sound to[o] good, someone told [me] a few days ago that you were very sick, so that made my suspicion worse enough to write this letter and find out what is happening."[44]

To lift Hamer's spirits, siblings wrote affectionate letters reminding her that she was loved by many. Right around the time of the mastectomy, Annie M. Townsend, her sister-in-law—the wife of Hamer's brother Ben—had sent a brief note: "sis i bin think about you very much i love my sis . . . our sweet sis i love you."[45]

By March 1977, Hamer was back in the hospital for the last time. She spent her days holding her body, crying and singing "Precious Lord" and other gospel favorites. Although she voiced concerns about leaving behind Pap and the girls, she told family and friends that her spiritual house was in order and that she was ready to go home to her god. Her sister Laura remembered that Hamer looked very tired and resigned to her fate: "I had never seen anybody in that much pain before. She cried, oh, how she cried. She was just ready to go to the Lord. She had helped a lot of peoples here. She did good work."[46] On March 14, 1977, Fannie Lou Hamer died from heart failure, leaving behind a record of "good work" matched by few others in her time.

Six days later, a throng of civil rights dignitaries gathered at Ruleville's Williams Chapel Missionary Baptist Church, the site of Hamer's first mass meeting. They came to say goodbye to a most esteemed daughter of the Mississippi Delta. Movement veterans Andrew Young, Ella Baker, Stokely Carmichael (Kwame Touré), and others spoke eloquently of Hamer's powerful persona and her enormous accomplishments as she lay in an open casket, dressed in white, her favorite color. Sadly, as hundreds paid tribute to Hamer inside the crowded church, there were hundreds of other mourners who were kept outside, against the wishes of her husband and family. They were not the big personalities from the movement. Instead, they were the "little folks" for whom Hamer fought so hard all of her years. Ironically, even at her funeral the battle for voice and representation of the marginalized continued. Some still had not gotten her message.

Conclusion:
A Movement and a Life

Undoubtedly, the civil rights movement changed the country in ways that were virtually unparalleled in its history. To the extent that movement activists radically altered the social and political landscape of America, they too were carried on a wave of change. This is certainly true for Fannie Lou Hamer, a lowly woman farmer who emerged to become one of the era's most well respected figures. We can only imagine the magnitude of such change for her personal life and sense of self. One of the most significant changes was her realization that she could take her destiny in her own hands. Her oft-told tale of voting for the first time conveyed an experience of empowerment never felt before. In addition, her travels added much to the personal meaning of change. It must have been overwhelming for Hamer to move from the cotton fields of the Mississippi Delta to the Democratic Party's national convention hall, or to the chamber of the House of Representatives. It must have been equally overwhelming to travel outside the confines of the South to other regions of the country, to places such as New York, California, and Wisconsin, where she spent a good deal of time. But the most significant and memorable of her trips out of Mississippi was her journey to Africa. And what about the various people whose paths crossed hers? It must have been an enormous sea change to go from negotiating and acceding to the demands and whims of landowners to meeting and interacting with some of the nationally and universally acclaimed figures of her day, from other civil rights leaders to elected officials and internationally recognized political leaders. Indeed, the changes that Hamer help wrought for the rest of the nation cut just as deeply into her own life.

But such change was not always overwhelmingly pleasant, exciting, and inspirational for her personal life. Much that was glorious about the movement was counterbalanced by its many difficult moments, and Hamer experienced some of these not-so-glorious times, particularly toward the end of her career. This had much to do with the pattern of change and continuity for Hamer's life and for the life of the movement. For Hamer, it seems that change was especially painful after 1964. It devastated her to lose momentum after the Freedom Democratic Party failed to unseat the Mississippi representatives to the national convention. It unnerved her and distorted her perspective to be disrespected and belittled at the height of SNCC's coming apart over questions of black separatism. It was equally tough to witness the Freedom Democrats dissolve into a party of moderates by 1968 without serious regard for her input. Devastating change pervaded her family life as well, with the death of her daughter Dorothy for reasons that appeared to be unnecessary and preventable. Most devastating of all, it was similarly difficult to endure having her body and mind betray her through unyielding bouts with depression, cancer, and other ailments during her last years. Change was not always good for Hamer or the movement, and yet this was their raison d'être—politically at least.

It is precisely because of these difficult changes and her small victories that we have come to embrace Hamer as a symbol and heroic figure, much as history embraced Martin Luther King Jr. without much departure until recently. There is certainly something to be said for Hamer the great survivor of tragedy and conqueror of personal difficulties. She had few peers when it came to enduring some of life's toughest challenges. But this sort of embracing of Hamer's legacy in some ways blinds us to an aspect of her personal history. Many people have memories of Hamer, and most are told in a fairly joyous and proud tone, with a slight tinge of sadness. Indeed, these accounts have been important to my study and to others. In an interesting way, however, these recollections have led me to reflect on the meaning of Hamer's life for Hamer. Understandably, most surviving activists who knew her recall and appreciate what she meant for our lives. In their remembrances, there is much emphasis on Hamer the victorious fighter for social change. Little is ever mentioned about the meaning of her defeats for her own life. It seems only fair and profitable to try to talk about her pain too, but not in a way in which we emphasize only her survival of that pain and those challenges.

Through this study, I have tried to suggest that returning that pain to Hamer's personal history gives us a more complete measure of what it meant to live her life. Too often, our study and research of black female historical figures yield depictions of yet another "strong black woman." While there was much that indicates strength and nobility in the lives of historic African-American women, there was also pain—pain that they learned to accommodate in their lives, yet never quite defeating or overtaking it. It was pain that continued to shape the thoughts and choices that these women made through the full duration of their lives. This was so for Fannie Lou Hamer. Her historical legacy is in no way diminished by acknowledging her ability to live with her pain. She sometimes tempered and used it and sometimes succumbed to it, but it never went away. This too was a part of her legacy. More than anything, Hamer taught others how to coexist with pain and challenge. In this regard, the abstract meaning of her story is not necessarily found in a story of triumph or defeat. It is simply a story of how best to live our lives with whatever we have been given, forever priming ourselves to push for a bit more.

Notes

Chapter 1: Delta Daughter

The chapter's epigraph is from Billie Holiday, "Billie's Blues," *Billie Holiday's Greatest Hits,* Polygram Records, 1985.

1. Danny Collum, "Stepping Out into Freedom," *Sojourners* 11, no. 11 (Dec. 1982): 11.

2. Lou Ella Townsend followed a community naming tradition by giving her children each an original first name but taking their middle names from family and community members who wanted namesakes. Consequently, Fannie Lou and her siblings each had anywhere from eight to sixteen names. For example, one of her sisters was named Jamilla Idella Juanita Ehtalete Tiny Sella Bell Ozin Liz Ann Alfred Jessie Dessie Bob Dett Burnett. Laura Ratliff, Hamer's sister, could not remember all of Fannie Lou's names, but she recalled that her full name was of similar length. Interview with Laura Ratliff by author, Dec. 21, 1985, Ruleville, Miss.

3. Fannie Lou Hamer, *To Praise Our Bridges: An Autobiography* (Jackson, Miss.: KIPCO, 1967), 5, 9; "Marked for Murder," *Sepia* 14, no. 4 (Apr. 1965): 33; "An Autobiography of Mrs. Fannie Lou Hamer," *Close-up* 4, no. 1 (Jan. 1969): 9.

4. According to U.S. census population schedules for Montgomery County, Mississippi, Lou Ella Bramlett and James Lee Townsend were born in October 1875 and July 1873, respectively. See U.S. Bureau of the Census, *Twelfth Census of the United States, 1900: Population Schedules* (Montgomery County, Mississippi). In this same census, Lou Ella Townsend is listed as simply Ella. However, I have decided to keep with her family tradition and refer to her as Lou Ella. See also State of Mississippi, Marriage Records, 1873, Choctaw County, book b, 572.

5. Hamer, *To Praise Our Bridges*, 5.

6. Fannie Lou Hamer, "It's in Your Hands," in *Black Women in White America: A Documentary History*, ed. Gerda Lerner (New York: Vintage, 1972), 613.

7. J. H. O'Dell, "Life in Mississippi: An Interview with Fannie Lou Hamer," *Freedomways* 5, no. 2 (Spring 1965): 232; Fannie Lou Hamer, "Songs My Mother Taught Me," *Voices of the Civil Rights Movement: Black American Freedom Songs, 1960–1966* (Washington, D.C.: Smithsonian Institution Folkways Recording, 1980), transcript in Civil Rights Collection, Jackson State University Library, Jackson, Miss., 2.

8. Phyl Garland, "Builders of a New South," *Ebony*, Aug. 1966, 28.

9. Ibid.

10. Hamer, *To Praise Our Bridges*, 1; "An Autobiography of Mrs. Fannie Lou Hamer," 6. Children were central to the household economy under sharecropping. Some scholars suggest that share tenancy did a better job at exploiting child labor than did slavery. See, for example, Edgar T. Thompson, ed., *Plantation Societies, Race Relations, and the South: The Regimentation of Populations* (Durham: Duke University Press, 1975), and Neil R. McMillen, *Dark Journey: Black Mississippians in the Age of Jim Crow* (Urbana: University of Illinois Press, 1989), 129.

11. June Jordan, *Fannie Lou Hamer* (New York: Crowell, 1972) 8–9; Susan Kling, *Fannie Lou Hamer: A Biography* (Chicago: Women for Racial and Economic Equality, 1979), 11.

12. The daily average for an adult of either sex was two hundred to three hundred pounds. See McMillen, *Dark Journey*, 130.

13. *Independent Eye*, Dec. 23, 1968–Jan. 20, 1969, n.p.; Austin Scott, "Fannie Lou Hamer, Civil Rights Leader, Dies," *Washington Post*, Mar. 17, 1977. On sharecroppers' mixed feelings of pride and resentment toward their work, see also Ned Cobb's story in Theodore Rosengarten, *All God's Dangers: The Life of Nate Shaw* (New York: Knopf, 1974), 188–203.

14. O'Dell, "Life in Mississippi," 231–32.

15. Franklynn Peterson, "Sunflowers Don't Grow in Sunflower County," *Sepia* 19 (Feb. 1970): 11; Kling, *Fannie Lou Hamer*, 11–12.

16. Jordan, *Fannie Lou Hamer*, 12.

17. O'Dell, "Life in Mississippi," 232. On school attendance rates in Mississippi, see McMillen, *Dark Journey*, 88–89, 95.

18. McMillen, *Dark Journey*, 73. See also various county tables for Mississippi in Charles S. Johnson, *Statistical Atlas of Southern Counties: Listing and Analysis of Socioeconomic Indices of 1104 Southern Counties* (Chapel Hill: University of North Carolina Press, 1941), 160–74. Reconstruction and Progressive Era educational reforms for the American South had little, if any, impact on the state of Mississippi. Where there were advances, needless to say, white pupils were the primary beneficiaries. Throughout most of this century (and up until very recently), Mississippi remained last in the country in school expenditures.

19. Fannie Lou Hamer, *Address to the Systematic Training and Redevelopment Program,* video tape, Sept. 17, 1969, Newsfilm Collection, 1954–1971 (video), Mississippi Department of Archives and History, Jackson, Miss.

20. Jordan, *Fannie Lou Hamer,* 10.

21. Kling, *Fannie Lou Hamer,* 12. Susan Kling notes that one of the things that Hamer did for her mother when she got older was to teach her how to read and write. However, according to the *Twelfth Census of the United States, 1900: Population Schedules* (Montgomery County), both of Hamer's parents were already literate. Perhaps the real questions center around what constituted literacy in 1900, the assumptions of illiteracy on behalf of historians/biographers, or, assuming that the Townsend parents were in fact literate, Hamer's recollection/depiction of her parents' condition.

22. Kling, *Fannie Lou Hamer,* 13–14; Leslie McLemore, "Fannie Lou Hamer: An Unfinished Political Portrait" (Paper presented at conference of National Council for Black Studies, Chicago, Ill., Mar. 17–20, 1982), 3; George Sewell, "Fannie Lou Hamer," *Black Collegian* 8, no. 5 (May/June 1978): 18.

23. Jordan, *Fannie Lou Hamer,* 12, 15.

24. Interview with Laura Ratliff.

25. Fannie Lou Hamer, "Fannie Lou Hamer Speaks Out," *Essence* 1, no. 6 (Oct. 1971): 53; idem, *To Praise Our Bridges,* 20.

26. Hamer, *To Praise Our Bridges,* 21; *Portrait in Black: Fannie Lou Hamer, Chronicle of a Movement* (film, Rediscovery Productions, 1972), Mississippi Department of Archives and History; Hamer, "It's in Your Hands," 609.

27. Interview with Laura Ratliff.

28. Hamer, "It's in Your Hands," 609–10.

29. McMillen, *Dark Journey,* 14.

30. Kling, *Fannie Lou Hamer,* 12. The term "outraged mother" is used by the literary historian Joanne M. Braxton to describe features and consequences of black mothering, particularly, but not exclusively, during the period of slavery. In her discussion of the mothering role of "Linda Brent" in *Incidents in the Life of a Slave Girl,* she writes: "The archetypal outraged mother travels alone through the darkness to impart a sense of identity and 'belongingness' to her child. She sacrifices and improvises to create the vehicles necessary for the survival of flesh and spirit. Implied in all her actions and fueling her heroic ones is abuse of her people and her person." See Joanne M. Braxton, *Black Women Writing Autobiography: A Tradition within a Tradition* (Philadelphia: Temple University Press, 1989), 21. On black motherhood, see also Patricia Hill Collins, "The Meaning of Motherhood in Black Culture and Black Mother/Daughter Relationships," *Sage* 4, no. 2 (Fall 1987): 3–10; and Elsa Barkley Brown, "Mothers of Mind," *Sage* 6 (Spring 1989): 4–11.

31. Hamer, "Songs My Mother Taught Me," 3–6.

32. Hamer, *To Praise Our Bridges,* 9; *Independent Eye,* Dec. 23, 1968–Jan. 20, 1969, n.p.; Hamer, "Songs My Mother Taught Me," 3.

33. Hamer, "Fannie Lou Hamer Speaks Out," 54; Hamer, *To Praise Our Bridges,* 11. At the age of fifty-three, Hamer proudly observed that she "never had a tooth pulled in my life." In spite of her indulgence in what the historian Jack Temple Kirby calls the "white food syndrome" typical of southern diets (i.e., pork fat; cornbread, or "pone," fried in pork grease; and corn or sorghum molasses), Hamer had relatively healthy teeth, which she attributed to eating what she referred to as "natural food" that her mother was able to gather up. See Jack Temple Kirby, *Rural Worlds Lost: The American South, 1920–1960* (Baton Rouge: Louisiana State University Press, 1987), 188.

34. Jordan, *Fannie Lou Hamer,* 1–3.

35. Ibid., 3–6; Kling, *Fannie Lou Hamer,* 12.

36. Jordan, *Fannie Lou Hamer,* 3.

37. Ibid., 17; Kling, *Fannie Lou Hamer,* 12.

38. Hamer, "Fannie Lou Hamer Speaks Out," 54.

39. Hamer, *To Praise Our Bridges,* 20. See also interview with Fannie Lou Hamer by Robert Wright, Aug. 9, 1968, Oral History Collection, Civil Rights Documentation Project (CRDP), Moorland-Spingarn Research Center, Howard University.

40. Cathy Aldridge, "What Makes Fannie Lou Hamer Run?" *Amsterdam News,* Sept. 13, 1969, Woman's World Section, 5; Fannie Lou Hamer Vertical File, Schomburg Center for Research in Black Culture, New York Public Library.

41. Hamer, "Fannie Lou Hamer Speaks Out," 53. The use of the phrase "black is beautiful" seems very historically specific, and thus Hamer's uses of them in 1969 and 1971 is somewhat anachronistic when we consider that she was referring to advice and encouragement imparted by her mother during the thirties, the period of Hamer's adolescent years. Here, the larger point about Hamer's use of "black is beautiful" and "black," in reference to what was then most commonly known as "coloreds" and "Negroes," is that her mother was a dedicated proponent of fostering racial pride. A figure of her own time, Hamer cannot help but remember her mother in terms that were so historically specific to the black power phase of the civil rights era.

42. On this tradition see, for example, Collins, "The Meaning of Motherhood," 3–5; and Deborah Gray White, *Ar'n't I a Woman? Female Slaves in the Plantation South* (New York: Norton, 1985), 105–6, 109–13, 159–60.

43. Interview with Fannie Lou Hamer by Wright.

44. L. C. Dorsey, "Fannie Lou Hamer," *Jackson Advocate,* Feb. 26–Mar. 6, 1981, section C, 1; O'Dell, "Life in Mississippi," 232.

45. Alice Walker, "'Can't Hate Anybody and See God's Face,'" *New York Times Book Review,* Apr. 26, 1973, 8; Kling, *Fannie Lou Hamer,* 14.

46. Hamer, "Fannie Lou Hamer Speaks Out," 54.

47. For information on the births and deaths of Ella Townsend's children up to 1900, see *Twelfth Census of the United States, 1900: Population Schedules* (Montgomery County) and interview with Laura Ratliff. Mrs. Ratliff says that some of the children did die, but she did not specify how many or which ones. I suspect more than two may have died.

48. Lawrence Levine, *Black Culture, Black Consciousness: Afro-American Folk Thought from Slavery to Freedom* (New York: Oxford University Press, 1977), 7–10, 208–9, 282–83.

49. Hamer, "Songs My Mother Taught Me," 5.

50. Levine, *Black Culture and Black Consciousness*, 212–17, 240, 297.

51. *Independent Eye*, Dec. 23, 1968–Jan. 20, 1969, n.p.

52. Jordan, *Fannie Lou Hamer*, 15.

53. Hamer, *To Praise Our Bridges*, 6; *Independent Eye*, Dec. 23, 1968–Jan. 20, 1969, n.p.; O'Dell, "Life in Mississippi," 232.

54. For a colorfully engaging account of the circumstances and motivation for such mobility, consult Rosengarten, *All God's Dangers*, 112–15, 124, 151, 164, 240–43, 280–81. Regarding the significance and potential of mobility, see also the vivid accounts cited in Gerald Jaynes, *Branches without Roots: Genesis of the Black Working Class in the American South, 1862–1882* (New York: Oxford University Press, 1986), 314–15. Economic mobility also included movement from farm labor to nonagricultural work and back to farm work. See Rosengarten, *All God's Dangers*, 186–87; and Bruce Schulman, *From Cotton Belt to Sunbelt: Federal Policy, Economic Development, and the Transformation of the South, 1938–1980* (New York: Oxford University Press, 1991), 4, 5, 235 n. 8. Illegal and extralegal labor-repression measures notwithstanding, the option to move was a transhistorical feature of farm tenancy, dating back to the origins of the system itself. See, for example, Roger Ransom and Richard Sutch, *One Kind of Freedom: The Economic Consequences of Emancipation* (Cambridge: Cambridge University Press, 1977), 62–66; Pete Daniel, *The Shadow of Slavery: Peonage in the South, 1901–1969* (Urbana: University of Illinois Press, 1990), 20, chap. 2, passim; idem, *Breaking the Land: The Transformation of Cotton, Tobacco and Rice Cultures Since 1880* (Urbana: University of Illinois Press, 1985), 5–6.

55. Hamer, "Fannie Lou Hamer Speaks Out," 53–54; Sewell, "Fannie Lou Hamer," 18. In "Songs My Mother Taught Me," Hamer says that the animals were poisoned with kerosene. All other accounts (including Hamer's) point to the insecticide Paris green.

56. Jordan, *Fannie Lou Hamer*, 17; Hamer, *To Praise Our Bridges*, 6; idem, "Songs My Mother Taught Me," 2.

57. Hamer, *To Praise Our Bridges*, 9; *Motive*, Dec. 1970, 44, Fannie Lou Hamer Vertical File, 1925–74, Schomburg Center.

58. Hamer, *To Praise Our Bridges*, 9; *Motive*, 44; McLemore, "Fannie Lou Hamer: An Unfinished Political Portrait," 3.

59. *Motive*, 44.

60. Hamer, *To Praise Our Bridges*, 7–9; O'Dell, "Life in Mississippi," 233–34; Peterson, "Sunflower Don't Grow in Sunflower County," 16.

61. O'Dell, "Life in Mississippi," 233.

62. Ibid., 234.

63. See McMillen, *Dark Journey*, passim, esp., 110–50. On "rural terrorism" in Mississippi, see Herbert Shapiro, *White Violence and Black Response: From Reconstruction*

to Montgomery (Amherst: University of Massachusetts Press, 1988), 223–24. Violent reprisal was not the sole preserve of crazed and spiteful individuals; sometimes retaliation against sharecroppers' defiant self-sufficiency took the form of organized raids and assaults, many times led by local law enforcement. In the case of legendary Alabama sharecropper, Ned Cobb, such retaliation took the form of a 1932 shootout between local sheriffs and farmers of the Sharecroppers Union, including Cobb. See Rosengarten, *All God's Dangers,* 310–35, 585–87.

64. Kirby, *Rural Worlds Lost,* 151–52; Robin D. G. Kelley, *Hammer and Hoe: Alabama Communists during the Great Depression* (Chapel Hill: University of North Carolina Press, 1990), chap. 3.

65. Kling, *Fannie Lou Hamer,* 14. It's not clear exactly when James Lee Townsend died. Cemetery records for Montgomery and Sunflower counties are incomplete, as are most county records for the South due to fires or mismanagement. Any other records of his death (e.g., a death certificate) are unavailable to nonrelatives. While there is, I am told, a Townsend family plot, there is no guarantee that his grave will be marked, and there are no immediate survivors.

66. Dorsey, "Fannie Lou Hamer," 1; O'Dell, "Life in Mississippi," 232; interview with Fannie Lou Hamer by Wright.

67. Kay Mills notes that the couple married in 1944, when Perry Hamer was thirty-two and Fannie Lou was twenty-six or twenty-seven. See Kay Mills, *This Little Light of Mine: The Life of Fannie Lou Hamer* (New York: Dutton, 1993), 14. June Jordan notes that they married in 1945, not 1944 (Jordan, *Fannie Lou Hamer,* 18), while other accounts have them married anywhere between 1942 and 1945. See, for example, Deborah LeSure and Deborah Bouton, "Fannie Lou Hamer, Remembered Well," *Southern Rural Women's Network Newsletter* 2 [Jan. 1984)] 5; "Fannie Lou Hamer, 60, Civil Rights Activist, Dies," *Bay State Banner,* Mar. 24, 1977, 1, 23; Kling, *Fannie Lou Hamer,* 14; Hamer, *To Praise Our Bridges,* 11; George Sewell, "Fannie Lou Hamer's Light Still Shines," *Encore American and Worldwide News,* July 18, 1977, 3. Sylvia Townsend suggested to me that Fannie Lou was Pap's second spouse (interview with Sylvia Townsend by author, May 18, 1990, New York City).

I did not find any marriage records under either name in Montgomery County. I have not been able to locate marriage records for Sunflower County, and it seems unlikely that the Hamers would have married in any other county. In a letter to me (Aug. 31, 1985), Clayborne Carson speculated that the Hamers were common-law spouses.

68. On the recognition of common-law marriages by the state of Mississippi, see McMillen, *Dark Journey,* 15.

69. United States Congress, "Hearing Before a Select Panel on Mississippi and Civil Rights, Testimony of Fannie Lou Hamer," *Congressional Record,* 88th Cong., 2d sess., June 4, 1964, to June 16, 1964, vol. 110, pt. 10, 14001; Milton Meltzer, *In Their Own Words: A History of the American Negro, 1916–1966* (New York: Crowell, 1967), 195.

70. Interview with Perry (Pap) Hamer by author, Dec. 21, 1985, Ruleville, Miss.; "An Autobiography of Mrs. Fannie Lou Hamer," 9; Garland, "Builders of a New South," 28.

71. Interview with Sylvia Townsend. There is something inconsistent and thus unsettling about this part of Mrs. Hamer's work experience in light of the exploitative nature of insurance sales to blacks during this period. While I know she must have needed the work, I wonder about her role in this.

72. Interview with Fannie Lou Hamer by Wright. The object Hamer refers to as a "pea" was a counterweight on the scale, or steelyard, as it was also called. See discussion in, for example, Rupert Vance, *Human Factors in Cotton Culture: A Study in the Social Geography of the American South* (Chapel Hill: University of North Carolina Press, 1929), 168–69; and Pete Daniel, *Breaking the Land: The Transformation of Cotton, Tobacco, and Rice Cultures since 1880* (Urbana: University of Illinois Press, 1985), 2.

73. Garland, "Builders of a New South," 29.

74. Interview with Fannie Lou Hamer by Wright; interview with Jacqueline (Cookie) Hamer by author, Dec. 21, 1985, Ruleville, Miss.

75. Kenneth O'Reilly, *"Racial Matters": The FBI's Secret File on Black America, 1960–1972* (New York: Free Press, 1989), 1–8; Federal Bureau of Investigation, File No. 44-48733, 44-31908, 9-49604, 157-3933 (Fannie Lou Hamer).

76. Hamer, *To Praise Our Bridges,* 11; interview with Fannie Lou Hamer by Wright. In a 1968 speech before the Mt. Zion Baptist Church in Lincoln Heights, Ohio, Hamer said that her mother was ninety-eight years old at the time of her death in 1961 (*Independent Eye,* Dec. 23, 1968–Jan. 20, 1969, n.p.). However, this places her mother's birth at around 1863, instead of 1875 as reported in the census returns for 1900. If Ella Townsend was ninety-eight at death, this means she was fifty-four at the time she gave birth to Hamer, which would have been very rare. In other accounts of her mother's age at death, Hamer notes that she was ninety, which would put Ella Townsend's birth date closer to 1875, which may not be the exact date either. It's probably safe to assume that Ella Townsend was between her late eighties and early nineties at the time of her death.

77. Kling, *Fannie Lou Hamer,* 14.

78. Hamer, "Fannie Lou Hamer Speaks Out," 56.

79. Ibid.

80. Interview with Fannie Lou Hamer by Wright.

81. Mills, *This Little Light,* 21; Collum, "Stepping Out into Freedom," 12; Kling, *Fannie Lou Hamer,* 15.

82. Mills, *This Little Light,* 21.

83. Dorothy Roberts, *Killing the Black Body: Race, Reproduction, and the Meaning of Liberty* (New York: Pantheon, 1997), 89–98, 213–14; *Great Speckled Bird,* Apr. 19, 1971, n.p., Fannie Lou Hamer Vertical File, 1925–74, Schomburg Center; Vicki Lynn Crawford, "We Shall Not Be Moved: Black Female Activists in the Mississippi Civil Rights Movement, 1960–1965" (Ph.D. diss., Emory University, 1986), 22–23; "Illegitimacy Bill," May 21, 1964, Student Nonviolent Coordinating Committee (SNCC) Papers (hereaf-

ter, SNCC Papers), box 32, Martin Luther King Jr. Library and Archives, Martin Luther King Jr. Center for Nonviolent Social Change, Atlanta; "Genocide in Mississippi," SNCC Papers, microfilm, reel 19, 3–4. According to *the Great Speckled Bird:* "In 1964 a black woman from Mississippi, Mrs. Fannie Lou Hamer, told a meeting of the Women's International League for Peace and Freedom (WILPF) that 'six out of every ten Negro women were taken to Sunflower City Hospital to be sterilized for no reason at all. Often the women were not told they had been sterilized until they were released from the hospital.'"

84. "Genocide in Mississippi."

85. *Portrait in Black.*

Chapter 2: Black Woman Leader

The chapter's first epigraph is an African proverb, quoted in an unattributed typescript, Fannie Lou Hamer Papers, Zenobia Coleman Library, Tougaloo College, Tougaloo, Miss. The second epigraph is from Aaron D. Greeson, "Beyond Selves Deferred: Langston Hughes' Style and the Psychology of Black Selfhood," *Langston Hughes Review* 4, no. 1 (Spring 1985): 47.

1. See Steven F. Lawson, *Black Ballots: Voting Rights in the South* (New York: Columbia University Press, 1976), 263–65; Pat Watters and Reese Cleghorn, *Climbing Jacob's Ladder: The Arrival of Negroes in Southern Politics* (New York: Harcourt, Brace and World, 1967), 48–49; Minion K. C. Morrison, *Black Political Mobilization, Leadership, Power, and Mass Behavior* (Albany: State University of New York Press, 1987), 47–49.

2. Lerone Bennett Jr., "SNCC: Rebels with a Cause," *Ebony,* July 1965, 147–49; Clayborne Carson, *In Struggle: SNCC and the Black Awakening of the 1960s* (Cambridge, Mass.: Harvard University Press, 1981), 82.

3. Carson, *In Struggle,* 30; Ellen Canterow, ed., *Moving the Mountain: Women Working for Social Change* (Old Westbury, N.Y.: Feminist Press, 1980), 53.

4. Kay Mills, *This Little Light of Mine: The Life of Fannie Lou Hamer* (New York: Dutton, 1993), 23–24.

5. Interview with Sylvia Townsend by author, May 18, 1990, New York City; interview with Pap Hamer by author, Dec. 21, 1985, Ruleville, Miss.; interview with Fannie Lou Hamer by Robert Wright, Aug. 9, 1968, Oral History Collection, Civil Rights Documentation Project (CRDP), Moorland-Spingarn Research Center, Howard University; Howell Raines, *My Soul Is Rested: Movement Days in the Deep South Remembered* (New York: Putnam, 1977), 249; Phyl Garland, "Builders of a New South," *Ebony,* Aug. 1966, 29.

6. Mills, *This Little Light,* 24.

7. Later on, Hamer noted that CORE's Dave Dennis and Amzie Moore, a Deltan, were also in attendance that night at Williams Church. See "Fannie Lou Hamer

Speech," Santa Fe Junior [Community] College, Gainesville, Florida, n.d., tape recording in author's possession.

8. Fannie Lou Hamer, *To Praise Our Bridges: An Autobiography* (Jackson, Miss.: KIPCO, 1967), 12; Raines, *My Soul Is Rested*, 249; John Egerton, *A Mind to Stay Here: Profiles from the South* (New York: Macmillan, 1970), 95; "Profiles of Typical Freedom Schools, Ruleville," Student Nonviolent Coordinating Committee (SNCC) Papers (hereafter, SNCC Papers), Martin Luther King Jr. Library and Archives, Martin Luther King Jr. Center for Nonviolent Social Change, Atlanta, microfilm, reel 13.

9. "Fannie Lou Hamer Speech"; George Sewell, "Fannie Lou Hamer's Light Still Shines," *Encore American and Worldwide News*, July 18, 1977, 3.

10. Hamer, *To Praise Our Bridges*, 12.

11. Deborah LeSure and Deborah Bouton, "Fannie Lou Hamer, Remembered Well," *ruralamerica* (Nov.–Dec. 1983): 24; Leslie McLemore, "Fannie Lou Hamer: An Unfinished Political Portrait" (Paper presented at conference of National Council for Black Studies, Chicago, Ill., Mar. 17–20, 1982), 6–7.

12. June Jordan, *Fannie Lou Hamer* (New York: Crowell, 1972), 24.

13. Raines, *My Soul Is Rested*, 249.

14. Ibid., 255.

15. Hamer, *To Praise Our Bridges*, 12.

16. Susan Kling, *Fannie Lou Hamer: A Biography* (Chicago: Women for Racial and Economic Equality, 1979), 17.

17. Jerry Demuth, "'Tired of Being Sick and Tired,'" *The Nation*, June 1, 1964, 549.

18. Interview with Fannie Lou Hamer by Wright; "Fannie Lou Hamer Speech."

19. While council members originally emerged as staunch advocates of school segregation, the organization eventually dedicated its efforts to upholding segregation in all areas of American public and private life. Comprised of the more "respectable" among segregationists, the council was nonetheless never above committing wanton acts of violence. See Neil R. McMillen, *The Citizens' Council: Organized Resistance to the Second Reconstruction, 1954–64* (Urbana: University of Illinois Press, 1971), and Numan V. Bartley, *The Rise of Massive Resistance: Race and Politics in the South during the 1950s* (Baton Rouge: Louisiana State University Press, 1969).

20. Interview with Fannie Lou Hamer by Wright; Kling, *Fannie Lou Hamer*, 17. Hamer sued Cecil B. Campbell three years later for unlawful interference with the elections held in Sunflower and Moorhead, Mississippi.

21. Egerton, *A Mind to Stay Here*, 97; interview with Fannie Lou Hamer by Wright; "Fannie Lou Hamer Speech."

22. Kling, *Fannie Lou Hamer*, 17; "Fannie Lou Hamer Speech."

23. Interview with Fannie Lou Hamer by Wright; George Sewell, "Fannie Lou Hamer," *Black Collegian* 8, no. 5 (May/June 1978): 18.

24. This Mississippi constitution was ratified in 1890 by a constitutional convention of 134 delegates, among whom 130 were disgruntled Democrats bent on rescind-

ing black gains made during Reconstruction. Unlike the Mississippi constitution of 1868, this later constitution severely limited the voting activities of blacks by introducing literacy and poll tax requirements. Voters had to be able to read any section or be able to understand it when it was read to them. One had to also give a "reasonable" interpretation of various sections of the constitution. The poll tax clause required that voters pay two dollars, due two years in advance of the election year, before the candidates or issues were known. Despite subsequent legal challenges, the constitution of 1890 was upheld later by the Mississippi Supreme Court and by the United States Supreme Court in the case of *Williams v. Mississippi* (1898). See Vernon Lane Wharton, *The Negro in Mississippi, 1865–1890* (Chapel Hill: University of North Carolina Press, 1947), 206–15; James W. Loewen and Charles Sallis, *Mississippi: Conflict and Change* (New York: Pantheon, 1974), 185–88.

25. Raines, *My Soul Is Rested,* 250; interview with Fannie Lou Hamer by Wright.

26. Kling, *Fannie Lou Hamer,* 18.

27. Interview with Fannie Lou Hamer by Wright; Raines, *My Soul Is Rested,* 250; Demuth, "'Tired of Being Sick and Tired,'" 550.

28. Charles McLaurin, "Voice of Calm," *Sojourners* 11, no. 11 (Dec. 1982): 12–13; Demuth, "'Tired of Being Sick and Tired,'" 550; Raines, *My Soul Is Rested,* 250. Bob Moses was the only one who was eventually arrested. He had accompanied the group on the ride as sort of a "morale booster." See Taylor Branch, *Parting the Waters: America in the King Years, 1954–63* (New York: Simon and Schuster, 1988), 636.

29. Interview with Fannie Lou Hamer by Wright.

30. Ibid.; Susan Johnson, "Fannie Lou Hamer: Mississippi Grassroots Organizer," *Black Law Journal* 2, no. 2 (Summer 1972): 158; "Fannie Lou Hamer Speech." Although it is incorrectly thought that Hamer and all of the people aboard the bus were arrested, Hamer gives two different versions of what happened on their way back to Ruleville. In her autobiography she says that they all were later arrested, taken to jail, and that she was bailed out later that night. However, apparently only Bob Moses was actually arrested. See Raines, *My Soul Is Rested,* 250.

31. Kling, *Fannie Lou Hamer,* 18.

32. U.S. Commission on Civil Rights, *Political Participation* (Washington, D.C.: Government Printing Office, 1968), 246; "Registration Efforts in Mississippi Continue Despite Violence and Terror," *Student Voice,* Oct. 1962. Voter registration figures for groups in the nonwhite category are hard to come by for the Delta before 1964. Compare these Sunflower County figures with those for the entire state: blacks represented 36 percent of the statewide voting age population but comprised only 5.3 percent of the registered voters. See also, U.S. Commission on Civil Rights, *Voting in Mississippi* (Washington, D.C.: Government Printing Office, 1965), 70–71; and Watters and Cleghorn, *Climbing Jacob's Ladder,* Appendix 2.

33. "Marked for Murder," *Sepia* 14, no. 4 (Apr. 1965): 28–33.

34. Interview with Fannie Lou Hamer by Wright; Raines, *My Soul Is Rested,* 250; United States Congress, "Hearing Before a Select Panel on Mississippi and Civil Rights,

Testimony of Fannie Lou Hamer," *Congressional Record,* 88th Cong., 2d sess., June 4, 1964, to June 16, 1964, vol. 110, pt. 10, 14001.

35. Jordan, *Fannie Lou Hamer,* 22.

36. Interview with Fannie Lou Hamer by Wright; Demuth, "'Tired of Being Sick and Tired,'" 550; Raines, *My Soul Is Rested,* 250–51.

37. Interview with Fannie Lou Hamer by Wright. Besides Hamer's insolence, another factor that seemed to weigh heavily on Marlow's mind was the thought of his being singled out for allowing an "agitator" to remain on his property. During his exchange with Hamer, he also pointed out: "They gon' worry me tonight. They gon' worry the hell outa me, and I'm gon' worry hell outa you. You got 'til in the mornin' to tell me." Although he never identified who "they" were, Hamer assumed he was referring to men in the White Citizens Council or the Ku Klux Klan. See Raines, *My Soul Is Rested,* 251.

38. Egerton, *A Mind to Stay Here,* 97–98.

39. Interview with Fannie Lou Hamer by Wright.

40. Andrew Young, *Eulogy for Mrs. Hamer, Fannie Lou Hamer Funeral* (Mar. 1977), video tape, Mississippi Department of Archives and History, Jackson, Miss.; Kling, *Fannie Lou Hamer,* 19; Jordan, *Fannie Lou Hamer,* 22.

41. Sewell, "Fannie Lou Hamer's Light Still Shines," 3; Kling, *Fannie Lou Hamer,* 20.

42. Hamer, *To Praise Our Bridges,* 13; Raines, *My Soul Is Rested,* 251; Branch, *Parting the Waters,* 636.

43. Hamer, *To Praise Our Bridges,* 13; Raines, *My Soul Is Rested,* 245–48, 251; "Fannie Lou Hamer Speech."

44. When Moses showed up at the hospital to get a report on the women's condition, the Ruleville mayor, Charles Dorrough, arrested him for allegedly planning the attacks that night as a part of a publicity stunt to draw sympathy for activists in the Delta. See Branch, *Parting the Waters,* 637–38.

45. "Two Negro Girls Shot in Home of Voter Registration Worker," SNCC news release, Sept. 11 (1962), SNCC Papers, microfilm, reel 13; "Registration Efforts in Mississippi Continue Despite Violence and Terror," *Student Voice,* Oct. 1962, 2, SNCC Papers, microfilm, reel 8; telegram to John F. Kennedy from James Forman, Sept. 10 [1962], SNCC Papers, microfilm, reel 10; untitled SNCC news release, Atlanta, Georgia, Sept. 20 [1962].

46. Raines, *My Soul Is Rested,* 245–46.

47. Interview with Fannie Lou Hamer by Wright.

48. Raines, *My Soul Is Rested,* 251.

49. Interview with Fannie Lou Hamer by Wright.

50. Ibid.

51. Ibid.

52. The conversion motif abounds in Western and non-Western life-writing. See, for example, Robert Elbaz, *The Changing Nature of the Self* (Iowa City: University of Iowa Press, 1987); Theodore Rosengarten, ed., *All God's Dangers: The Life of Nate Shaw*

(New York: Knopf, 1974); Nellie Y. McKay, "Nineteenth-Century Black Women's Spiritual Autobiographies: Religious Faith and Self-Empowerment," in *Interpreting Women's Lives: Feminist Theory and Personal Narratives,* ed. Personal Narratives Group (Urbana: University of Illinois Press, 1989), 1397–54. Perhaps the most well-known example in African-American life-writing is Malcolm X (with Alex Haley), *The Autobiography of Malcolm X* (New York: Grove Press, 1965).

53. Raines, *My Soul Is Rested,* 251; interview with Fannie Lou Hamer by Wright.

54. Charles McLaurin, "Memories of Fannie Lou Hamer," *Jackson Advocate,* Feb. 26–Mar. 4, 1981, section C, 1. For information about SNCC's Fall Institute and Hamer's participation, see the following: Memo from Charles McDew on Combination Fall Coordinating Committee Meeting and Leadership Training Institute, n.d., SNCC Papers, microfilm, reel 11; 1962 Fall Coordinating Committee Meeting Leadership Training Institute application for Fannie Lou Hamer, SNCC Papers, microfilm, reel 11; Politics and Voting Workshop sign-up sheet for Leadership Training Institute [in longhand], SNCC Papers, microfilm, reel 11. The institute hoped to achieve the following: "students, the nation over, shall have an opportunity to communicate problems and solutions to each other and to dramatize the comprehensive unity of *the Movement.* It is hoped that the students . . . will return to their respective tasks with additional information, with a revitalized commitment and with a new sense of community and good will." Memo from Charles McDew, Chairman, to Dear Friend, n.d., SNCC Papers, microfilm, reel 11.

55. Garland, "Builders of a New South," 30.

56. Fieldwork application of Fannie Lou Hamer, SNCC Papers, microfilm, reel 12; interview with Fannie Lou Hamer by Wright.

57. Raines, *My Soul Is Rested,* 252; Sewell, "Fannie Lou Hamer's Light Still Shines," 3.

58. See, for example, Henry Louis Gates Jr., "Frederick Douglass and the Language of the Self," in Gates, *Figures in Black: Words, Signs, and the "Racial" Self* (New York: Oxford University Press, 1987), 98–124. The act of self-imaging by historical figures seems universal in that it crosses parameters of gender, class, culture, place, and time. For example, see also, Georges Gusdorf, "Conditions and Limits of Autobiography," in *Autobiography: Essays Theoretical and Critical,* ed. James Olney (Princeton: Princeton University Press, 1980), 28–48; Timothy Dow Adams, *Telling Lies in Modern American Autobiography* (Chapel Hill: University of North Carolina Press, 1990), esp. ix–xi, 1–16.

59. "Fannie Lou Hamer Speech," Gainesville, Florida, n.d.

60. Raines, *My Soul Is Rested,* 252. In spite of their many contributions, citizenship school organizers did not explicitly challenge literacy as a condition of voter registration. In part, this was because literacy was not taught just to satisfy a condition of registration, but because people like Clark believed it opened up other avenues to power and self-improvement.

61. McLemore, "Fannie Lou Hamer: An Unfinished Political Portrait," 9; Demuth, "'Tired of Being Sick and Tired,'" 550; Garland, "Builders of a New South," 34.

62. "Marked for Murder"; Egerton, *A Mind to Stay Here*, 98; Demuth, "'Tired of Being Sick and Tired,'" 550; Kling, *Fannie Lou Hamer*, 20.

63. Raines, *My Soul Is Rested*, 252; Johnson, "Fannie Lou Hamer: Mississippi Grassroots Organizer," 158.

64. Jordan, *Fannie Lou Hamer*, 24; Kling, *Fannie Lou Hamer*, 20.

65. Hamer, *To Praise Our Bridges*, 13.

66. Interview with Fannie Lou Hamer by Wright; Egerton, *A Mind to Stay Here*, 98–99.

67. "Hearing Before a Select Panel on Mississippi and Civil Rights, Testimony of Fannie Lou Hamer"; interview with Fannie Lou Hamer by Wright. Fannie Lou Hamer noted that he was named so also because he bore a striking resemblance to the legendary nineteenth-century outlaw the Sundance Kid, who terrorized the American West in the late 1880s and 1890s with his robbing and rustling.

68. Interview with Fannie Lou Hamer by Wright.

69. Ibid.

70. Ibid.; Egerton, *A Mind to Stay Here*, 98–99; "Fannie Lou Hamer Speech."

71. Here it is interesting to note how the rules and customs of southern, transracial patriarchy defined ultimate liability in such cases. Even though it was clear to the mayor that Fannie Lou actually "stole" the water, Pap Hamer was deemed ultimately liable, and consequently only he would receive the punishment for *her* allegedly illegal behavior. Perhaps this had to do with the bill's being in his name, but, again, the transgression for which he was arrested did not involve an outstanding debt, but the "stolen water." The other ironic and curious fact was that the mayor sought out only Fannie Lou (the accused) to notify of a theft charge and to get her response; the summons was for her, not Pap, even though he would be the one to go to jail. Ironically, it was this same mayor who, as Hamer neared death, declared her a "champion of her people" at a Fannie Lou Hamer Day in Ruleville. See, Raines, *My Soul Is Rested*, 254–55.

72. Interview with Fannie Lou Hamer by Wright.

73. "Hearing Before a Select Panel on Mississippi and Civil Rights, Testimony of Fannie Lou Hamer."

74. Branch, *Parting the Waters*, 637–38; Egerton, *A Mind to Stay Here*, 90.

75. James Forman to Mattie Bivins, Nov. 16, 1962, SNCC Papers, reel 5; SNCC news release, Sept. 17 [1962], Ruleville, Miss., SNCC Papers, microfilm, reel 13.

76. Telegram to Attorny [*sic*] Gen. Robert F. Kennedy, Justice Dept., Dec. 22 [1962], from Charles McDew, Chairman, Student Nonviolent Coordinating Committee; SNCC news release, Dec. 22 [1962], Atlanta, Georgia, SNCC Papers, microfilm, reel 13.

77. Hamer, *To Praise Our Bridges*, 13; Jordan, *Fannie Lou Hamer*, 24.

78. Fannie Lou Hamer to James Forman, Nov. 6, 1963, SNCC Papers, microfilm, reel 6.

79. Egerton, *A Mind to Stay Here*, 92, 99; Cathy Aldridge, "What Makes Fannie Lou Hamer Run?" *New York Amsterdam News*, Sept. 13, 1969, Women's World Section, 5.

80. Inconsistencies in her self-constructions point to what psychoanalysts, psychohistorians, and psychobiographers call the phenomenon of "leaking."

81. Jordan, *Fannie Lou Hamer*, 22.

82. Raines, *My Soul Is Rested*, 252; Demuth, "'Tired of Being Sick and Tired,'" 550; Garland, "Builders of a New South," 30.

83. McLemore, "Fannie Lou Hamer: An Unfinished Political Portrait," 9; Bernice Reagon, "The Cultural Impact of Freedom Songs upon the Civil Rights Movement" (Paper presented at Fannie Lou Hamer Memorial Symposium Lecture Series, Jackson State University, Nov. 15, 1984).

84. On Greenwood as an active spot in the Delta, see Charles M. Payne, *I've Got the Light of Freedom: The Organizing Tradition and the Mississippi Freedom Struggle* (Berkeley: University of California Press, 1995).

85. Interview with June Johnson, July 22, 1979, Tom Dent Oral History Collection (TDC), Tougaloo Civil Rights Collection, Tougaloo College, Tougaloo, Miss.

86. Minutes from SNCC Staff Meeting, Oct. 11, 1964, 3, SNCC Papers, microfilm, reel 11.

87. Interview with Lawrence Guyot by author, Jan. 6, 1986, Washington, D.C.; Joyce A. Ladner, "Fannie Lou Hamer: In Memoriam," *Black Enterprise* (May 1977): 56.

88. Garland, "Builders of a New South," 34.

89. McLemore, "Fannie Lou Hamer: An Unfinished Political Portrait," 6–7; interview with Fannie Lou Hamer by Wright.

90. Charles Flint Kellogg, *NAACP: A History of the National Association for the Advancement of Colored People* (Baltimore: Johns Hopkins University Press, 1967); Mark V. Tushnet, *The NAACP's Legal Strategy against Segregated Education, 1925–1950* (Chapel Hill: University of North Carolina Press, 1987); Robert Zangrando, *The NAACP Crusade against Lynching, 1909–1950* (Philadelphia: Temple University Press, 1980); Kenneth Goings, *The NAACP Comes of Age* (Bloomington: Indiana University Press, 1990).

91. I am indebted to George Lipsitz for this idea. He introduces this concept, among others regarding the emergence of grass-roots leaders, in *A Life in the Struggle: Ivory Perry and the Culture of Opposition* (Philadelphia: Temple University Press, 1988), 227–47.

Chapter 3: Winona

The chapter's opening epigraph is from Charles Dorrough, mayor of Ruleville, Mississippi, *Jackson Clarion-Ledger*, Aug. 16, n.d., quoted in Shirley Tucker, *Mississippi from Within* (New York: Arco, 1976), 107.

1. Interview with June Johnson, Tom Dent Collection (TDC), Zenobia Coleman Library, Tougaloo College, Tougaloo, Miss.

2. Ibid.; "The Winona Incident, An Interview with Annelle Ponder and Fannie Lou Hamer, June 1963," reprinted in Pat Watters and Reese Cleghorn, *Climbing Jacob's*

Ladder: The Arrival of Negroes in Southern Politics, (New York: Harcourt, Brace and World, 1967), Appendix I, 364.

3. In September 1955, the Interstate Commerce Commission (ICC) issued a regulation outlawing racial separation in all vehicles and terminals involved in interstate travel. It went into effect in November of the same year. In September 1961, the ICC prohibited any interstate carriers from using segregated terminals, although many southern communities continued ignoring both the 1955 and 1961 rulings. See Harvard Sitkoff, *The Struggle for Black Equality, 1954–1980* (New York: Hill and Wang, 1981), 49, 110.

4. Interview with June Johnson (TDC).

5. Ibid.; June Johnson, "Broken Barriers and Billy Sticks," *Sojourners* 11, no. 11 (Dec. 1982): 16.

6. Interview with June Johnson (TDC).

7. Ibid.; Johnson, "Broken Barriers and Billy Sticks."

8. Hamer probably learned of this second-hand since, as noted, she remained on the bus while others went into the cafe. Johnson, "Broken Barriers and Billy Sticks," 17; "The Winona Incident," 364.

9. "The Winona Incident," 364.

10. Ibid.

11. United States Congress, "Hearing Before a Select Panel on Mississippi and Civil Rights, Testimony of Fannie Lou Hamer," *Congressional Record,* 88th Cong., 2d sess., June 4, 1964, to June 16, 1964, vol. 110, pt. 10, 14001–2; interview with Fannie Lou Hamer by Robert Wright, Aug. 9, 1968, Oral History Collection, Civil Rights Documentation Project (CRDP), Moorland-Spingarn Research Center (CRDP), Howard University; interview with June Johnson (TDC).

12. "The Winona Incident," 364–65; interview with June Johnson (TDC).

13. Interview with Fannie Lou Hamer by Wright; see also, "The Winona Incident," 365, 370.

14. "Hearing Before a Select Panel on Mississippi and Civil Rights, Testimony of Fannie Lou Hamer"; interview with Fannie Lou Hamer by Wright.

15. Interview with June Johnson (TDC).

16. "The Winona Incident," 365.

17. John Egerton, *A Mind to Stay Here: Profiles from the South* (New York: Macmillan, 1970), 100; interview with June Johnson (TDC).

18. Interview with June Johnson (TDC).

19. Sally Belfrage, *Freedom Summer* (New York: Viking, 1965), 123–24; Taylor Branch, *Parting the Waters: America in the King Years, 1954–63* (New York: Simon and Schuster, 1988), 819.

20. "The Winona Incident," 365.

21. Interview with June Johnson (TDC).

22. Ibid.

23. Ibid.

24. Ibid.; interview with Fannie Lou Hamer by Wright; Johnson, "Broken Barriers and Billy Sticks," 17.

25. Interview with June Johnson (TDC).

26. "The Winona Incident," 365.

27. Ibid.

28. Ibid., 366.

29. Ibid.

30. Ibid.

31. Ibid.

32. Howard Zinn, "The Battle-Scarred Youngsters," *The Nation,* Oct. 5, 1963, n.p., Student Nonviolent Coordinating Committee (SNCC) Papers (hereafter, SNCC Papers), Martin Luther King Jr. Library and Archives, Martin Luther King Jr. Center for Nonviolent Social Change, Atlanta, microfilm, reel 13.

33. "The Winona Incident," 370.

34. Interview with Fannie Lou Hamer by Wright; "Hearing Before a Select Panel on Mississippi and Civil Rights, Testimony of Fannie Lou Hamer."

35. Interview with June Johnson (TDC).

36. "Hearing Before a Select Panel on Mississippi and Civil Rights, Testimony of Fannie Lou Hamer"; interview with Fannie Lou Hamer by Wright.

37. "The Winona Incident," 370.

38. "Jury Frees Officers," *Student Voice,* Dec. 9, 1963, 1.

39. Interview with Fannie Lou Hamer by Wright.

40. "The Winona Incident," 371. When Hamer recounted this part of the story some three days later in an interview, she still seemed to be quite angry and unforgiving of the two black men for their part in her beating. In fact, she told her coworkers that this part of the beating hurt her feelings a great deal. However, later on in a 1968 interview, she expressed sorrow for these men: "See a lot of people would say . . . I wouldn't done that, but if they had of seen the shape the cat was in that beat me they would have done what he done because they had done near killed him anyway." See interview with Fannie Lou Hamer by Wright.

41. "The Winona Incident," 371; see also, "Hearing Before a Select Panel on Mississippi and Civil Rights, Testimony of Fannie Lou Hamer," and Fannie Lou Hamer, *To Praise Our Bridges: An Autobiography* (Jackson, Miss.: KIPCO), 14.

42. Hamer revealed this in a 1971 interview with Gil Noble. See "Mrs. Fannie Lou Hamer," Gil Noble, producer, WABC-TV (New York City, 1979; videotape reissued, 1992).

43. Howell Raines, *My Soul Is Rested: Movement Days in the Deep South Remembered* (New York: Putnam, 1977), 253; Branch, *Parting the Waters,* 819.

44. Interview with June Johnson (TDC).

45. Austin Scott, "Fannie Hamer, Civil Rights Leader, Dies," *Washington Post,* Mar. 17, 1977.

46. Hamer, *To Praise Our Bridges*, 14; Franklynn Peterson, "Sunflowers Don't Grow in Sunflower County," *Sepia* 19 (Feb. 1970): 12.

47. Prov. 26:26 reads: "Though his hatred covers itself with guile, His wickedness will be revealed before the Assembly." And Acts 7:26 reads: "Hath made of one blood all nations of men for to dwell on all the face of the earth, and hath determined the times before appointed, and the bounds of their habitation."

48. Susan Kling, *Fannie Lou Hamer: A Biography* (Chicago: Women for Racial and Economic Equality, 1979), 22–23; George Sewell, "Fannie Lou Hamer's Light Still Shines," *Encore American and Worldwide News,* July 18, 1977, 3.

49. Interview with June Johnson (TDC).

50. "Jury Frees Officers," *Student Voice,* Dec. 9, 1963, 2.

51. Howard Zinn, *SNCC: New Abolitionists* (Boston: Beacon, 1964), 95; interview with June Johnson (TDC).

52. "The Winona Incident," 374; Jerry Demuth, "'Tired of Being Sick and Tired,'" *The Nation,* June 1, 1964, 550; Hamer, *To Praise Our Bridges,* 14.

53. Interview with Fannie Lou Hamer by Wright.

54. "Hearing Before a Select Panel on Mississippi and Civil Rights, Testimony of Fannie Lou Hamer."

55. "The Winona Incident," 373.

56. Ibid.

57. Ibid., 367.

58. Kay Mills, *This Little Light of Mine: The Life of Fannie Lou Hamer* (New York: Dutton, 1993), 62.

59. Interview with June Johnson (TDC); "Jury Frees Officers," *Student Voice,* Dec. 9, 1963, 2.

60. Telegram to Attorney General Robert F. Kennedy, Justice Dept., from Julian Bond, Student Nonviolent Coordinating Committee, June 9 [1963], SNCC Papers, microfilm, reel 10; Clarence Clyde Ferguson Jr., General Counsel, United States Commission on Civil Rights, to Julian Bond, June 14, 1963, SNCC Papers, microfilm, reel 12. See also Horace Julian Bond, SNCC, to Asa J. Merrill, Director, Interstate Commerce Commission, June 12, 1963, SNCC Papers, microfilm, reel 12.

61. "The Winona Incident," 368–69; Branch, *Parting the Waters,* 826. Some accounts say that as many as five FBI investigators came to the Winona jail during the group's detention. In *Parting the Waters,* Branch notes that John Doar was the only representative from the Justice Department to ever reach Winona. It was a well-established fact that the FBI had a shortage of agents throughout the state of Mississippi, so perhaps some of the men who identified themselves as agents were actually impostors. In FBI activities in Mississippi, see also, Seth Cagin and Philip Dray, *We Are Not Afraid: The Story of Goodman, Schwerner, and Chaney and the Civil Rights Campaign for Mississippi* (New York: Macmillan, 1988), and Kenneth O'Reilly, *"Racial Matters": The FBI's Secret File on Black America, 1960–1972* (New York: Free Press, 1989).

62. "The Winona Incident," 373.

63. Telegram to Attorney General Robert F. Kennedy, Justice Dept., from Julian Bond, Student Nonviolent Coordinating Committee, June 9 [1963], SNCC Papers, microfilm, reel 10; Clarence Clyde Ferguson Jr., General Counsel, United States Commission on Civil Rights, to Julian Bond, June 14, 1963, SNCC Papers, microfilm, reel 12. Julian Bond got little help from the Interstate Commerce Commission. See Horace Julian Bond, SNCC, to Asa J. Merrill, Director, Interstate Commerce Commission, June 12, 1963, SNCC Papers, microfilm, reel 12.

64. Interview with June Johnson (TDC).

65. Danny Collum, "Stepping Out into Freedom," *Sojourners* 11, no. 11 (Dec. 1982): 13; interview with Fannie Lou Hamer by Wright; Phyl Garland, "Builders of a New South," *Ebony,* Aug. 1966, 34.

66. Interview with June Johnson (TDC).

67. Ibid.

68. Branch, *Parting the Waters,* 818; Kling, *Fannie Lou Hamer,* 23.

69. Egerton, *A Mind to Stay Here,* 101.

70. Interview with Laura Ratliff by author, Dec. 21, 1985, Ruleville, Miss.

71. "Jury Frees Officers," *Student Voice,* Dec. 9, 1963, 1. Hamer's FBI file includes records about the case, including photos of Hamer and Ponder and diagrams of the jail. See FBI file no. 44-22262, sections 1–3.

72. Branch, *Parting the Waters,* 826; Egerton, *A Mind to Stay Here,* 101.

73. J. H. O'Dell, "Life in Mississippi: An Interview with Fannie Lou Hamer," *Freedomways* 5, no. 2 (Spring 1965): 238.

74. "Negro Testifies Later Arrested," *Student Voice,* Dec. 16, 1963, 2. Less than a week later, one of the two men, twenty-three-year-old Roosevelt Knox, out free at the time, was rearrested on a trumped-up charge of passing a bad check. He allegedly committed this crime during the same period he was locked up in the Winona jail (ibid., 1).

75. Egerton, *A Mind to Stay Here,* 101.

76. Jacquelyn Dowd Hall, "'The Mind That Burns in Each Body': Women, Rape, and Racial Violence," in *Powers of Desire: The Politics of Sexuality,* ed. Ann Snitow, Christine Stansell, and Sharon Thompson (New York: Monthly Review Press, 1983), 329.

77. Interview with Sylvia Townsend by author, May 18, 1990, New York City.

78. On black women and the phenomenon of dissemblance, see Darlene Clark Hine, "Rape and the Inner Lives of Black Women in the Middle West: Preliminary Thoughts on the Culture of Dissemblance," *Signs* 14 (Summer 1989): 912–20.

79. Myrlie B. Evers, *For Us, the Living* (Garden City, N.Y.: Doubleday, 1967), 302.

80. Lisa Cron, "Fannie Lou Hamer, an American Freedom Fighter," information sheet (Organization for Equal Education of the Sexes, 1987), 2; Kling, *Fannie Lou Hamer,* 24; Garland, "Builders of a New South," 36.

81. George Sewell, "Fannie Lou Hamer," *Black Collegian* 8, no. 5 (May/June 1978): 20; Collum, "Stepping Out into Freedom," 10.

Chapter 4: Local Need and Electoral Politics

The chapter's first epigraph comes from Charles Cobb, "Deprivation and Dissatisfaction in the Mississippi Delta, Winter, 1964," Civil Rights Collection, box 3, Mississippi folder, Special Collections, UCLA. The second epigraph is from a remark quoted in Charles Evers, *Evers* (New York: World, 1971), 92.

1. Field Report, Jan. 5–10, 1964, Ruleville, Miss., 1, Student Nonviolent Coordinating Committee (SNCC) Papers (hereafter, SNCC Papers), Martin Luther King Jr. Library and Archives, Martin Luther King Jr. Center for Nonviolent Social Change, Atlanta, microfilm, reel 15. Also see Field Office Telephones and Address lists for 1965, SNCC Papers, microfilm, reel 12.

2. Karen Brodkin Sacks, *Caring by the Hour: Women, Work, and Organizing at Duke Medical Center* (Urbana: University of Illinois Press, 1988), 120–21. In her study of women hospital workers at Duke Medical Center, Sacks describes the women union organizers as "centers and sustainers of workplace networks" and "key actors in network formation and consciousness-shaping." Centerwomen are grass-roots activists whose leadership roles usually place them outside the limelight or center of national attention. Their efforts are key to successful completion of an operation or activity. They are pivotal players in disseminating information; in mobilizing community members who are unknown to each other but who are participating in similar protest activities areawide; in arranging the logistics of public protest or other group activities; in acting as political troubleshooters when events do not go as planned; and in serving as spiritual guides or advisers to other activists during inevitably trying times. In performing these functions, they receive little national visibility but assume lots of importance within their immediate sphere of influence. Hamer did this and more for the civil rights movement in various Delta counties, from her own Sunflower County to surrounding Bolivar, Leflore, Holmes, and Tallahatchie counties. On the question of black women's leadership styles and civil rights contributions, see also Belinda Robnett, *How Long? How Long? African-American Women in the Struggle for Civil Rights* (New York: Oxford University Press, 1997).

3. U.S. Department of Agriculture, *Statistical Bulletin, 1964* (Washington, D.C.: Government Printing Office, 1964). Nationally the median incomes of blacks and whites were $1,362 and $2,088, respectively. U.S. Department of Commerce, *Statistical Abstract of the United States, 1966* (Washington, D.C.: Government Printing Office, 1966), 338; U.S. Department of Commerce, Bureau of the Census, *Current Population Reports,* (Washington, D.C.: Government Printing Office, 1965), Series P-20, no. 145, and Series P-60, no. 47.

4. U.S. Bureau of the Census, *Statistical Abstract of the United States: 1967* (Washington, D.C.: Government Printing Office, 1967).

5. Ibid.

6. Action Memo from Jim [James A.] Dombrowski, Executive Director, Southern Conference Educational Fund, Inc., to Friends Everywhere, Jan. 23, 1964, SNCC Papers, microfilm, reel 9. The participation of the Southern Conference Educational Fund (SCEF) in economic assistance projects during the movement was entirely consistent with SCEF's mission. SCEF was set up in 1948 as a tax-exempt sister organization to the Southern Conference of Human Welfare, a southern white liberal organization founded in 1938. The SCHW championed racial equality and fairness by taking on inequality of pay and condition between black and white schools and teachers. SCHW also championed the cause of black and white tenant farmers. An interracial organization, SCHW was bent on uplifting the South economically by eradicating racial inequality, which it believed retarded the progress of the South as a whole. See Linda Reed, *Simple Decency and Common Sense: The Southern Conference Movement, 1938–1963* (Bloomington: Indiana University Press, 1991); Thomas Krueger, *And Promises to Keep: The Southern Conference for Human Welfare, 1938–1948* (Nashville: Vanderbilt University Press, 1967).

7. WATS Report, Mar. 13, 1964, Ruleville, Miss., SNCC Papers, microfilm, reel 15.

8. Ibid.

9. The freedom schools were among the key institutions established, along with community centers and voter registration projects, during the Freedom Summer campaign. They were formed to redress inequalities in Mississippi education and to empower students by encouraging them to ask and answer questions about their immediate surroundings.

10. Tracy Sugarman, *Stranger at the Gates: A Summer in Mississippi* (New York: Hill and Wang, 1966), 117.

11. Ibid.

12. Ibid., 119.

13. Some received food and clothing through theft.

14. Field Report from Rick Seifert, Jackson, Miss., to Joyce Barrett, Apr. 23, 1964, 1, SNCC Papers, microfilm, reel 15.

15. Ibid.

16. Joanne Grant, "Way of Life in Mississippi," *National Guardian* 16, no. 19 (Feb. 13, 1964): 12.

17. Field Report, Jan. 10, 1964, 1, SNCC Papers, microfilm, reel 15.

18. WATS Report, June 24, [1964], 7, SNCC Papers, microfilm, reel 15.

19. WATS Report, Mar. 20, 1964, SNCC Papers, microfilm, reel 15.

20. Nan Robertson, "Mississippian Relates Struggle of Negro in Voter Registration," *New York Times*, Aug. 24, 1964, 17.

21. Ibid.

22. "Hearing Before a Select Panel on Mississippi and Civil Rights, Testimony of Fannie Lou Hamer," *Congressional Record*, 88th Cong., 2d sess., June 4, 1964, to June 16, 1964, vol. 110, pt. 10, 14001–2.

23. Grant, "Way of Life in Mississippi."

24. Danny Collum, "Stepping Out into Freedom," *Sojourners* 11, no. 11 (Dec. 1982): 16.

25. WATS Line Report, Feb. 29, 1964, State of Mississippi, SNCC Papers, microfilm, reel 15.

26. Ibid.

27. The other candidates included Victoria Gray and John Earle Cameron of Hattiesburg, Mississippi, for the Fifth Congressional District seats; James M. Houston of Vicksburg, Mississippi, for the Third Congressional District; Amelia P. Boynton for the Fourth Congressional District in Alabama; and attorney C. B. King for the Second District, also in Alabama. See SNCC news release, "Six Negroes Qualify in Deep South States," [Apr. 1964], SNCC Papers, microfilm, reel 14; "Congressional Candidates Spur Deep South Registration Drives," *Student Voice,* Apr. 28, 1964, reprinted in *The Student Voice, 1960–1965: Periodical of the Student Nonviolent Coordinating Committee,* ed. Clayborne Carson (Westport, Conn.: Meckler Corporation, 1990), 140–41. Interestingly, Hamer was the only one to come from the ranks of farm laborers. All of the other individuals had roots firmly planted in the southern black middle class.

28. Susan Kling, *Fannie Lou Hamer: A Biography* (Chicago: Women for Racial and Economic Equality, 1979), 26.

29. *Student Voice,* Apr. 28, 1964, in Carson, *The Student Voice,* 2; Fannie Lou Hamer and Victoria Gray campaign flyer, SNCC Papers, microfilm, reel 10.

30. SNCC news release, "Mississippi Negro Candidate Has Strong Rights Platform," Apr. 1, 1964, SNCC Papers, microfilm, reel 14.

31. Sue Cronk, "They've Already Lost Election," *Washington Post,* Apr. 7, 1964.

32. Ibid.; *Student Voice,* Apr. 28, 1964, in Carson, *The Student Voice,* 140; affidavits (1–8), Columbus, Mississippi, beatings, SNCC Papers, microfilm, reel 14. COFO's expectation of trouble was soundly based on the widespread incidents of violence and intimidation that marred the 1963 Freedom Vote campaign, a mock election than ran a biracial gubernatorial ticket to demonstrate that black Mississippians would vote if given a chance. Many white politicians, including the infamous James O. Eastland, had defended their own continual reelection and black disfranchisement by arguing that blacks were not interested in voting.

33. In his letter, Bond asks Whitten "to speak out on the floor of the House against such arrests of political workers and to ask you to request and [*sic*] investigation of their street by the United States Department of Justice." Julian Bond to Representative Jamie Whitten, Mar. 21, 1964, SNCC Papers, microfilm, reel 13. While it may appear ironic, it was only appropriate that Bond asked Whitten to ensure a fair election by addressing the hostile political climate in his district. In her campaign speeches Hamer also made similar appeals to Whitten. See, for example, SNCC news release, "Mississippi Negro Candidate Has Strong Rights Platform."

34. Horace Julian Bond to Representative Jamie Whitten, Mar. 21, 1964, SNCC Papers, microfilm, reel 13.

35. John Lewis to Jamie L. Whitten, Mar. 31, 1964, SNCC Papers, microfilm, reel 1.

36. Ibid.

37. "Miss. Negro Vote Curtailed in Congressional Primary," *Student Voice,* June 9, 1964, 1, SNCC Papers, microfilm, reel 10. A *Washington Post* report on the election notes that there were 422,256 eligible black voters and 28,000 of them were registered. *Washington Post,* Mar. 17, 1977.

38. "Miss. Negro Vote Curtailed in Congressional Primary," 1.

39. Ibid., 3.

40. Meeting minutes, June 9, 1964, 6, SNCC Papers, microfilm, reel 3.

41. Ibid. Amelia Boynton was a prominent middle-class black woman who was also running for office in the state of Alabama.

42. Ibid., 7.

43. The close relationship between Hamer and McLaurin is remembered by many who knew her. Johnnie Walls to Chana Lee, June 20, 1985; interview with Charles Tisdale by author, Dec. 21, 1985, Jackson, Miss.

44. Meeting minutes, Wednesday, June 10, 1964, 12, SNCC Papers, microfilm, reel 3.

45. Interview with Bobbi Betts by author, June 3, 1986, Los Angeles, Calif.

46. "Incidents Reported to the Jackson Office during a 24-Hour Period," SNCC Papers, microfilm, reel 15; [field report], June 25, [1964].

47. "Incidents Reported to the Jackson Office during a 24-Hour Period," SNCC Papers, microfilm, reel 15; WATS Report, June 25, 1964, SNCC Papers, microfilm, reel 15; [field report], June 25 [1964].

48. "Incidents Reported to the Jackson Office during a 24-Hour Period," SNCC Papers, microfilm, reel 14; WATS Report, Saturday, July 25, 1964, SNCC Papers, microfilm, reel 15.

49. Doug McAdam, *Freedom Summer* (New York: Oxford University Press, 1988), 7.

50. "Freedom Summer Planned in Miss.," *Student Voice,* Special Issue, Spring 1964, quoted in Carson, *The Student Voice, 1960–1965,* 133.

51. Sugarman, *Stranger at the Gates,* 113.

52. Ibid.

53. Ibid.

54. Ibid., 114.

55. Ibid.

56. Ibid.

57. See, for example, [SNCC] New York Steering Committee Meeting Minutes, Jan. 23, 1964, SNCC Papers, microfilm, reel 6; Field Report [Summer 1964], 5, SNCC Papers, microfilm, reel 15; WATS Report, July 20, 1964, SNCC Papers, microfilm, reel 15.

58. *Student Voice,* July 29, 1964, reprinted in Carson, *The Student Voice, 1960–1965,* 178.

59. "Legal Barriers to Greet Workers," *Student Voice,* June 9, 1964, 2; SNCC news release, "Mississippi Legislates to Outlaw Summer Civil Rights Project," n.d., SNCC Papers, microfilm, reel 13.

60. Louis Allen was the key witness to the 1961 murder of Herbert Lee, a voter registration worker brutally slain by a Mississippi state representative, E. H. Hurst. Hurst

claimed to a grand jury that he killed Lee in self-defense because Lee was threatening him with a tire iron. Initially, fearing for his life, Allen corroborated Hurst's version of the incident. However, just after the jury freed Hurst, Allen signed a statement charging that Hurst murdered Lee "without provocation." Allen was subsequently warned to leave his home town of Liberty, Mississippi. After the threats and an encounter with a deputy sheriff that resulted in his jaw being broken, Allen asked for federal protection, but to no avail. Allen finally decided to leave Mississippi for Milwaukee, but twelve hours before his scheduled departure, he was shot down in his front yard (reportedly, his head was blown off), while his terrified wife and children witnessed the incident from inside the Allen house. For a full account of the Lee and Allen murders see Clayborne Carson, *In Struggle: SNCC and the Black Awakening of the 1960s* (Cambridge, Mass.: Harvard University Press, 1981), 48–49.

61. News release, June 1, 1964, Council of Federated Organizations, SNCC Papers, microfilm, reel 14; *Student Voice*, June 9, 1964, 1, SNCC Papers, microfilm, reel 10; "Hearing Before a Select Panel on Mississippi and Civil Rights, Testimony of Fannie Lou Hamer."

62. *Student Voice*, June 9, 1964, 1, SNCC Papers, microfilm, reel 10; "Summary of Major Points in Testimony by Citizens of Mississippi," SNCC Papers, microfilm, reel 1.

63. Regarding SNCC's operating premise during its early years, Julian Bond observed that SNCC staff members planned around "the theory that here was a problem, you expose it to the world, the world says 'How horrible!' and moves to correct it." Carson, *In Struggle*, 54.

64. "Hearing Before a Select Panel on Mississippi and Civil Rights, Testimony of Fannie Lou Hamer," June 8, 1964, Washington, D.C., audiotape, MFDP Collection, King Library and Archives, Martin Luther King Jr. Center for Nonviolent Social Change, Atlanta, Ga.

65. Ibid.

66. Ibid.

67. Ibid.

68. "Genocide in Mississippi," SNCC Papers, microfilm, reel 19.

69. Harold Taylor, chairman of the panel of citizens, to Lyndon B. Johnson, June 11, 1964, SNCC Papers, microfilm, reel 19.

70. Ibid.

71. Ibid.

72. [WATS Report], June 20, 1964, SNCC Papers, microfilm, reel 15.

73. *Mrs. Victoria Jackson Gray, et al. v. The State of Mississippi*, 1964.

74. Ibid., 5.

75. Ibid., 6–7.

76. Ibid., 7–8.

77. Ibid., 10–11.

78. Ibid., 11.

79. Ibid., 11–12.

80. Ibid., 14.

81. WATS Report, July 10, 1964, SNCC Papers, microfilm, reel 15.

82. WATS Report, Aug. 3, 1964, SNCC Papers, microfilm, reel 15.

83. "Judge Dismisses Protection Suit," *Student Voice,* Aug. 12, 1964, quoted in Carson, *The Student Voice, 1960–1965,* 183–84.

84. WATS Report, Aug. 3, 1964, SNCC Papers, microfilm, reel 15.

Chapter 5: The National Stage

The chapter's first epigraph is a remark quoted during an interview with Joseph Rauh conducted by Anne Romaine, Nov. 1966, Washington, D.C., transcript, Anne Romaine Papers, Martin Luther King Jr. Library and Archives, Martin Luther King Jr. Center for Nonviolent Social Change, Atlanta, Ga. The second epigraph is from Fannie Lou Hamer, *To Praise Our Bridges: An Autobiography* (Jackson, Miss.: KIPCO, 1967), 16–17.

1. Interview with Fannie Lou Hamer by Robert Wright, Aug. 9, 1968, Oral History Collection, Civil Rights Documentation Project (CRDP), Moorland-Spingarn Research Center, Howard University; Leslie McLemore, "The Mississippi Freedom Democratic Party: A Case Study of Grassroots Politics" (Ph.D diss., University of Massachusetts, Amherst, 1971), 107–8.

2. "Ella Baker, Organizing for Civil Rights," in *Moving the Mountain: Women Working for Social Change,* ed. Ellen Cantarow with Susan Gushee O'Malley and Sharon Hartman Strom (Old Westbury, N.Y.: Feminist Press, 1980), 88–90; Susan Kling, *Fannie Lou Hamer: A Biography* (Chicago: Women for Racial and Economic Equality, 1979), 25–26.

3. Interview with Joseph Rauh.

4. Taylor Branch, *Pillar of Fire: America in the King Years, 1963–65* (New York: Simon and Schuster, 1998), 457.

5. Interview with Walter Tillow by Anne Romaine, Sept. 1966, Knoxville, Tenn., Anne Romaine Papers (hereafter ARP), King Library and Archives, Martin Luther King Jr. Center for Nonviolent Social Change, Atlanta, Ga. On the print media coverage see especially issues of these newspapers for the week Aug. 23–27, 1964.

6. Robert Dallek, *Flawed Giant: Lyndon Johnson and His Times, 1961–1973* (New York: Oxford University Press, 1998), 162–64.

7. John Dittmer, *Local People: The Struggle for Civil Rights in Mississippi* (Urbana: University of Illinois Press, 1994), 292; Dallek, *Flawed Giant,* 162.

8. On Hamer's doubts about winning, see interview with Fannie Lou Hamer by Wright. Two years prior to her interview with Wright, Hamer admitted to being quite hopeful: "And I thought with all of my heart that the people would have been unseated in Atlantic City. I believed that, because if the Constitution of this United States means something to all of us, then I know they would unseat them." Interview with Fannie Lou Hamer by Anne Romaine, Nov. 1966, Ruleville, Miss., ARP. Bob Moses, Dave

Dennis, and Ella Baker were also among those with little optimism at the beginning of the convention. Dittmer, *Local People,* 286–87.

9. On the worksheets, see Mississippi Freedom Democratic Party Records, 1962–71, mss 586, microfilm 788, reel 1, Social Action Collection, State Historical Society of Wisconsin, Madison.

10. Interview with Mendy Samstein by Anne Romaine, Nov. 1966, Knoxville, Tenn., ARP.

11. Ibid.

12. Ibid.

13. Clayborne Carson, *In Struggle: SNCC and the Black Awakening of the 1960s* (Cambridge, Mass.: Harvard University Press, 1981), 123.

14. "Brief Submitted by the Mississippi Freedom Democratic Party," Joseph Rauh Papers, MFDP Folder, Library of Congress, Washington, D.C.

15. Dittmer, *Local People,* 287–88; "Democrats Too Placid, as of Now, for Palmistry," *New York Times,* Aug. 24, 1964.

16. Interview with Samstein; interview with Tillow.

17. The MFDP challenge was not the first of its kind. Dating back to 1836, there had been several major credentials contests. "Content of Previous Challenges," Mississippi Freedom Democratic Party Papers, box 20, folder 8, King Library and Archives, the Martin Luther King Jr. Center for Nonviolent Social Change, Atlanta, Ga.

18. Arthur I. Waskow, "Notes on the Democratic National Convention, Atlantic City, August, 1964," 6, ARP; "Mississippi Factions Clash Before Convention Panel," *New York Times,* Aug. 23, 1964.

19. Interview with Tillow.

20. "Mississippi Factions Clash Before Convention Panel"; Kay Mills, *This Little Light of Mine: The Life of Fannie Lou Hamer* (New York: Dutton, 1993), 118–21.

21. Branch, *Pillar of Fire,* 461.

22. Waskow, "Notes on the Democratic National Convention," 193.

23. Interview with Joseph Rauh by Anne Romaine, Joseph Rauh Papers (hereafter, JRP), Library of Congress, Washington, D.C.

24. Waskow, "Notes on the Democratic National Convention," 9.

25. Ibid., 10. Hamer first raised the sterilization issue during the Jackson hearing that spring in Mississippi.

26. Interview with Samstein (ARP).

27. Ibid.; interview with Rauh (ARP).

28. Waskow, "Notes on the Democratic National Convention," 13–14.

29. Ibid., 13.

30. Interview with Samstein (ARP).

31. Interview with Tillow (ARP); Mississippi Freedom Democratic Party Press Release, Aug. 24, 1964, MFDP Papers, folder 1, Zenobia Coleman Library, Tougaloo College, Tougaloo, Miss. According to Samstein's interview, the number throughout the convention actually hovered around 15 out of 110 credential committee members.

32. Waskow, "Notes on the Democratic National Convention, Atlantic City, August, 1964," 13.

33. Ibid.

34. Congress of Racial Equality Press Release, "Round-the-Clock Vigil Supports Freedom Delegation," Aug. 27, 1964, Student Nonviolent Coordinating Committee (SNCC) Papers (hereafter, SNCC Papers), Martin Luther King Jr. Library and Archives, Martin Luther King Jr. Center for Nonviolent Social Change, Atlanta, microfilm, reel 21.

35. "Mississippi Factions Clash Before Convention Panel."

36. Waskow, "Notes on the Democratic National Convention"; interview with Rauh (JRP); interview with Samstein (ARP).

37. Interview with Rauh (JRP).

38. Interview with Fannie Lou Hamer by Wright; interview with Edwin King by Anne Romaine, Aug. 1966, Knoxville, Tenn. (ARP).

39. Interview with Rauh (JRP).

40. Waskow, "Notes on the Democratic National Convention," 18.

41. Ibid.

42. Ibid.; interview with Tillow (ARP).

43. Waskow, "Notes on the Democratic National Convention," 22.

44. Ibid.

45. Interview with Fannie Lou Hamer by Anne Romaine.

46. Interview with Rauh (JRP); interview with Samstein (ARP).

47. Ibid.

48. Events during the convention often took place in such a rapid, spontaneous, and decentralized fashion that it is not inconceivable that Moses was unaware that Hamer had been deliberately excluded by those who called the meeting.

49. Interview with Tillow (ARP).

50. Interview with King (ARP).

51. Interview with Tillow (ARP).

52. Interview with Samstein (ARP).

53. Waskow, "Notes on the Democratic National Convention," 25.

54. Ibid.

55. Interview with Tillow (ARP).

56. Interview with Samstein (ARP).

57. Waskow, "Notes on the Democratic National Convention," 28.

58. Ibid., 29.

59. Ibid., 32; interview with Ella Baker by Anne Romaine, Mar. 25, 1967, New York City (ARP).

60. Waskow, "Notes on the Democratic National Convention," 30.

61. Rita Schwerner continued working in the movement after her husband's death, thus the reason for her presence at the convention as a MFDP supporter. She and Hamer were friends and there was much respect and admiration between the two. During the convention "sneak-in," Hamer pointed out that if there was anybody de-

serving a seat in the convention hall it was Rita Schwerner because, as Hamer put it later, "She [had] lost as much as anybody in Mississippi." Interview with Fannie Lou Hamer by Anne Romaine, Mar. 25, 1967, New York City (ARP).

62. Waskow, "Notes on the Democratic National Convention," 31.

63. Interview with Fannie Lou Hamer by Wright.

64. Interview with Baker (ARP).

65. Waskow, "Notes on the Democratic National Convention," 32.

66. Interview with Ivanhoe Donaldson by Anne Romaine, Mar. 1967, Washington, D.C. (ARP).

67. Waskow, "Notes on the Democratic National Convention," 33.

68. Interview with Baker (ARP).

69. Interview with Hamer by Romaine (ARP); interview with Fannie Lou Hamer by Wright.

70. McLemore, "The Mississippi Freedom Democratic Party," 163, 165.

71. Interview with Fannie Lou Hamer by Romaine (ARP).

72. Interview with Fannie Lou Hamer by Wright.

73. "Hypocrisy on Rights Denounced," *Atlanta Constitution,* Apr. 20, 1968.

74. Phyl Garland, "Builder of a New South," *Ebony,* Aug. 1966, 35–36.

75. Hamer, *To Praise Our Bridges,* 16–17.

76. See for example, David Garrow, *Protest at Selma: Martin Luther King, Jr., and the Voting Rights Act of 1965* (New Haven: Yale University Press, 1978), passim.

Chapter 6: Returning Home

The chapter's epigraph is from Fannie Lou Hamer, "Fannie Lou Hamer Speaks Out," *Essence* 1, no. 6 (Oct 1971): 57.

1. James Forman, *The Making of Black Revolutionaries: A Personal Account* (New York: Macmillan, 1972), 408; meeting minutes, Sept. 4, 1964, 9, Student Nonviolent Coordinating Committee (SNCC) Papers (hereafter, SNCC Papers), Martin Luther King Jr. Library and Archives, Martin Luther King Jr. Center for Nonviolent Social Change, Atlanta, microfilm, reel 3.

2. Forman, *The Making of Black Revolutionaries,* 408; John Lewis with Michael D'Orso, *Walking with the Wind: A Memoir of the Movement* (New York: Simon and Schuster, 1998), 284; Clayborne Carson, *In Struggle: SNCC and the Black Awakening of the 1960s* (Cambridge, Mass.: Harvard University Press, 1981), 134.

3. Forman, *The Making of Black Revolutionaries,* 408.

4. Ibid.

5. Ibid.

6. Ibid., 410.

7. Ibid., 409.

8. Ibid., 409–10.

9. Fannie Lou Hamer, *To Praise Our Bridges: An Autobiography* (Jackson, Miss.: KIPCO, 1969), 21–22

10. Ibid., 21; Carson, *In Struggle,* 134.

11. Hamer, *To Praise Our Bridges,* 23.

12. Ibid., 24.

13. Ibid., 23.

14. J. H. O'Dell, "Life in Mississippi: An Interview with Fannie Lou Hamer," *Freedomways* 5, no. 2 (Spring 1965): 235.

15. Hamer, *To Praise Our Bridges,* 24; "An Autobiography of Mrs. Fannie Lou Hamer," *Close-up* 4, no. 1 (Jan. 1969): 9.

16. Hamer, *To Praise Our Bridges,* 23.

17. Leslie McLemore, "The Mississippi Freedom Democratic Party: A Case Study of Grassroots Politics" (Ph.D. diss., University of Massachusetts, Amherst, 1971), 174–75, 176; Steven F. Lawson, *Black Ballots: Voting Rights in the South, 1944–1969* (New York: Columbia University Press, 1976), 325. Interestingly, in a SNCC meeting during fall 1964, this same question of legality was raised about the participation of Hamer and Devine in the challenge. One meeting attendee named Sandy pointed out that Hamer's second run for the same post she lost was illegal according to Mississippi law. Someone in attendance named Doug then noted how Hamer and Gray could run as independents after running as Democrats. It was also noted in this same meeting that "anyone who falsly [*sic*] signs as a qualified elector is [subject] to a perjury change." SNCC meeting minutes, n.d. [ca. Fall 1964], 4, SNCC Papers, microfilm, reel 3. Although this possibility did not deter the MFDP challengers, it did become the basis of opposition to the challenge by congressmen sympathetic to the "regular" Mississippi Democratic Party.

18. McLemore, "The Mississippi Freedom Democratic Party," 176; "Freedom Vote Is Open to All," *Student Voice,* Oct. 28, 1964, SNCC Papers, microfilm, reel 19; Lawson, *Black Ballots,* 322.

19. McLemore, "The Mississippi Freedom Democratic Party," 176.

20. Betty Garman to Richard M. Dudley, Oct. 27, 1964, SNCC Papers, microfilm, reel 28.

21. McLemore, "The Mississippi Freedom Democratic Party," 177.

22. Betty Garman to Richard M. Dudley, Oct. 27, 1964, SNCC Papers, microfilm, reel 28.

23. "MFDP Gives Live Lesson in Democracy," *Bay Area Student Nonviolent Coordinating Committee* (newsletter), Nov. 1964, SNCC Papers, microfilm, reel 28. In the event of a defeat or dismissal of their challenge, the MFDP planned to request that the National Democratic caucus take seniority away from the incumbents on the grounds of voting discrimination and state and national party disloyalty.

24. McLemore, "The Mississippi Freedom Democratic Party," 178.

25. Ibid., 180–81.

26. Ibid.

27. Fannie Lou Hamer to Friend(s) of SNCC, n.d. [ca. Dec. 1964–Jan. 1965], SNCC Papers, microfilm, reel 24.

28. Telephone interview with Annie Devine by author, Nov. 1991, Jackson, Miss.

29. McLemore, "The Mississippi Freedom Democratic Party," 189.

30. Press release, Jan. 5, 1965, Mississippi Freedom Democratic Party, SNCC Papers, microfilm, reel 28; McLemore, "The Mississippi Freedom Democratic Party," 189.

31. The MFDP made this state challenge on the basis of an 1851 federal law. *Sacramento Friends of SNCC* (newsletter), Jan. 22, 1965, SNCC Papers, microfilm, reel 28.

32. Betty Garman to Sandy Seigel, Dec. 5, 1964, SNCC Papers, microfilm, reel 28.

33. Betty Garman to Sandy Seigel, Davis Friends of SNCC, Jan. 13, 1965, SNCC Papers, microfilm, reel 28. In one of her letters Garman indicated how busy Hamer actually was due to her work on behalf of MFDP and even SNCC: "She definitely speaks in Chicago on Feb. 14th at some big fund event for SNCC and presumably is pretty busy before that doing MFDP challenge work. So suggest you make it after the Feb. 14th date if you can. . . . Then, at the same time, send me a copy of the letter to her and I'll try to reach her by phone to see if she says ok." Betty Garman to Sandy Seigel, Dec. 5, 1964, SNCC Papers, microfilm, reel 28.

34. Betty Garman to Viola M. Brooks, Feb. 21, 1965, SNCC Papers, microfilm, reel 28.

35. Fred Hirsch to Betty [Garman], Apr. 3, 1965, SNCC Papers, microfilm, reel 28.

36. Statement of Funds Received and Disbursed, Marin Friends of SNCC, May 15, 1965, SNCC Papers, microfilm, reel 24.

37. McLemore, "The Mississippi Freedom Democratic Party," 196.

38. Esther Heifetz to Jan Phillips, Aug. 14, 1965, SNCC Papers, microfilm, reel 29.

39. Karen Morgan to Esther Hefeitz [*sic*], Aug. 20, 1965, SNCC Papers, microfilm, reel 24.

40. McLemore, "The Mississippi Freedom Democratic Party," 227.

41. Ibid.

42. Ibid., 228.

43. Here, it is not clear whether she was referring to sexual discrimination within the movement, or sexual promiscuity—particularly interracial sex—among movement activists. Both of these subjects remained concerns of key local activists after the issues surfaced in summer 1964.

44. COFO Convention Minutes, Mar. 7, 1965, Charles Horwitz Collection, box 2, folder 32, Tougaloo Civil Rights Collection, Tougaloo College, Tougaloo, Miss.

45. Ibid.

46. Ibid.

47. Ibid.

48. Ibid.

49. Ibid.

50. Ibid.

51. Ibid.

52. *Newsweek*, Apr. 12, 1965. The primary focus of this article was the matter of al-

leged "communist infiltration" in SNCC. Hamer was not alone in receiving the negative attention this source gave to activists considered to be left of center. (This holds true for this particular issue of *Newsweek* and for others preceding and succeeding it.) In fact, on the subject of outside agitation in the civil rights movement, the MFDP was deemed guilty because of its mere association with SNCC. In this same article, *Newsweek* referred to the party as "SNCC's political offspring," which was not entirely untrue. The charge of communist ties was a popular one leveled at SNCC, in spite of SNCC leadership's many attempts (including its own brand of red-baiting) to give another impression prior to 1965.

53. Andrew Kopkind, "New Radicals in Dixie: Those 'Subversive' Civil Rights Workers," *New Republic*, Apr. 10, 1965, 13–16. It is not clear from Kopkind's article whom he considered to be these more "respected" leaders. My guess is that he was referring to those individuals from moderate mainstream organizations like the NAACP and perhaps even the Southern Christian Leadership Conference (SCLC). Nonetheless, on the matter of respect, he clearly miscalculated the nature and extent of respect Hamer commanded, locally and nationally. Depending on one's frame of reference, she too was one of those "respected" leaders.

54. This is hardly an original observation on my part. Consider the following excerpt from a SNCC staff meeting as recorded in a John Lewis memo: "The MFDP-SNCC problem was not unique, some said: it related to the basic nature of SNCC as a band of organizers. It would come up again in other states (such as Alabama) when other political parties initiated by SNCC developed. The problem was compared to that of a child becoming independent of its parents. A weaning process. At what point should SNCC withdraw? And if SNCC organized something which developed in a way that SNCC didn't like, what should SNCC do?" SNCC Memo, John Lewis to Executive Committee of the MFDP, n.d. [ca. 1965–66], SNCC Papers, microfilm, reel 12.

55. Executive Committee Meeting transcript, Holly Springs, Miss., Apr. 12–14, 1965, SNCC Papers, microfilm, reel 3.

56. *ERAP Newsletter*, Mar. 11, 1965, 4, SNCC Papers, microfilm,, reel 21.

57. Ibid.

Chapter 7: The Mississippi Freedom Labor Union

The chapter's epigraph is from Nola May Coleman, "New Hope in the Delta—The Mississippi Freedom Labor Union," draft of typescript circular, c. Apr. 1965, Special Collection on Civil Rights Struggle and Black Power Movement in the United States, 1950s to the Present, UCLA, box 3, folder 9.

1. "Shaw, Mississippi: New Sounds in the Delta," n.d., Student Nonviolent Coordinating Committee (SNCC) Papers (hereafter, SNCC Papers), Martin Luther King Jr. Library and Archives, Martin Luther King Jr. Center for Nonviolent Social Change, Atlanta, microfilm, reel 20.

2. Mary Hawkins to Sir, n.d. [ca. May 1965], SNCC Papers, microfilm, reel 24; "Cotton Workers Form Labor Union," SNCC news release, n.d. [ca. Apr. 9–16, 1965], SNCC Papers, microfilm, reel 14. In its solicitation letters to its supporters after June 1965, SNCC and its chairman, John Lewis, relied heavily on their connection to the MFLU and the MFDP. This reflected the close association between corollary movements during the period. In fact, the SNCC leadership was proud of the MFLU and its relative successes; John Lewis wrote about the union as "evidence of SNCC's continuing work and activity." This was a bit of an overstatement. The MFLU was more autonomous and independent than Lewis's claim implied. The larger point here is that SNCC, in soliciting funds throughout the spring, summer, and fall of 1965, found it advantageous to claim the relatively successful MFLU as one of its many "local projects." In actuality, MFLU was more independent in creation and activities than its political counterpart, the Mississippi Freedom Democratic Party, which, it could be argued fairly persuasively, was more of a SNCC offshoot organization. Lewis's less-than-accurate claim reflected the general anxiety SNCC felt over the erosion of its influence in the Delta after 1964. On the Lewis claim, see John Lewis to Friends [of SNCC], July 1965, SNCC Papers, microfilm, reel 24. However, in fairness, it most be noted that MFLU also made the best of its connection to SNCC, even though there never existed a formal association between organizations. For example, MFLU used the SNCC organ, *Student Voice*, to make written appeals to unorganized plantation workers and other exploited laborers. See, for example, "Union Members Talk Strike," *Student Voice*, June 6, 1965, as reprinted in "Sampling of Articles from Community Organizations' Newsletter," n.d., SNCC Papers, microfilm, reel 24.

3. "Negroes Win ASCS Post, But Irregularities Charged," *Student Voice*, Dec. 20, 1965, in *The Student Voice, 1960–1965: Periodical of the Student Nonviolent Coordinating Committee,* ed. Clayborne Carson (Westport, Conn.: Meckler Corporation, 1990), 231, 233.

4. "Cotton Workers Form Labor Union."

5. This observation draws on contemporary black feminist theory on multiple oppressions and identities. For a fuller and precisely elaborated discussion of the topic, see the following: Patricia Hill Collins, *Black Feminist Thought: Knowledge, Consciousness, and the Politics of Empowerment* (Boston: Unwin Hyman, 1990); Evelyn Brooks Higginbotham, "Afro-American Women's History and the Metalanguage of Race," *Signs* 17 (Winter 1992): 251–74; Deborah King, "Multiple Jeopardy, Multiple Consciousness: The Context of a Black Feminist Ideology," *Signs* 13 (Autumn 1988): 42–72.

6. "Union Members Talk Strike."

7. Ibid.

8. SNCC WATS Reports, June 4, 1965, Leadership Conference on Civil Rights Collection, series F, box 5, Mississippi Folder, 1963–64, Library of Congress, Washington, D.C.

9. From 1960 to 1965 the SNCC newspaper was titled *The Student Voice*. In December 1965 the newspaper appeared as *The Voice* and subsequently ceased publication. Clayborne Carson, "Introduction," in *The Student Voice, 1960–1965,* vii.

10. "Union Members Talk Strike."

11. Mary Hawkins to Sir, n.d.; "Cotton Workers Form Labor Union."

12. "Shaw, Mississippi: New Sounds in the Delta."

13. Ibid.

14. Gavin Wright, "Economic Consequences of the Southern Protest Movement," in *New Directions in Civil Rights Studies*, ed. Armstead L. Robinson and Patricia Sullivan (Charlottesville: University Press of Virginia, 1991), 176; Bruce J. Schulman, *From Cotton Belt to Sunbelt: Federal Policy, Economic Development, and the Transformation of the South, 1938–1980* (New York: Oxford University Press, 1991), 20, 29–30, 102–3; James C. Cobb, "'Somebody Done Nailed Us on the Cross': Federal Farm and Welfare Policy and the Civil Rights Movement in the Mississippi Delta," *Journal of American History* 77, no. 3 (Dec. 1990), 912–13, 916–18, 920; Roger D. Tate Jr., "Easing the Burden: The Era of Depression and New Deal in Mississippi" (Ph.D. diss., University of Tennessee, Knoxville, 1978), 28–29, 108–9, 176, 188–89.

15. Carol Stevens, "Hope in Sunflower," *Southern Patriot*, Mar. 1966, Fannie Lou Hamer Papers (hereafter FLH Papers), box 7, folder 18, Amistad Research Center, Tulane University, New Orleans; "Negro Walkouts in Delta Spurred," *New York Times*, June 7, 1965.

16. "Shaw, Mississippi: New Sounds in the Delta." See also, Cobb, "'Somebody Done Nailed Us on the Cross,'" 915.

17. "Shaw, Mississippi: New Sounds in the Delta."

18. The citywide workshops were held to prepare an agenda (specific to the needs and concerns of a particular town) for discussion at the statewide meeting. Also at the city or town workshops, committees were elected and rules created. The statewide workshop was a big event attended by activists from a number of nearby towns, including Glenallen, Winstonville, Louise, Greenville, Batesville, Vicksburg, Thorn, and Marks, Mississippi. "Union Members Talk Strike."

19. Ibid.

20. Ibid.

21. "Cotton Workers Form Labor Union."

22. "Shaw, Mississippi: New Sounds in the Delta." Without any collateral or security, day laborers most often did not qualify for FHA loans, and the interest rates for loans offered by private finance companies were astronomical—as much as 33⅓ percent, according to a union organizer. The plight of the black day laborer was best summed up by the observation of one MFLU organizer: "I've taken people to Greenville to get loans and must [have] come back just as they left—with nothing. But if you borrow it, you get to pay it back and with what? If you got a dark skin you're in trouble." "Shaw, Mississippi: New Sounds in the Delta."

23. Federal minimum wage laws did not apply to farm labor.

24. There were other demands as well. "Cotton Workers Form Labor Union"; "Shaw, Mississippi: New Sounds in the Delta."

25. The context of MFLU's creation was a very rich one in terms of the rise of self-sufficiency projects. In part this was due to the spread of black nationalism and its call to provide and empower oneself (community). On the proliferation of unions and co-ops on the heels of civil rights activities in the Delta, see "Mississippi Freedom Labor Union," report from George Shelton, State Chairman, n.d. [ca. Sept. 1965]; Minutes of Statewide Meeting, MFLU, Sept. 4, 1965, box 3, folder 9, Special Collection on Civil Rights Struggle and Black Movement in the United States, 1950s to the Present, UCLA; Vickie Lynn Crawford, "Beyond the Human Self: Grassroots Activists in the Mississippi Civil Rights Movement," in *Trailblazers and Torchbearers: Black Women in the Civil Rights Movement*, ed. Vicki Lynn Crawford, Jacqueline Rouse, and Barbara Woods (New York: Carlson Publishing, 1990), 14–16.

26. "Cotton Workers Form Labor Union"; "Union Members Talk Strike."

27. "Union Members Talk Strike."

28. Minutes of Statewide Meeting, MFLU, Sept. 4, 1965.

29. Memo to Friends of SNCC, Oct. 28, 1965, SNCC Papers, microfilm, reel 24. The MFLU sponsored and participated in a number of protests and activities that defined it as both a labor union and a pseudo–social welfare organization. As the latter, it organized and contributed to a number of food and clothing drives, a continuation of work initiated by SNCC and Hamer during the early stages of the civil rights movement. See also, Margaret Lauren to [SNCC] Northern Offices, n.d., box 3, folder 9, Special Collections, UCLA.

30. See, for example, "Running Summary of the Events Concerning the Strike of the Mississippi Freedom Labor Union," SNCC Papers, microfilm, reels 14 and 24; "Shaw, Mississippi: New Sounds in the Delta"; John Lewis to Friends [of SNCC], July 1965, SNCC Papers, microfilm, reel 24.

31. SNCC Research Paper, "Why Are Farm Laborers Poor?" June 7, 1965, SNCC Papers, microfilm, reel 24.

32. Ibid.

33. Ibid.

34. Mary Hawkins to Sir, n.d. [ca. May 1965], SNCC Papers, microfilm, reel 24; "Running Summary of Events."

35. "Union Members Talk Strike."

36. Memo on Bail, June 14, 1965, SNCC papers, microfilm, reel 24. The memorandum issued the following directive: "P.S. With the recent growth of the Mississippi Freedom Labor Union, expansion of summer projects in Mississippi, Alabama, Arkansas, and Georgia, and anticipated action by the Mississippi Freedom Democratic Party (such as demonstrations in Jackson today, which resulted in 500 arrests), we can predict a great need for bail money this summer. Please get to work now!"

37. "15 Strikers Walk off Senator James O. Eastland's Plantation," SNCC news release, June 5, 1965, box 3, folder 9, Special Collections, UCLA.

38. "Negro Walkouts in Delta Spurred."

39. Ibid.

40. John Lewis to Friends [of SNCC], July 1965, SNCC Papers, microfilm, reel 24.

41. "Negro Walkouts in Delta Spurred."

42. "Running Summary of Events."

43. Ibid.

44. "Negro Walkouts in Delta Spurred."

45. Ibid.

46. The periodization for the black power phase of the civil rights era varies. Some scholars date the beginning of this phase to 1966, with the public introduction of the slogan "Black Power" by Stokely Carmichael and Willie Ricks in Mississippi. However, as Clayborne Carson has pointed out in his SNCC history, there were discussions about whites and black self-determination as early as November 1964. See Carson, *In Struggle: SNCC and the Black Awakening of the 1960s* (Cambridge, Mass.: Harvard University Press, 1981), 144–52.

47. Haig A. Bosmajian and Hamida Bosmajian, *The Rhetoric of the Civil Rights Movement* (New York: Random House, 1969), 6–7; Leonard Broom and Norval Gleen, "Occupation and Income," in *Roots of Rebellion: The Evolution of Black Politics and Protest since World War II*, ed. Richard P. Young (New York: Harper and Row, 1970), 83, passim; Nathan Wright, *Black Power and Urban Unrest: Creative Possibilities* (New York: Hawthorn, 1967), 46–54. On the "rising expectations" theory, see Doug McAdam, *Political Process and the Development of Black Insurgency, 1930–1950* (Chicago: University of Chicago Press, 1982); Manning Marable, *Race, Reform and Rebellion: The Second Reconstruction in Black America, 1945–1982* (Jackson: University Press of Mississippi, 1984), 103–4.

48. Robert L. Scott and Wayne Brockriede, *The Rhetoric of Black Power* (New York: Harper and Row, 1969), 5–7. On self-determination, see also, Robert L. Scott and Wayne Brockriede, "The Rhetoric of Black Power: Order and Disorder in the Future," ibid., 194–201. For a comprehensive discussion of black power and its principles see, Stokely Carmichael and Charles V. Hamilton, *Black Power: The Politics of Liberation in America* (New York: Random House, 1967), 34–57, passim; and John T. McCartney, *Black Power Ideologies: An Essay in African-American Political Thought* (Philadelphia: Temple University Press, 1992), 111–90.

49. Bosmajian and Bosmajian, *The Rhetoric of the Civil Rights Movement*, 3–32.

50. SNCC WATS Report, June 4, 1965, Leadership Conference on Civil Rights Collection, series F, box 5, Mississippi Folder, 1963–64, Library of Congress, Washington, D.C.; "Running Summary of Events."

51. SNCC WATS Reports, June 4, 1965; "Running Summary of Events."

52. "Running Summary of Events."

53. SNCC WATS Reports, June 4, 1965.

54. See "15 Strikers Walk Off"; SNCC WATS Reports, June 4, 1965; "Running Summary of Events."

55. SNCC WATS Report, June 4, 1965; "Running Summary of Events."

56. Minutes of Statewide Meeting, MFLU, Sept. 4, 1965; Mississippi Freedom Labor Union Financial Report, "Report on Locals and Money Distributed," box 3, folder 9, Special Collections, UCLA; "Miss. Freedom Labor Union Strikes Again," SNCC news release, Sept. 14, 1965, box 3, folder 9, Special Collections, UCLA.

57. "Maid Strike, Join Freedom Union," SNCC news release, July 31, 1965, box 3, folder 9, Special Collections, UCLA; Minutes of Statewide Meeting, MFLU, [Sept. 4, 1965]; "SNCC Program: A Report for 1965," 3, SNCC Papers, microfilm, reel 24.

58. "Mississippi Freedom Labor Union," report from George Shelton, State Chairman, n.d. [ca. Sept. 1965]; "Miss. Freedom Labor Union Strikes Again."

59. "Appeals from the South: The Mississippi Freedom Labor Union and Natchez Boycott," box 3, folder 9, Special Collections, UCLA.

60. "What's New in Mississippi," *Delta Ministry* 3 (Jan. 1966), Charles Horwitz Collection, box 2, folder 39, Tougaloo Civil Rights Collection, Tougaloo College, Tougaloo, Miss.

61. Ibid.

62. *MFDP Newsletter,* Dec. 20, 1965, Charles Horwitz Collection, box 3, folder 51, Tougaloo Civil Rights Collection, Tougaloo College.

63. Ibid.

64. This is speculation based on a few SNCC sources. See, for example, Margaret Lauren to [SNCC] Northern Offices, n.d., box 3, folder 9, Special Collections, UCLA; Memo to Friends of SNCC, Oct. 28, 1965, SNCC Papers, microfilm, reel 24; *Nonviolent Notes,* Nov. 15, 1965, SNCC Papers, microfilm, reel 29. Mostly, these sources indicate SNCC's profound frustration with what it identified as poor record keeping on the part of MFLU. According to the Lauren letter: "The Northern office has been disturbed by the lack of information about the Mississippi Freedom Labor Union and by rumors of mismanagement of funds and factions within the union." It appears that SNCC leaders wanted to be helpful to the union, but both SNCC and the sparsely available MFLU records indicate a strong degree of protectiveness of the union by its local organizers.

65. Some historians and other scholars have maintained that the changing political climate had much to do with the demise of local organizations; that is, white liberals were less inclined to give to organizations perceived to be nationalist. On this point, see Steven Lawson, *Running for Freedom: Civil Rights and Black Politics in America since 1941* (Philadelphia: Temple University Press, 1991), 121; Carson, *In Struggle,* 229–43. The social scientist Herbert H. Haines takes issue with the correlation between the withdrawal of white support and strident calls for black power. He argues that radicalism actually helped the more moderate causes in the movement because outside financial resources poured in even more from elite interests opposed to black power. See Herbert H. Haines, *Black Radicals and the Civil Rights Mainstream, 1954–1970* (Knoxville: University of Tennessee Press, 1988), 1–14, 77–128, 172–86.

Chapter 8: Poverty Politics and the Freedom Farm

The chapter's first epigraph is from Charles Cobb, "Deprivation and Dissatisfaction in the Mississippi Delta," Special Report, Winter 1964, Special Collection on Civil Rights Struggle and Black Power Movement in the United States, 1950s to the Present, UCLA, box 3, folder 9. The second epigraph is from Phineas Israeli, "Hard-hitting Hamer, Exclusive Interview," *Berkeley Tribe*, Oct. 27, 1969, Fannie Lou Hamer Vertical File, Schomburg Center for Research in Black Culture, New York Public Library.

1. Clayborne Carson, *In Struggle: SNCC and the Black Awakening of the 1960s* (Cambridge, Mass.: Harvard University Press, 1981), 149, 180.

2. Ibid., 151; Executive Committee Meeting Minutes, Atlanta, Ga., Aug. 23, 1965, Student Nonviolent Coordinating Committee (SNCC) Papers (hereafter, SNCC Papers), box 32, Martin Luther King Jr. Library and Archives, Martin Luther King Jr. Center for Nonviolent Social Change, Atlanta, microfilm, reel 3; Executive Committee Meeting Minutes, Atlanta, Ga., Feb. 1965, SNCC Papers, microfilm, reel 3.

3. Carson, *In Struggle*, 191–99.

4. Ibid., 240.

5. James Forman, *The Making of Black Revolutionaries: A Personal Account* (New York: Macmillan, 1972), 475–79.

6. Interview with Fannie Lou Hamer by Anne Romaine, Nov. 1966, Ruleville, Miss., Anne Romaine Papers (hereafter ARP), Martin Luther King Jr. Library and Archives, Martin Luther King Jr. Center for Nonviolent Social Change, Atlanta. Regarding her closeness to SNCC, see also Fannie Lou Hamer, "Foreword," in Tracy Sugarman, *Stranger at the Gates: A Summer in Mississippi* (New York: Hill and Wang, 1966), viii.

7. *Mrs. Fannie Lou Hamer, et al. v. Cecil C. Campbell, Circuit Clerk and Registrar of Sunflower County,* U.S. Court of Appeals, Fifth Circuit.

8. Kay Mills, *This Little Light of Mine: The Life of Fannie Lou Hamer* (New York: Dutton, 1993), 176.

9. Ibid., 179.

10. Ibid., 180.

11. John Dittmer, *Local People: The Struggle for Civil Rights in Mississippi* (Urbana: University of Illinois Press, 1994), 412.

12. Robert Analavage, "Bitter Defeat in Sunflower," *National Guardian*, May 13, 1967.

13. *Fannie Lou Hamer et al. v. Sam J. Ely et al.,* U.S. Court of Appeals, Fifth Circuit.

14. See Frank Parker, *Black Votes Count: Political Empowerment in Mississippi after 1965* (Chapel Hill: University of North Carolina Press, 1990); Leslie McLemore, "The Mississippi Freedom Democratic Party: A Case Study of Grassroots Politics" (Ph.D. diss., University of Massachusetts, Amherst, 1971).

15. Susan Kling, *Fannie Lou Hamer: A Biography* (Chicago: Women for Racial and Economic Equality, 1979), 32–33; Joyce Ladner, "Fannie Lou Hamer: In Memoriam,"

Black Enterprise (May 1977): 56; *Independent Eye,* Dec. 23, 1968–Jan. 20, 1969, n.p., Tougaloo Civil Rights Collection, Tougaloo College, Tougaloo, Miss.

16. Mills, *This Little Light,* 190.

17. Ibid., 204–6; Dittmer, *Local People,* 369.

18. Richard D. Chesteen, "Change and Reaction in a Mississippi Delta Civil Community" (Ph.D diss., University of Mississippi, 1976), 314.

19. Ibid., 316–17 n. 18.

20. Mills, *This Little Light,* 205.

21. Ibid., 210.

22. Ibid., 211.

23. Dittmer, *Local People,* 378.

24. Ibid., 378.

25. Mills, *This Little Light,* 213.

26. Report from the Jackson, Miss., office of the FBI, on the attempted firebombing of the residence of Mrs. Fannie Lou Hamer, Feb. 18, 1971, FBI file no. 44-48733-3 (Fannie Lou Hamer).

27. Franklynn Peterson, "Pig Banks Pay Dividends," *Commercial Appeal Mid-South Magazine,* Jan. 7, 1973, 32, Fannie Lou Hamer Vertical File, Mississippi Department of Archives and History, Jackson, Miss.

28. James M. Fallows, "Mississippi Farmers Fight for Co-Op," *Harvard Crimson,* Jan. 27, 1969.

29. FFC Proposal for Funding, 1975, Fannie Lou Hamer Papers (hereafter FLH Papers), box 11, older 23, Amistad Research Center, Tulane University, New Orleans.

30. Peterson, "Pig Banks Pay Dividends," 33.

31. "Brief History of the Freedom Farm," 4, FLH Papers, box 11, folder 23.

32. Northern Sunflower County Memorandum (ca. Nov. 1971), 5, FLH Papers, box 11, older 22. See also, Freedom Farm Proposal [ca. Nov. 1971], FLH Papers, box 11, folder 24; Peterson, "Pig Banks Pay Dividends"; Freedom Farm Progress Report, n.d. [1972–73], "Projects," FLH Papers, box 11, folder 23; "Freedom Farm Corporation," 2 [ca. Mar. 1973], FLH Papers, box 10, folder 7.

33. Northern Sunflower County Memorandum (ca. Nov. 1971), 5–6.

34. Progress Report (Mar. 1973), "Farming Operation," FLH Papers, box 11, folder 23; Freedom Farm Corporation Status Report and Request for Funds, Mar. 1973, 7, FLH Papers, box 11, folder 24; ibid., July 1973, 7; Freedom Farm Corporation Proposal for Funding, 1975, FLH Papers, box 11, folder 23.

35. Proposal for Financial Support, Madison Measure for Measure [ca. Aug. 25, 1973], 2, FLH Papers, box 10, folder 12.

36. Northern Sunflower County Memorandum (ca. Nov. 1971), 1–4.

37. Fannie Lou Hamer to Friend, May, 15, 1970, FLH Papers, box 10, folder 2.

38. Progress Report (Mar. 1973), "Farming Operation"; Freedom Farm Corporation Status Report and Request for Funds, Mar. 1973, 6–7; Proposal for Financial Support, Madison Measure for Measure [ca. Aug 25, 1973], 3.

39. "Brief History of the Freedom Farm," 2.

40. Peterson, "Pig Banks Pay Dividends," 34.

41. "Brief History of the Freedom Farm," 4.

42. Peterson, "Pig Banks Pay Dividends," 34.

43. Ibid.

44. Mills, *This Little Light,* 262.

45. Progress Report, n.d. [1972–73], "Projects."

46. Freedom Farm Corporation Status Report and Request for Funds, Mar. 1973, 10.

47. 1969 Annual Report on Sunflower County by Joseph Harris, County Project Director, FLH Papers, box 3, folder 19.

48. Freedom Farm Corporation Progress Report [ca. 1973], "Past Projects," FLH Papers, box 11, folder 23; Freedom Farm Corporation Status Report and Request for Funds, Mar. 1973, 11; ibid., July 1973, 11.

49. Freedom Farm Corporation Progress Report [ca. 1973], "Past Projects"; Freedom Farm Corporation Status Report and Request for Funds, Mar. 1973, 9; ibid., July 1973, 9; Freedom Farm Corporation Proposal for Funding, 1975.

50. Fannie Lou Hamer to Robert S. Brown, Director, BERC, Aug. 23, 1971, FLH Papers, box 10, folder 3.

51. David M. Landry, Domestic Project Coordinator, American Freedom from Hunger Foundation, to Fannie Lou Hamer, Dec. 1, 1971, FLH Papers, box 10, folder 3.

52. Progress Report (Mar. 1973), "Farming Operation"; Freedom Farm Status Report and Request for Funds, July 1973, FLH Papers, 8.

53. Freedom Farm Status Report and Request for Funds, July 1973, 8.

54. Ibid.

55. Freedom Farm Corporation Proposal for Funding, 1975.

56. Freedom Farm Corporation Application for Minority Group Self-Determination Fund, Commission on Religion and Race, United Methodist Church, June 6, 1973, FLH Papers, box 10, folder 10.

57. Freedom Farm Corporation Proposal for Funding, 1975.

58. Ibid.

59. Fallows, "Miss. Farmers Fight for Co-op."

60. "Brief Historical Background of Freedom Farm Corporation," 1, FLH Papers, box 11, folder 1.

61. Northern Sunflower County Memorandum (ca. Nov. 1971), 6.

62. "Brief Historical Background of Freedom Farm Corporation," 1.

63. Freedom Farm Corporation Status Report and Request for Funds, Mar. 1973.

64. Freedom Farm Corporation Proposal for Funding, 1975.

65. Delta Ministry Employment Application for Joseph Harris, Mar. 7, 1968, FLH Papers, box 3, folder 19; Joseph Harris résumé, Nov. 7, 1972, FLH Papers, box 3, folder 19.

66. Freedom Farm Corporation Proposal, June 1970, 6–8, FLH Papers, box 11, folder 24.

67. Meeting minutes, Freedom Farm Board of Directors, Mar. 2, 1972, FLH Papers, box 11, folder 14.

68. Freedom Farm Corporation Proposal for Funding, 1975.

69. Peterson, "Pig Banks Pay Dividends," 33.

70. Progress Report (Mar. 1973), "Farming Operation"; Freedom Farm Corporation Status Report and Request for Funds, July 1973, 8.

71. Roger Yockey, "King Co. 'Adopts' Sunflower Co., Miss.," unidentified newspaper article, Mar. 7, 1969, FLH Papers, box 3, folder 13.

72. Ibid.

73. Fallows, "Miss. Farmers Fight for Co-op."

74. Tom Windham to Freed. Farm Coop and Fannie Hamer, Nov. 21, 1969, FLH Papers, box 10, folder 1.

75. Harry Belafonte to Dear Friend, May 1969, FLH Papers, box 10, folder 1.

76. "Jim" [Frederick W. Bassett] to Mrs. Hamer, 3 May 1969, FLH Papers, box 10, folder 19.

77. Kelly James to Fannie Lou Hamer, May 15, 1969, FLH Papers, box 10, folder 19.

78. Michael C. Ferguson, Attorney [Berkeley, Calif.] to Freedom Farm Corporation, Nov. 3, 1972, FLH Papers, box 10, folder 4.

79. Grace Mitchell to David Frost, Oct. 3, 1969, FLH Papers, box 10, folder 20. See also the following letters in response to Hamer's appearance: Erma O. Williams to David Frost, Oct. 4, 1969, and Rosa E. Green to Fannie Lou Hamer, Oct. 9, 1969, both in FLH Papers, box 10, folder 20.

80. Marguerite Rabbitt to Fannie Lou Hamer, July 15, 1973, FLH Papers, box 10, folder 11.

81. Jeff [Lowenstine] to Fannie Lou Hamer, Oct. 21, 1970, FLH Papers, box 10, folder 2; (Mrs.) Fannie Lou Hamer to Dear Friend, Madison Measure for Measure, Nov. 13, 1970, FLH Papers, box 10, folder 2.

82. On the importance of the 1970 Milwaukee contribution, see Hamer's letter of thanks to Measure for Measure: Fannie Lou Hamer to Mrs. [Helen] Finney [Treasurer], Madison Measure for Measure, Inc., July 26, 1971, FLH Papers, box 10, folder 3; annie Lou Hamer to Jeffrey Lowenstine, Madison Measure for Measure, Jan. 19, 1971, FLH Papers, box 10, folder 3.

83. "Brief History of the Freedom Farm," 3–4.

84. Helen Finney, Treasurer, Madison Measure for Measure, to Fannie Lou Hamer [ca. July 23, 1971], FLH Papers, box 10, folder 3.

85. (Mrs.) Fannie Lou Hamer to Harry [sic] Si[l]ver, Project Director, America Hungry for Freedom Foundation [American Freedom from Hunger Foundation], Sept. 28, 1970, FLH Papers, box 10, folder 2.

86. David M. Landry, Domestic Projects Coordinator, American Freedom from Hunger Foundation, to Fannie Lou Hamer, FLH Papers, box 10, folder 3.

87. Harvey Silver, Projects Director, American Freedom from Hunger Foundation,

Inc., to Fannie Lou Hamer, Freedom Farm Corporation, Aug. 11, 1971, Sept. 21, 1971, and Nov. 26, 1971, all in FLH Papers, box 10, folder 3; David M. Landry to Fannie Lou Hamer, Dec. 1, 1971, FLH Papers, box 10, folder 3; Harvey Silver, Projects Director, American Freedom from Hunger Foundation, to Fannie Lou Hamer, FFC, Apr. 27, 1972, FLH Papers; David M. Landry, Domestic Project Coordinator, American Freedom from Hunger Foundation, Inc., to Fannie Lou Hamer, n.d., FLH Papers, box 10, folder 3.

88. Harvey Silver, Projects Director, American Freedom from Hunger Foundation, to Robert Browne, Director, Black Economic Research Center, Dec. 28, 1971, FLH Papers, box 10, folder 3; Rev. A. J. McKnight, C.S. Sp. President, to Mrs. Fannie Lou Hammer [sic], Freedom Farm Co-op, Nov. 30, 1970, FLH Papers, box 10, folder 2.

89. Fannie Lou Hamer to Leslie Dunbar, Field Foundation, Nov. 16, 1971, FLH Papers, box 10, folder 3.

90. Joseph Harris to [Michael] C. Ferguson, Nov. 10, 1972, FLH Papers, box 10, folder 4; Freedom Farm Corporation application for Minority Group Self-Determination Fund, Commission on Religion and Race, United Methodist Church, June 6, 1973.

91. Fannie Lou Hamer to Leah Carver Toabe, July 5, 1973, FLH Papers, box 10, folder 21.

92. Joseph Harris, Committee Chairman, Fannie Lou Hamer Anniversary Committee, to Dear Friend, May 29, 1974, FLH Papers, box 10, folder 14; Clanton Beamon to Dick Lewis, treasurer, Madison Measure for Measure, Oct. 22, 1974, FLH Papers, box 10, folder 14.

93. Meeting minutes, Freedom Farm Corporation, Board of Directors, Mar. 2, 1972, pp. 2–3, box 11, folder 14.

94. Joseph Harris to Nora L. Campbell, May 10, 1973, FLH Papers, box 10, folder 10.

95. Nora L. Campbell to Joseph Harris, May 11, 1973, FLH Papers, box 10, folder 10.

96. Progress Report (Mar. 1973), "Farming Operation"; Freedom Farm Corporation Status Report and Request for Funds, July 1973, 9.

97. Proposal for Financial Support, Madison Measure for Measure [ca. Aug. 25, 1973], 2–3; Certification of Losses Caused by Major of Natural Disaster, Freedom Farm Corporation, Oct. 1972, FLH Papers, box 11, folder 22; Progress Report (Mar. 1973), "Introduction," FLH Papers, box 11, folder 23; Freedom Farm Corporation Status Report and Request for Funds, July 1973, 1.

98. Progress Report (Mar. 1973), "Reorganization," FLH Papers, box 11, folder 23; Freedom Farm Corporation Status Report and Request for Funds, Mar. 1973, 5.

99. Progress Report (Mar. 1973), "Reorganization."

100. Joseph Harris, Committee Chairman, Fannie Lou Hamer Anniversary Committee to Dear Friend, May 29, 1974, FLH Papers, box 10, folder 14.

101. [Helena] Bunny Wilkening, chairman, Madison Measure for Measure, to Joe Harris, Aug. 29, 1973, FLH Papers, box 10, folder 12.

102. Memo, Proposal for a "Poor Peoples Land Corporation," Stokely Carmichael, Bob Mants, Tina Harris, Alabama Staff to [SNCC] Staff, n.d., SNCC Papers, microfilm, reel 2.

103. Proposal for Financial Support, Madison Measure for Measure, 3 [ca. Aug 25, 1973].

104. Fallows, "Miss. Farmers Fight for Co-op."

Chapter 9: Last Days

The chapter's first epigraph is from L. C. Dorsey, "Fannie Lou Hamer," *Jackson Advocate*, Feb. 26–Mar. 6, 1981, section C, 1. The second epigraph is from Jamaica Kincaid, *The Autobiography of My Mother* (New York: Farrar, Straus and Giroux, 1997), 82–83.

1. The Mississippi Young Democrats came together out of a number of Young Democrat clubs on white college campuses in the state. Members included young, ambitious individuals with an interest in mainstream political affairs and high hopes for a professional political career someday. See John Dittmer, *Local People: The Struggle for Civil Rights in Mississippi* (Urbana: University of Illinois Press, 1994), 348–49.

2. Interview with Fannie Lou Hamer by Robert Wright, Aug. 9 1968, Oral History Collection, Civil Rights Documentation Project (CRDP), Moorland-Spingarn Research Center, Howard University; Kay Mills, *This Little Light of Mine: The Life of Fannie Lou Hamer* (New York: Dutton, 1993), 223, 226.

3. After Mississippi activists abolished COFO in July 1965, the MFDP, in effect, was left alone to maintain some level of political organization among the still largely disfranchised poor.

4. Dittmer, *Local People,* 421.

5. Mills, *This Little Light,* 234.

6. "Issues of MFDP Platform,"Proposed Program of Mississippi Freedom Democratic Party," [c. July 1968], Fannie Lou Hamer Papers (hereafter FLH Papers), box 5, folder 10, Amistad Research Center, Tulane University, New Orleans.

7. Mills, *This Little Light,* 233.

8. For Hamer's remarks about her telegram to Lyndon Johnson, see the *Worker,* July 13, 1965, Fannie Lou Hamer Vertical File, Schomburg Center for Research in Black Culture, New York Public Library.

8. Ibid., 232.

9. Mills, *This Little Light,* 232.

10. Ibid.

11. "We Have to Fight These Battles Together," Fannie Lou Hamer campaign flyer, Oct. 1968, FLH Papers, box 9, folder 29.

12. Mills, *This Little Light,* 238.

13. Ibid., 238, 240.

14. "Fannie Lou Hamer Backs Boycott," *Delta-Democrat-Times,* Feb. 13, 1969; "Student-Faculty Accord Ends Boycott at MVSC," *Delta-Democrat-Times,* Feb. 14, 1969.

15. "Nobody Knows the Trouble She's Seen," *Washington Post,* July 14, 1968.

16. See Mills, *This Little Light,* chap. 13, passim.

17. Fannie Lou Hamer Platform for 1971 Campaign, FLH Papers, box 9, folder 13. In anticipation of her 1967 run, Hamer had printed some business-card-size campaign cards that read: "Vote for Mrs. Fannie Lou Hamer for State Senator, Sunflower County, Nov. 7, 1967, FAIR*HONEST*IMPARTIAL." FLH Papers, box 9, folder 29.

18. "Megro Girl Is Slain; Whites Held in South," *New York Times*, May 27, 1971.

19. Mills, *This Little Light*, 282.

20. Memo to Bank of Ruleville from Trustees of the Jo Etha Collier Building Fund, Sept. 13, 1971, FLH Papers, box 10, folder 3.

21. Mills, *This Little Light*, 284.

22. Interview with Annette Samuels by author, Jan. 7, 1986, Washington, D.C.

23. Mills, *This Little Light*, 277.

24. "Women Organize for Political Power," *New York Times*, July 11, 1971, 1.

25. Ibid.

26. Ibid., 22.

27. Mills, *This Little Light*, 278.

28. Fannie Lou Hamer, "It's in Your Hands," in *Black Women in White America: A Documentary History*, ed. Gerda Lerner (New York: Vintage, 1972), 609–14.

29. Mills, *This Little Light*, 274.

30. "Goals Set by Women's Political Caucus," *New York Times*, July 13, 1971.

31. "Caucus to Seek Equal Number of Women Convention Delegates," *New York Times*, Nov. 10, 1971.

32. Mills, *This Little Light*, 286–87.

33. Ibid., 288–89; Richard D. Chesteen, "Change and Reaction in a Mississippi Delta Civil Community" (Ph.D. diss., University of Mississippi, 1976), 520.

34. Telephone interview with June Johnson by author, Apr. 4, 1991; Fannie Lou Hamer to Jean Sweet, Jan. 29, 1976, FLH Papers; Mills, *This Little Light*, chap. 16, passim.

35. Louise Mitchell to Soror Fannie Lou Hamer, July 24, 1972, FLH Papers, box 1, folder 19.

36. Joseph Harris to Louise Mitchell, Aug. 31, 1972, FLH Papers, box 1, folder 19, record 1.

37. Mills, *This Little Light*, 295.

38. Interview with Fannie Lou Hamer by Neil McMillen, Apr. 14, 1972, Ruleville, Miss., Oral History Collection, University of Southern Mississippi, Hattiesburg.

39. "The Official Proceedings of the Democratic National Convention, 1972," July 13, 1972, 435.

40. (Mrs.) Fannie Lou Hamer to Mr. Alan S. Walker, President, Program Corporation of America, Feb. 22, 1973, FLH Papers, box 1, folder 19.

41. Eleanor Holmes Norton to Perry Hamer, Mar. 1, 1977, FLH Papers, box 2, folder 9, record 1; see also Eleanor Holmes Norton to Mrs. Hamer [ca. Feb. 4, 1977], FLH Papers, box 1, folder 17.

42. Telephone interview with June Johnson by author, Apr. 4, 1991. See also, Mills, *This Little Light*, 302.

43. Vickie to Fannie Lou, Jan. 23, 1977, FLH Papers, box 1, folder 17.

44. Linnie Smoote to Mom and Dad, Jan. 10, 1976, FLH Papers, box 1, folder 7.

45. Annie M. Townsend to [Fannie Lou Hamer], [c. Apr. 9, 1976], FLH Papers, box 1, folder 8.

46. Interview with Laura Ratliff by author, Dec. 21, 1985, Ruleville, Miss.

Selected Bibliography

Manuscript Collections

Amistad Research Center, Tulane University, New Orleans
    Fannie Lou Hamer Papers
    Free Southern Theater Records, 1963–78
    Poor Peoples Corporation Records, 1960–67
    Southern Civil Rights Litigation Records
Howard University, Washington, D.C.
    Oral History Collection, Civil Rights Documentation Project, Moorland-Spingarn Research Center
Library of Congress, Washington, D.C.
    Congress of Racial Equality Papers
    Joseph Rauh Papers
    Leadership Conference on Civil Rights Collection
    NAACP Papers
Martin Luther King Jr. Center for Nonviolent Social Change, Archives Department, Atlanta, Georgia
    Anne Romaine Papers
    Congress of Racial Equality Papers
    Delta Ministry Papers
    Hazel Gregory Papers
    James Forman Tapes
    Johnnie Carr Papers
    Martin Luther King Oral History Collection
    SNCC Papers

Mary McLeod-Bethune Museum and Archives, Washington, D.C.
    Fannie Lou Hamer File
    National Council of Negro Women Records
Mississippi Department of Archives and History, Jackson, Mississippi
    Fannie Lou Hamer Vertical File
    Fannie Lou Hamer Funeral (videotape)
    Newsfilm Collection, 1954–71
    Marriage Records, 1873, Choctaw County, Mississippi
    Marriage Records, 1942–46, Montgomery County, Mississippi
    Marriage Records, 1942–46, Sunflower County, Mississippi
    Portrait in Black: Fannie Lou Hamer, Chronicle of A Movement, film, Rediscovery
        Productions, 1972
Schomburg Center for Research in Black Life and Culture, New York City
    Clippings File, 1925–74, Fannie Lou Hamer
    Clippings File, 1925–74, SNCC
State Historical Society of Wisconsin, Madison, Wisconsin
    Civil Rights Collection
    Highlander Research and Education Center Papers
Tougaloo College, Zenobia Coleman Library, Tougaloo, Mississippi
    Aaron Henry Papers
    Annie C. Rankin Papers
    Charles Horwitz Collection
    Ed King Papers
    Fannie Lou Hamer Collection
    Mississippi Freedom Democratic Party Papers
    Tom Dent Oral History Collection
University of California at Los Angeles, Special Collections
    Special Collections on Civil Rights Struggle and Black Movement in the United
        States, 1950s to the present

Interviews and Oral Histories

Personal Interviews

Bobbie Betts, June 3, 1986, Los Angeles
Septima Clark, Apr. 30, 1987, Los Angeles
Annie Devine, Oct. 31, 1990, Canton, Mississippi (phone)
L. C. Dorsey, Dec. 20, 1985, Jackson, Mississippi (phone)
Lawrence Guyot, Jan. 6, 1986, Washington, D.C.
Jacqueline Hamer, Dec. 21, 1985, Ruleville, Mississippi
Perry Hamer, Dec. 21, 1985, Ruleville, Mississippi
June Johnson, Apr. 4, 1991, Washington, D.C.(phone)

Joyce Ladner, Jan. 6, 1986, Washington, D.C.
Leslie McLemore, Dec. 18, 1985, Jackson, Mississippi
Laura Ratliff, Dec. 21, 1985, Ruleville, Mississippi
Annette Samuels, Jan. 7, 1986, Washington, D.C.
Charles Tisdale, Dec. 27, 1985, Jackson, Mississippi
Sylvia Townsend, May 18, 1990, New York City

Interview Collections

Anne Romaine Collection, Martin Luther King Library and Archives, Martin Luther
King Jr. Center for Nonviolent Social Change, Atlanta, Ga.
    Ella Baker
    Annie Devine
    Ivanhoe Donaldson
    Lawrence Guyot
    Fannie Lou Hamer
    Aaron Henry
    Bill Higgs
    Edwin King
    Sandy Leigh
    Allard Lowenstein
    Robert Moses
    Joseph Rauh
    Mendy Samstein
    John Stewart
    Walter Tillow
    Arthur Waskow
Civil Rights Documentation Project, Moorland-Spingarn Collection, Howard Uni-
versity, Washington, D.C.
    Unita Blackwell
    Owen Brooks
    Hodding Carter III
    Annie Devine
    Fannie Lou Hamer
    Aaron Henry
    Margaret Kibbitt
    Annie Mae King
    Mary Lane
    Joseph Rauh
    George Raymond
    Emma Sanders
    Henry Sias

Pacifica Radio Archives, Los Angeles, California
    "Fannie Lou Hamer on the Mississippi Freedom Democratic Party" (audiotaped
    interview)

Government Collections, Documents, and Publications

Central Intelligence Agency Files
    Fannie Lou Hamer
    SNCC
Federal Bureau of Investigation Files
    Fannie Lou Hamer
    Highlander Folk School
    SNCC
Mississippi Population Characteristics. Starkville, Miss.: Mississippi State University
    Social Science Research Center, 1964.
U.S. Bureau of the Census. *Population Reports.* Washington, D.C.: Government
    Printing Office, 1964.
———. *Statistical Abstract of the United States, 1963.* Washington, D.C.: Government
    Printing Office, 1963.
———. *Statistical Abstract of the United States, 1966.* Washington, D.C.: Govern-
    ment Printing Office, 1966.
———. *Twelfth Census of the United States, 1900: Population Schedules* (Montgom-
    ery County, Mississippi). Washington, D.C.: Government Printing Office, 1901–2.
U.S. Commission on Civil Rights. *Civil Rights: Report of the United States Commis-
    sion on Civil Rights in Mississippi.* Washington, D.C.: Government Printing
    Office, 1963.
———. *Political Participation.* Washington, D.C.: Government Printing Office,
    1968.
———. *Report of the Mississippi Advisory Committee.* Washington, D.C.: Govern-
    ment Printing Office, 1969.
U.S. Congress. *Congressional Record.* Vol. 109, pt. 13 (Sept. 13–20, 1963), 2544–57.
    Washington, D.C.: Government Printing Office, 1963.
———. *Congressional Record.* Vol. 110, pt. 10 (June 4–16, 1964), 13996–14002. Wash-
    ington, D.C.: Government Printing Office, 1964.
U.S. Department of Agriculture. *Statistical Bulletin, 1964.* Washington, D.C.: Gov-
    ernment Printing Office, 1964.

Newspapers and Periodicals

Amsterdam News
Atlanta Constitution

Atlanta Daily World
Atlanta Voice
Bay State Banner
Be Reconciled
Berkeley Gazette
Bilalian News
Birmingham News
Birmingham Post
Black Enterprise
Claremont Press-Telegraph
Close-up
Delta-Democrat Times
The Drummer
Ebony
Freedomways
Great Speckled Bird
Independent Eye
Jackson Advocate
Jackson Daily News
Jet
Motive
Muhammad Speaks
Nation
National Guardian
New Republic
New York Times
Sojourners
Southern Patriot
Student Voice
Washington Post
Underground Newspapers Collection, University of Missouri, Columbia (microfilm edition)

Books

Adams, Timothy Dow. *Telling Lies in Modern American Autobiography.* Chapel Hill: University of North Carolina Press, 1990.
Ahmann, Matthew, H., ed. *The New Negro.* Notre Dame, Ind.: Fides Publishers, 1969.
Allen, Robert. *Reluctant Reformers.* Washington, D.C.: Howard University Press, 1974.
Anderson, James. *The Education of Blacks in the South, 1860–1935.* Chapel Hill: University of North Carolina Press, 1988.

Ascher, Carol, Louise DeSalvo, and Sara Ruddick. *Between Women: Biographers, Novelists, Critics, Teachers, and Artists Write About Their Work on Women.* Boston: Beacon, 1984.

Bartley, Numan. *The Rise of Massive Resistance: Race and Politics in the South during the 1950s.* Baton Rouge: Louisiana State University Press, 1969.

Bass, Jack, and Walter De Vries. *The Transformation of Southern Politics: Social Change and Political Consequences since 1945.* New York: Basic Books, 1976.

Bates, Daisy. *The Long Shadow of Little Rock.* New York: David McKay, 1962.

Beardslee, William. *The Way Out Must Lead In: Life Histories in the Civil Rights Movement.* Atlanta: Center for Research in Social Change, Emory University, 1977.

Belfrage, Sally. *Freedom Summer.* New York: Viking, 1965.

Black, Earl, and Merle Black. *Politics and Society in the South.* Cambridge, Mass.: Harvard University Press, 1987.

Bloom, Jack. *Class, Race and the Civil Rights Movement.* Bloomington: Indiana University Press, 1987.

Bosmajian, Haig A., and Hamida Bosmajian. *The Rhetoric of the Civil Rights Movement.* New York: Random House, 1969.

Branch, Taylor. *Parting the Waters: America in the King Years, 1954–63.* New York: Simon and Schuster, 1988.

———. *Pillar of Fire: America during the King Years, 1963–65.* New York: Simon and Schuster, 1998.

Brandfon, Robert L. *Cotton Kingdom of the New South: A History of the Yazoo Mississippi Delta from Reconstruction to the Twentieth Century.* Cambridge, Mass.: Harvard University Press, 1967.

Brauer, Carl M. *John F. Kennedy and the Second Reconstruction.* New York: Columbia University Press, 1977.

Braxton, Joanne M. *Black Women Writing Autobiography: A Tradition within a Tradition.* Philadelphia: Temple University Press, 1989.

Braxton, Joanne, and Andree Nicola McLaughlin. *Wild Women in the Whirlwind: Afra-American Culture and the Contemporary Literary Renaissance.* New Brunswick, N.J.: Rutgers University Press, 1989.

Brisbane, Robert. *Black Activism: Racial Revolution in the United States, 1954–1970.* Valley Forge, Pa.: Judson Press, 1974.

Cagin, Seth, and Philip Dray. *We Are Not Afraid: The Story of Goodman, Schwerner and Chaney and the Civil Rights Campaign for Mississippi.* New York: Macmillan, 1988.

Campbell, Clarice T. *Mississippi: The View from Tougaloo.* Jackson: University Press of Mississippi, 1979.

Cantarow, Ellen, ed. *Moving the Mountain: Women Working for Social Change.* Old Westbury, Conn.: Feminist Press, 1980.

Carmichael, Stokely, and Charles V. Hamilton. *Black Power: The Politics of Liberation in America.* New York: Random House, 1967.

Carson, Clayborne. *In Struggle: SNCC and the Black Awakening of the 1960s.* Cambridge, Mass.: Harvard University Press, 1981.

———, ed. *The Student Voice, 1960–1965: Periodical of the Student Non-violent Coordinating Committee.* Westport, Conn.: Meckler Corporation, 1990.

Carson, Josephine. *Silent Voices: The Southern Negro Woman Today.* New York: Delacorte, 1969.

Chafe, William. *Civilities and Civil Liberties: Greensboro, North Carolina, and the Black Struggle for Freedom.* New York: Oxford University Press, 1980.

———. *Never Stop Running: Allard Lowenstein and the Struggle to Save American Liberalism.* New York: Basic Books, 1993.

Clark, Septima. *Echo in My Soul.* New York: Dutton, 1962.

Clark, Septima, with Cynthia Stokes Brown. *Ready from Within: Septima Clark and the Civil Rights Movement.* Navarro, Calif.: Wild Trees Press, 1986.

Collins, Patricia H. *Black Feminist Thought: Knowledge, Consciousness, and the Politics of Empowerment.* Boston: Unwin Hyman, 1990.

Conklin, Nancy Faires. *The Culture of Southern Black Women: Approaches and Materials.* Tuscaloosa: University of Alabama, Archive of American Minority Cultures and Women Studies Program, 1983.

Conner, Douglass L., with John Marsalck. *A Black Physician's Story: Bringing Hope to Mississippi.* Jackson: University Press of Mississippi, 1985.

Crawford, Vicki, Jacqueline Rouse, and Barbara Woods. *Trailblazers and Torchbearers: Black Women in the Civil Rights Movement.* New York: Carlson, 1990.

Dallek, Robert. *Flawed Giant: Lyndon Johnson and His Times, 1961–1973.* New York: Oxford University Press, 1998.

Daniel, Pete. *Breaking the Land: The Transformation of Cotton, Tobacco, and Rice Cultures since 1880.* Urbana: University of Illinois Press, 1985.

———. *The Shadow of Slavery: Peonage in the South, 1901–1969.* Urbana: University of Illinois Press, 1990.

Davis, Allison. *Deep South: A Social Anthropological Study of Caste and Class.* Chicago: University of Chicago Press, 1941.

Dollard, John. *Caste and Class in a Southern Town.* Garden City, N.Y.: Doubleday, 1949.

Egerton, John. *A Mind to Stay Here: Profiles from the South.* New York: Macmillan, 1970.

Elbaz, Robert. *The Changing Nature of the Self: A Critical Study of the Autobiographics Discourse.* Iowa City: University of Iowa Press, 1987.

Evans, Sara. *Personal Politics: The Roots of Women's Liberation in the Civil Rights Movement and the New Left.* New York: Vintage, 1980.

Evers, Charles. *Evers.* New York: World, 1971.

Evers, Myrlie B. *For Us, the Living.* Garden City, N.Y.: Doubleday, 1967.

Farmer, James. *Lay Bare the Heart: An Autobiography of the Civil Rights Movement.* New York: Arbor House, 1985.

Fax, Elton C. *Contemporary Black Leaders.* New York: Dodd, Mead, 1970.

Forman, James. *The Making of Black Revolutionaries: A Personal Account.* New York: Macmillan, 1972.

Frazier, Thomas R. *Afro-American History: Primary Sources.* New York: Harcourt, Brace and World, 1970.

Garrow, David. *Protest at Selma: Martin Luther King, Jr., and the Voting Rights Act of 1965.* New Haven: Yale University Press, 1978.

Goings, Kenneth. *The NAACP Comes of Age.* Bloomington: Indiana University Press, 1990.

Haines, Herbert H. *Black Radicals and the Civil Rights Mainstream, 1954–1970.* Knoxville: University of Tennessee Press, 1988.

Hall, Jacquelyn Dowd. *Revolt against Chivalry: Jessie Daniel Ames and the Women's Campaign against Lynching.* New York: Columbia University Press, 1979.

Hamer, Fannie Lou. *To Praise Our Bridges.* Jackson, Miss.: KIPCO, 1967.

Jaynes, Gerald. *Branches without Roots: Genesis of the Black Working Class in the American South, 1862–1882.* New York: Oxford University Press, 1986.

Johnson, Charles S. *Statistical Atlas of Southern Counties: Listing and Analysis of Socioeconomic Indices of 1104 Southern Counties.* Chapel Hill: University of North Carolina Press, 1941.

Jordan, June. *Fannie Lou Hamer.* New York: Crowell, 1972.

Katz, William Loren, ed. *Eyewitness: The Negro in American History.* New York: Pitman, 1967.

Kelley, Robin D. G. *Hammer and Hoe: Alabama Communists during the Great Depression.* Chapel Hill: University of North Carolina Press, 1990.

Kellogg, Charles Flint. *NAACP: A History of the National Association for the Advancement of Colored People.* Baltimore: Johns Hopkins University Press, 1967.

King, Mary. *Freedom Song: A Personal Story of the 1960s Civil Rights Movement.* New York: Morrow, 1987.

Kirby, Jack Temple. *Rural Worlds Lost: The American South, 1920–1960.* Baton Rouge: Louisiana State University Press, 1987.

Kling, Susan. *Fannie Lou Hamer: A Biography.* Chicago: Women for Racial and Economic Equality, 1979.

Krueger, Thomas. *And Promises to Keep: The Southern Conference for Human Welfare, 1938–1948.* Nashville: Vanderbilt University Press, 1967.

Ladd, Everett. *Negro Political Leadership in the South.* Ithaca, N.Y.: Cornell University Press, 1966.

Lawson, Steven F. *Black Ballots: Voting Rights in the South, 1944–1969.* New York: Columbia University Press, 1976.

Leiserson, Avery, ed. *The American South in the Sixties.* New York: Praeger, 1964.

Lerner, Gerda, ed. *Black Women in White America: A Documentary History.* New York: Vintage, 1972.

Lewis, John, with Michael D'Orso. *Walking with the Wind: A Memoir of the Movement.* New York: Simon and Schuster, 1998.

Lipsitz, George. *A Life in the Struggle: Ivory Perry and the Culture of Opposition.* Philadelphia: Temple University Press, 1988.

Litwack, Leon, and August Meier, ed. *Black Leaders of the Nineteenth Century.* Urbana: University of Illinois Press, 1988.

Loewen, James W., and Charles Sallis. *Mississippi: Conflict and Change.* New York: Pantheon, 1974.

Louis, Debbie. *We Are Not Saved: A History of the Movement as People.* Garden City, N.Y.: Doubleday, 1970.

Malcolm X, with Alex Haley. *The Autobiography of Malcolm X.* New York: Grove Press, 1965.

Mazlish, Bruce. *The Leader, the Led, and the Psyche: Essays in Psychohistory.* Middletown, Conn.: Wesleyan University Press, 1990.

McAdam, Doug. *Freedom Summer.* New York: Oxford University Press, 1988.

McCartney, John T. *Black Power Ideologies: An Essay in African-American Political Thought.* Philadelphia: Temple University Press, 1992.

McCord, William. *Mississippi: The Long, Hot Summer.* New York: Norton, 1965.

McMillen, Neil R. *The Citizens' Council: Organized Resistance to the Second Reconstruction, 1954–64.* Urbana: University of Illinois Press, 1971.

———. *Dark Journey: Black Mississippians in the Age of Jim Crow.* Urbana: University of Illinois Press, 1989.

Meltzer, Milton. *In Their Own Words: A History of the American Negro, 1916–1966.* New York: Crowell, 1967.

Mills, Kay. *This Little Light of Mine: The Life of Fannie Lou Hamer.* New York: Dutton, 1993.

Moody, Anne. *Coming of Age in Mississippi.* New York: Dial, 1968.

Morris, Aldon. *The Origins of the Civil Rights Movement: Black Communities Organizing for Change.* New York: Free Press, 1984.

Morrison, Minion K. C. *Black Political Mobilization, Leadership, Power, and Mass Behavior.* Albany: State University of New York Press, 1987.

Norrell, Robert. *Reaping the Whirlwind: The Civil Rights Movement in Tuskegee.* New York: Knopf, 1985.

Olney, James. *Metaphors of Self: The Meaning of Autobiography.* Princeton: Princeton University Press, 1972.

O'Reilly, Kenneth. *"Racial Matters": The FBI's Secret File on Black America, 1960–1972.* New York: Free Press, 1989.

Political Profiles: The Johnson Years. Vol. 4. New York: Facts on File, 1976.

Raines, Howell. *My Soul Is Rested: Movement Days in the Deep South Remembered.* New York: Putnam, 1977.

Ransom, Roger, and Richard Sutch. *One Kind of Freedom: The Economic Consequences of Emancipation.* Cambridge: Cambridge University Press, 1977.

Reed, Linda. *Simple Decency and Common Sense: The Southern Conference Movement, 1938–1963.* Bloomington: Indiana University Press, 1991.

Reilly, Philip R. *The Surgical Solution: A History of Involuntary Sterilization in the United States.* Baltimore: Johns Hopkins University Press, 1991.

Roberts, Dorothy. *Killing the Black Body: Race, Reproduction, and the Meaning of Liberty.* New York: Pantheon, 1997.

Robinson, Armstead R., and Patricia Sullivan, eds. *New Directions in Civil Rights Studies.* Charlottesville: University Press of Virginia, 1991.

Robinson, Jo Ann Gibson. *The Montgomery Bus Boycott and the Women Who Started It: The Memoir of Jo Ann Robinson.* Knoxville: University of Tennessee Press, 1987.

Rosengarten, Theodore. *All God's Dangers: The Life of Nate Shaw.* New York: Knopf, 1974.

Rothschild, Mary. *A Case of Black and White: Northern Volunteers and the Southern Freedom Summers, 1964–1965.* Westport, Conn.: Greenwood, 1982.

Rubel, David. *Fannie Lou Hamer: From Sharecropping to Politics.* New York: Silver Burnett, 1990.

Sacks, Karen Brodkin. *Caring by the Hour: Women, Work, and Organizing at Duke Medical Center.* Urbana: University of Illinois Press, 1988.

Salter, John. *Jackson, Mississippi: An American Chronicle of Struggle and Schism.* Malabar, Fla.: R. E. Krieger, 1987.

Schulman, Bruce. *From Cotton Belt to Sunbelt: Federal Policy, Economic Development, and the Transformation of the South, 1938–1980.* New York: Oxford University Press, 1991.

Scott, Robert L., and Wayne Brockriede, eds. *The Rhetoric of Black Power.* New York: Harper and Row, 1969.

Sellers, Cleveland. *The River of No Return: The Autobiography of a Black Militant and the Life and Death of SNCC.* Jackson: University Press of Mississippi, 1973.

Shapiro, Herbert. *White Violence and Black Response: From Reconstruction to Montgomery.* Amherst: University of Massachusetts Press, 1988.

Sheftall, Beverly Guy. *"Daughters of Sorrow": Attitudes Toward Black Women, 1880–1920.* New York: Carlson, 1990.

———, ed. *Words of Fire: An Anthology of African-American Feminist Thought.* New York: New Press, 1995.

Silberman, Charles E. *Crisis in Black and White.* New York: Random House, 1964.

Silver, James. *Mississippi: The Closed Society.* New York: Harcourt, Brace and World, 1964.

Sitkoff, Harvard. *The Struggle for Black Equality, 1954–1980.* New York: Hill and Wang, 1981.

Smead, Howard. *Blood Justice: The Lynching of Mack Charles Parker.* New York: Oxford University Press, 1986.

Snitow, Ann, Christine Stansell, and Sharon Thompson, eds. *Powers of Desire: The Politics of Sexuality.* New York: Monthly Review Press, 1983.

Sugarman, Tracy. *Stranger at the Gates: A Summer in Mississippi.* New York: Hill and Wang, 1966.

Sutherland, Elizabeth, ed. *Letters from Mississippi.* New York: McGraw-Hill, 1965.

Thompson, Edgar T., ed. *Plantation Societies, Race Relations, and the South: The Regimentation of Populations.* Durham: Duke University Press, 1975.

Tushnet, Mark V. *The NAACP's Legal Strategy against Segregated Education, 1925–1950.* Chapel Hill: University of North Carolina Press, 1987.

Vance, Rupert. *Human Factors in Cotton Culture: A Study in the Social Geography of the American South.* Chapel Hill: University of North Carolina Press, 1929.

Walker, Alice. *In Search of Our Mother's Gardens: Womanist Prose.* San Diego: Harcourt Brace Jovanovich, 1983.

Watters, Pat, and Reese Cleghorn. *Climbing Jacob's Ladder: The Arrival of Negroes in Southern Politics.* New York: Harcourt, Brace and World, 1967.

White, Deborah Gray. *Ar'n't I a Woman? Female Slaves in the Plantation South.* New York: Norton, 1985.

White, Theodore H. *The Making of the President, 1964.* New York: Atheneum, 1965.

Whitfield, Stephen. *A Death in the Delta: The Story of Emmett Till.* New York: Free Press, 1988.

Wright, Gavin. *Old South, New South: Revolutions in the Southern Economy since the Civil War.* New York: Basic Books, 1986.

Yates, Gayle Graham. *Mississippi Mind: A Personal Cultural History of An American State.* Knoxville: University of Tennessee Press, 1990.

Yette, Samuel. *The Choice: The Issue of Black Survival in America.* New York: Putnam, 1971.

Young, Richard P., ed. *Roots of Rebellion: The Evolution of Black Politics and Protest since World War II.* New York: Harper and Row, 1970.

Zangrando, Robert. *The NAACP Crusade against Lynching, 1909–1950.* Philadelphia: Temple University Press, 1980.

Zinn, Howard. *SNCC: New Abolitionists.* Boston: Beacon, 1964.

Articles

Ajanaku, Mzee O. "We Have to Take for Ourselves." *Jackson Advocate,* Oct. 3–9, 1985, 1b.

Aldridge, Cathy. "What Makes Fannie Lou Hamer Run?" *New York Amsterdam News,* Sept. 13, 1969, Woman's World Section, 5.

Alley, Harmon. "Mississippi Farmers Helping Themselves with Machinery Cooperative." *News for Farmer Cooperatives,* Feb. 1966, 7–8.

Archer, Doug. "'Send Troops to Mississippi, Not Vietnam,' Says Mrs. Hamer." *Worker,* July 13, 1965.

"An Autobiography of Mrs. Fannie Lou Hamer." *Close-up* 4, no. 1. (Jan. 1969): 9.

Baker, Ella. "Bigger Than a Hamburger." *Southern Patriot* 18, no. 4 (May 1960): 4.

———. "Developing Community Leadership." In *Black Women in White America,* ed. Gerda Lerner, 345–52. New York: Vintage, 1972.

Barry, Kathleen. "Biography and the Search for Women's Subjectivity." *Women's Studies International Forum* 12, no. 6 (1989): 561–77.

Bennett, Lerone, Jr. "SNCC: Rebels with a Cause." *Ebony,* July 1965, 146–53.

Braden, Anne. "The SNCC Trends Challenge to White America." *Southern Patriot* 24, no. 5 (May 1966):1–3.

Bramlett-Solomon, Sharon. "Civil Rights Vanguard in the Deep South: Newspaper Portrayal of Fannie Lou Hamer, 1964–1977." *Journalism Quarterly* (Fall 1991): 515–21.

Branton, Wiley A. "To Register to Vote in Mississippi." *New South* 20, no. 2 (Feb. 1965): 10–15.

Brown, Elsa Barkley. "Mothers of Mind." *Sage* 6 (Spring 1989): 4–11.

Burroughs, Margaret, and Eugene Feldman. "Book Review of *Fannie Lou Hamer, A Biography* by Susan Kling." Freedomways 20, no. 1 (1980): 50–51.

Cadmere, Dwight. "Mrs. Fannie Lou Hamer: [illegible] Struggles for Freedom." *Muhammad Speaks,* Aug. 2, 1968, 5.

Carson, Clayborne. "Black Power after Ten Years." In *A History of Our Time: Readings in Postwar America,* ed. William Chafe and Harvard Sitkoff, 197–204. New York: Oxford Univ. Press, 1987.

"Civil Rights Leader Fannie Hamer Dies." *McComb Enterprise-Journal,* Mar. 16, 1977, 13.

Cleghorn, Reese. "Who Speaks for Mississippi?" *The Reporter,* Aug. 13, 1964, 31–34.

Cobb, James C. "'Somebody Done Nailed Us on the Cross': Federal Farm and Welfare Policy and the Civil Rights Movement in the Mississippi Delta." *Journal of American History* 77, no. 3 (Dec., 1990): 912–36.

Coles, Robert. "The Protesters." *New South* 22, no. 2 (Spring 1967): 2–40.

Collier-Thomas, Bettye. "Fannie Lou Hamer and the Struggle for Human Rights." *Legacy* 3, no. 1 (Spring 1990): 3.

Collins, Patricia Hill. "The Meaning of Motherhood in Black Culture and Black Mother/Daughter Relationships." *Sage* 4, no. 2 (Fall 1987): 3–10.

———. "The Social Construction of Black Feminist Thought." *Signs* 14 (Summer 1989): 745–73.

Collum, Danny. "Prophet of Hope for the Sick and Tired." *Sojourners* 11, no. 11 (Dec. 1982): 18–21.

———. "Stepping Out into Freedom." *Sojourners* 11, no. 11 (Dec. 1982): 11–16.

Cortez, Jayne. "Big Fine Woman from Ruleville (For Fannie Lou Hamer)." *Black Collegian* 9, no. 5 (May/June 1979): 90.

Cribbs, Arthur, Jr. "Canton, Mississippi Site Where Black Activists Remember the Sixties." *Harambee* 20 (Oct. 11, 1984): 4.

Cron, Lisa. "Fannie Lou Hamer, an American Freedom Fighter." Information sheet. Organization of Equal Education of the Sexes, Inc., 1987.

Dalfiume, Richard. "The Forgotten Years of the Negro Revolution." *Journal of America History* 55 (June 1968): 90–106.

Demuth, Jerry. "Summer in Mississippi: Freedom Moves in to Stay." *The Nation,* Sept. 14, 1964, 104–10.

———. "'Tired of Being Sick and Tired.'" *The Nation,* June 1, 1964, 548–51.

Dent, Tom. "Annie Devine Remembers." *Freedomways* 22, no. 2 (1982): 81–92.

"Dialogue, Fannie Lou Hamer and Hodding Carter III, Caucus of the Loyal Democrats of Mississippi Chicago—Via Southern Media Tape." *Close-up* 4, no. 1 (Jan. 1969): 9.

"Dixie Picket Lines: No Place for Negro Women." *Sepia* 14 (Apr. 1965): 42–47.

Dorsey, L. C. "Fannie Lou Hamer." *Jackson Advocate,* Feb. 26–Mar. 6, 1981, section C, 1.

———. "A Prophet Who Believed." *Sojourners* 11, no. 11 (Dec. 1982): 21.

Dumas, Rhetaugh Graves. "Dilemmas of Black Females in Leadership." In *The Black Woman,* ed. La Frances Rodgers-Rose, 203–45. Beverly Hills: Sage Publications, 1980.

Egerton, John. "Fannie Lou Hamer." *The Progressive* 41 (May 1977): 7.

Fairclough, Adam. "The Preachers and the People: The Origins and Early Years of the Southern Christian Leadership Conference, 1955–1959." *Journal of Southern History* 52 (Aug. 1986): 403–40.

Fallows, James. "Mississippi Farmers Fight for Co-op." *Harvard Crimson,* Jan. 27, 1969.

"Fannie Lou Hamer at King Observance." *Berkeley Gazette,* Jan. 1, 1971.

"Fannie Lou Hamer, 60, Civil Rights Activist, Dies." *Bay State Banner,* Mar. 24, 1977, 1, 23.

"Fighting Cancer, Fannie Lou Hamer to Be Released from Mississippi Hospital." *Jet,* Mar. 24, 1977, 5.

Fletcher, Bob. "Sunflower County: We Gonna Rule." *The Movement,* June 1967, 5–8.

Foster, E. C. "Time of Challenge: Afro-Mississippi Political Developments since 1965." *Journal of Negro History* 68 (Spring 1983): 185–200.

Garland, Phyl. "Builders of a New South." *Ebony,* Aug. 1966, 27–37.

Gates, Henry Louis, Jr. "Frederick Douglass and the Language of the Self." In Gates, *Figures in Black: Words, Signs, and the "Racial" Self,* 98–124. New York: Oxford University Press, 1987.

Gilliam, Dorothy. "An Activist Recalls—and Assesses." *Washington Post,* Jan. 19, 1987, 83.

Grant, Joanne. "Mississippi and 'The Establishment.'" *Freedomways* 5, no. 2 (1965): 294–300.

———. "Way of Life in Mississippi." *National Guardian* 16, no. 19 (Feb. 13, 1964): 12.

"Grassroots Action, the Freedom Democrats." *Southern Patriot* 22, no. 8 (Oct. 1964): 1, 3.

Greeson, Aaron D. "Beyond Selves Deferred: Langston Hughes' Style and the Psychology of Black Selfhood." *Langston Hughes Review* 4, no. 1 (Spring 1985): 47–54.

Gusdorf, Georges. "Conditions and Limits of Autobiography." In *Autobiography: Essays Theoretical and Critical,* ed. James Olney, 28–48. Princeton: Princeton University Press, 1980.

Guyot, Lawrence, and Mike Thelwell. "The Politics of Necessity and Survival in Mississippi." *Freedomways* 6, no. 2 (1966): 120–32.

———. "Toward Independent Political Power." *Freedomways* 6, no. 3 (1966): 246–54.

Hall, Jacquelyn Dowd. "'The Mind That Burns in Each Body': Women, Rape, and Racial Violence." In *Powers of Desire: The Politics of Sexuality,* ed. Ann Snitow, Christine Stansell, and Sharon Thompson, 328–49. New York: Monthly Review Press, 1983.

Hamer, Fannie Lou. "Fannie Lou Hamer Speaks Out." *Essence* 1, no. 6 (Oct. 1971): 53–75.

———. "It's in Your Hands." In *Black Women in White America: A Documentary History,* ed. Gerda Lerner, 609–14. New York: Vintage, 1972.

Harrist, Ron. "Civil Libertarian Makes Last Trip Through Ruleville." *Jackson Daily News,* Mar. 21, 1977, 1B.

Herron, Jeannine. "Mississippi: Underground Election." *The Nation,* Dec. 7, 1963, 387–89.

Higginbotham, Evelyn Brooks. "Afro-American Women's History and the Metalanguage of Race." *Signs* 17 (Winter 1992): 251–74.

Hine, Darlene Clark. "Rape and the Inner Lives of Black Women in the Middle West: Preliminary Thoughts on the Culture of Dissemblance." *Signs* 14 (Summer 1989): 912–20.

Hodes, Martha. "The Sexualization of Reconstruction Politics: White Women and Black Men in the South after the Civil War." *Journal of the History of Sexuality* 3 (Jan. 1993): 402–17.

Houghton, Genevieve. "Sweat Equity and the Freedom Farms Cooperative, An Exclusive Interview with Fannie Lou Hamer." *Berkeley Monitor,* Nov. 1, 1969, 1–4.

Howe, Florence. "Mississippi's Freedom Schools: The Politics of Education." *Harvard Educational Review* 34 (Spring 1965): 144–60.

Israeli, Phineas. "Hard-Hitting Hamer, Exclusive Interview." *Berkeley Tribe,* Oct. 27, 1969.

Jencks, Christopher. "Mississippi: From Conversion to Coercion." *New Republic* 15, no. 9 (Aug. 22, 1964): 17–21.

Johnson, June. "Broken Barriers and Billy Sticks." *Sojourners* 11, no. 11 (Dec. 1982): 16–17.

Johnson, Susan. "Fannie Lou Hamer: Mississippi Grassroots Organizer." *Black Law Journal* 2, no. 2 (Summer 1972): 154–62.

King, Deborah. "Multiple Jeopardy, Multiple Consciousness: The Context of a Black Feminist Ideology." *Signs* 13 (Autumn 1988): 42–72.

King, Mae. "Oppression and Poverty: The Unique Status of the Black Woman in the American Political Scene." *Social Science Quarterly.* 56 (June 1975): 116–28.

King, Martin Luther, Jr. "The Drum Major Instinct." In *Martin Luther King, Jr.: A Documentary . . . Montgomery to Memphis,* ed. Flip Schulke, 22. New York: Norton, 1976.

Kopkind, Andrew. "New Radicals in Dixie: Those 'Subversive' Civil Rights Workers." *New Republic,* Apr. 10, 1965, 13–16.

Ladner, Joyce A. "Fannie Lou Hamer: In Memoriam." *Black Enterprise* (May 1977): 56.

———. "What Black Power Means to Negroes in Mississippi." *Trans-action* 5 (Nov. 1967): 7–15.

Lawson, Steven. "Freedom Then, Freedom Now: The Historiography of the Civil Rights Movement." *American Historical Review* 96 (Apr. 1991): 456–71.

LeSure, Deborah, and Deborah Bouton. "Fannie Lou Hamer, Remembered Well." *ruralamerica* (Nov.–Dec. 1983): 24.

Locke, Mamie. "The Role of African-American Women in the Civil Rights and Women's Movements in Hinds County and Sunflower County, Mississippi." *Journal of Mississippi History* 53 (Aug. 1991): 229–39.

Lynd, Staughton. "The Freedom Schools: Concept and Organization." *Freedomways* 5, no. 2 (1965): 302–9.

Marable, Manning. "Black Nationalism in the 1970s: Through the Prism of Race and Class." *Socialist Review* 10 (Mar.–June 1980): 57–108.

"Marked for Murder." *Sepia* 14, no. 4 (Apr. 1965): 28–33.

McKay, Nellie Y. "Nineteenth-Century Black Women's Spiritual Autobiographies: Religious Faith and Self-Empowerment." In *Interpreting Women's Lives: Feminist Theory and Personal Narratives,* ed. Personal Narratives Group, 139–54. Urbana: University of Illinois Press, 1989.

McLaurin, Charles. "Voice of Calm." *Sojourners* 11, no. 11 (Dec. 1982): 12–13.

McMillen, Neil. "Black Enfranchisement in Mississippi: Federal Enforcement and Black Protest in the 1960s." *Journal of Southern History* 43 (Aug. 1977): 357–58.

———. "Development of Civil Rights 1956–1970." In *A History of Mississippi,* ed. Richard A. McLemore, vol. 2, 154–70. Hattiesburg: University and College Press of Mississippi, 1973.

Miles, Michael. "Black Cooperatives." *New Republic* 159, no. 12 (Sept. 21, 1968): 21–23.

Miller, Char, ed. "The Mississippi Summer Project Remembered—The Stephen Mitchell Bingham Letter." *Journal of Mississippi History* 47 (Nov. 1985): 284–307.

Minnis, Jack. "The Mississippi Freedom Democratic Party: A New Declaration of Independence." *Freedomways* 5, no. 2 (1965): 264–78.

"Mississippi, Freedom Rally Series Subject." *New York Amsterdam News,* July 25, 1964, 35.

"Mississippi Movement: Interview with Ella Jo Baker and Fannie Lou Hamer." *Southern Exposure* 9, no. 1 (Sept. 1981): 40–42, 47–49.

Moody, Anne. "All I Could Think of Was How Sick Mississippi Whites Were." In *Black Women in White America: A Documentary History,* ed. Gerda Lerner, 425–31. New York: Vintage, 1972.

"Morehouse Cites Nobility of Mrs. Fannie Lou Hamer." *Jet,* June 26, 1969, 20.

Norton, Eleanor Holmes. "A Memory of Fannie Lou Hamer." *Black Scholar* 6 (July 1977): 51.

O'Dell, J. H. "Life in Mississippi: An Interview with Fannie Lou Hamer." *Freedomways* 5, no. 2 (Spring 1965): 231–42.

Oppenheimer, Martin. "Current Negro Protest Activities and the Concept of Social Movement." *Phylon* 24 (Summer 1963): 154–60.

Painter, Nell Irvin. "Of Lily, Linda Brent, and Freud: A Non-Exceptionalist Approach to Race, Class, and Gender in the Slave South." *Georgia Historical Quarterly* 76 (Summer 1992): 241–59.

———. "'Social Equality,' Miscegenation, Labor, and Power." In *The Evolution of Southern Culture,* ed. Numan Bartley, 47–67. Athens: University of Georgia Press, 1988.

———. "Sojourner Truth in Life and Memory: Writing the Biography of an American Exotic." *Gender and History* 2 (Spring 1990): 3–16.

"Panola Land Buyers Association." *Southern Co-Op News* 1 (Aug. 1968): 1.

Peterson, Franklynn. "Fannie Lou Hamer: Mother of 'Black Women's Lib.'" *Sepia* 21 (Dec. 1972): 16–24.

———. "Sunflowers Don't Grow in Sunflower County." *Sepia* 19 (Feb. 1970): 8–18.

Poussaint, Alvin. "The Stresses of the White Female Workers in the Civil Rights Movement in the South." *American Journal of Psychiatry* 123 (Oct 1966): 401–7.

Price, William. "Mrs. Hamer 'Briefs' U.S. on Sunflower Election." *National Guardian,* Mar. 18, 1967, 5.

"Rally Attendance Exceeds 3,000." *Daily Californian,* Oct 16, 1969, 1.

Rampersad, Arnold. "Biography, Autobiography, and Afro-American Culture." *Yale Review* 73 (Autumn 1983): 1–16.

———. "Psychology and Afro-American Biography." *Yale Review* 78 (Autumn 1988): 1–18.

Reagon, Bernice. "African Diaspora Women: The Making of Cultural Workers." *Feminist Studies* 12 (Spring 1986): 77–90.

———. "On Beginning a Cultural Autobiography." *Feminist Studies* 8 (Spring 1982): 81–96.

Richards, Dona. "With Our Minds Set on Freedom." *Freedomways* 5, no. 2 (1965): 340.

Rickman, Geraldine. "A Natural Alliance: The New Role for Black Women." *Civil Rights Digest* 6 (Spring 1974): 57–65.

Roberton, Craig. "Fannie Lou Hamer Remembered." *Delta Democrat Times,* Mar. 16, 1977, 1.

"A Salute to Black Women." *Jackson Advocate,* Mar. 27–28, 1984 (entire issue).

"Secret Crisis in the Delta." *Newsweek,* Mar. 7, 1966, 28–29.

Sewell, George. "Fannie Lou Hamer." *Black Collegian* 8, no. 5 (May/June 1978): 18–20.

———. "Fannie Lou Hamer's Light Still Shines." *Encore American and Worldwide News,* July 18, 1977, 3.

"Sharecropper's Daughter Has Seen Horizons Widen." *Clarion-Ledger,* Sept. 12, 1980, 13A.

Simpson, William. "The Birth of the Mississippi 'Loyalist Democrats' (1965–1968)." *Journal of Mississippi History* 44, no. 1 (Feb. 1982): 27–45.

Sitton, Claude. "Inquiry into the Mississippi Mind." *New York Times Magazine,* Apr. 28, 1963, 13, 104–7.

"Spotlight on People: Fannie Lou Hamer." *Blacks in American History to the Present. Vol. 2, 1877 to the Present.* Englewood Cliffs, N.J.: Globe Book Company, 1989.

Stembridge, Jane. "New Directions in Mississippi." *Southern Patriot* 22, no. 2 (Feb. 1964): 1–3.

Strickland, William. "The Movement and Mississippi." *Freedomways* 5, no. 2 (1965): 310–13.

Strong, Augusta. "Negro Women in Freedom's Battles." *Freedomways* 7, no. 4 (1967): 302–15.

Surace, Samuel, and Melvin Seeman. "Some Correlates of Civil Rights Activism." *Social Forces* 46 (1967): 197–207.

"Two Poems in Memory of Fannie Lou Hamer (1917–1977)." *Freedomways* 17, no. 2 (1977): 91–92.

Washington, Cynthia. "We Started at Different Ends of the Spectrum." *Southern Exposure* 4 (Winter 1977): 14–15.

Watriss, Wendy. "It's Something Inside You: Interview with Anna Mae Dickson." *Southern Exposure* 4 (Winter 1977): 24–30.

Wigginton, Eliot, and Sue Thrasher. "To Make the World We Want: An Interview with Dorothy Cotton." *Southern Exposure* 10 (Sept.–Oct. 1982): 25–31.

Wright, Beverly Hendrix. "Ideological Change and Black Identity during the Civil Rights Movement." *Western Journal of Black Studies* 5, no. 3 (Fall 1981): 186–98.

Wright, Marion. "The Right to Protest." *New South* 17, no. 2 (Feb. 1962): 6–13.

Theses, Dissertations, and Unpublished Papers

Behel, Sandra K. "The Mississippi Home Front during World War II: Tradition and Change." Ph.D. diss., Mississippi State University, 1989.

Chesteen, Richard D. "Change and Reaction in a Mississippi Delta Civil Community." Ph.D diss., University of Mississippi, 1976.

Crawford, Vicki Lynn. "We Shall Not Be Moved: Black Female Activists in the Mississippi Civil Rights Movement, 1960–1965." Ph.D. diss., Emory University, 1986.

Hodes, Martha Elizabeth. "Sex across the Color Line: White Women and Black Men in the Nineteenth-Century American South." Ph.D. diss., Princeton University, 1991.

McLemore, Leslie. "Fannie Lou Hamer: An Unfinished Political Portrait." Paper presented at conference of National Council for Black Studies. Chicago, Illinois, Mar. 17–20, 1982.

———. "The Mississippi Freedom Democratic Party: A Case Study of Grassroots Politics." Ph.D. diss., University of Massachusetts, Amherst, 1971.

Reagon, Bernice. "The Cultural Impact of Freedom Songs upon the Civil Rights Movement." Paper presented at Fannie Lou Hamer Memorial Symposium Lecture Series, Jackson State University, Oct. 1984.

Richards, Johnetta. "The Southern Negro Youth Congress: A History." Ph.D. diss., University of Cincinnati, 1987.

Romaine, Anne. "The Mississippi Freedom Democratic Party through 1964." Master's thesis, University of Virginia, 1971.

Tate, Roger D., Jr. "Easing the Burden: The Era of Depression and New Deal in Mississippi." Ph.D. diss., University of Tennessee, Knoxville, 1978.

Williams, Kenneth H. "Mississippi and Civil Rights, 1945–1954." Ph.D. diss., Mississippi State University, 1985.

Woods, Barbara. "Black Woman Activist in Twentieth-Century South Carolina: Modjeska Montieth Simpkins." Ph.D. diss., Emory University, 1978.

Index

Chana Kai Lee is an associate professor of history and women's studies at the University of Georgia.

Women in American History

Typeset in 10.5/13 Minion
with Gill Sans Bold display
Designed by Dennis Roberts
Composed by Celia Shapland
for the University of Illinois Press
Manufactured by Thomson-Shore, Inc.